At the Sign of the Swan of the

Don G.

Detail from Merian's View of London, 1638, showing the old Swan Playhouse. (From the Art Collection of the Folger Shakespeare Library. By permission of the Folger Shakespeare Library.)

At the Sign of the Swan

An Introduction to Shakespeare's Contemporaries

JUDITH COOK

Foreword by Trevor Nunn

HARRAP

LONDON

For Richard Butterworth
who has guided me
through my theatre books

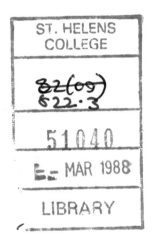
First published in Great Britain 1986
by HARRAP LIMITED
19 – 23 Ludgate Hill, London EC4M 7PD

ISBN 0 245-54263-9 (cased)
ISBN 0 245-54387-2 (paper)

Designed by Roger King Graphic Studios
Printed and bound in Great Britain
by Robert Hartnoll (1985), Bodmin

Contents

Acknowledgments

I would like to thank most of all my husband, Martin Green, for the encouragement he gave me during the time I worked on this project.
I would like to thank the helpful staff of the British Library, the Shakespeare Centre, the Shakespeare Institute and the Royal Shakespeare Theatre. Thanks also to Angela Barker for typing most of my own annotated typescript to make it legible.

Model of the new Swan Theatre at Stratford (RSC Press Office)

Foreword by Trevor Nunn

Stratford on Avon is the acknowledged world centre for Shakespeare studies and for the continuous performance of his plays. Gradually, a season which used to terminate in mid-October turned into the current reality of an eleven-months-of-the-year operation. It is easy enough to proclaim that Stratford is the world centre — nobody would particularly challenge this — but it has got to be real and palpable, a Shakespeare centre that is full of excitement and that has a curiosity value for anybody who visits it.

So what has to be going on in Stratford is main-house productions of Shakespeare that do not lose their sense of topicality, or relevance or originality or experimentation. By that I do not mean that the main house should become more secure. I think the Royal Shakespeare Company has got to go on being a company that does Shakespeare as if the plays had just come through the letter box that morning so that we can see what they mean for us now, at this moment in time.

But what we now have under the same roof is another building that does con-textual plays that research into the drama which directly influenced Shakespeare and the plays which he himself directly influenced, in the first instance, and then, in slightly more general terms, presents a neglected repertoire from the very greatest period of English dramatic literature. All this will be providing a context for Shakespeare which should lure people to spend a longer period of time in Stratford's centre.

What we should aim to be presenting in the Swan Theatre at the widest range is plays from 1570 to 1750 because we think that it is a mightily neglected area. There is a terrific published outlet that most theatre audiences have never come across. We think that this will create a very special interest and that it will not be only a scholarly interest or an interest which is confined to sixth formers and people doing Shakespeare studies.

We think that anybody and everybody interested in the theatre will be turned on to it. The dream is that there is such a huge overflow audience at Stratford beating on the door to get into the main house and finding it can't that it is going to go next door into the Swan Theatre and discover a whole world of new plays. People are going to discover things they had no idea existed and they are going to be thrilled and want to come back for more.

There is another reason for having a new building in which to put the plays on and that is the economic one. Over the years we have tried to pay tribute to the

Elizabethan and Jacobean writers by including them in occasional seasons in the main house. But it is impossibly difficult to fill a 1600-seat theatre with a play by Middleton or a play by Beaumont and Fletcher. At least at a time of economic stringency it would be a lunatic gamble although it does work sometimes. It was just such a gamble that Peter Hall took when he asked me to do Tourneur's *Revenger's Tragedy*. It just so happened that it did fill the seats for two years running, albeit for a very small number of performances. We also did a production of *Dr Faustus* directed by Clifford Williams which sold very well. But there were others for which the same thing could not be claimed and if the only way you can do Elizabethan and Jacobean plays is to look around for one that will fill 1600 seats then you are not going to do anything at all. Certainly you are not going to help scholarship or improve the consciousness of what is in the national literary locker. That is not to say that from time to time we will not come up with a gem which people will get extremely excited about, and if that happens and they want to see it in large numbers then we can transfer it to another theatre which has a larger number of seats, so there will be a forcing-house element in all this.

I think we should do the occasional piece of Shakespeare apocrypha where it is fairly clear he was collaborating with one or two other dramatists. For example there is *The Two Noble Kinsmen*, there is some evidence he had a hand in *Thomas More* and there is the *Edward III* play which John Barton, for instance, is convinced has sections of Shakespeare in it. Of course *Henry VIII* should really be in the Shakespeare apocrypha but then you see it would be very good if we could establish by the work we do at the Swan Theatre that it is foolish for us in the twentieth century to want to identify Shakespeare and Shakespeare-only masterpieces when it was so obvious that collaboration was a method of work that the Elizabethans and Jacobeans enthusiastically embraced.

Three or four dramatists would work together on the plays and obviously Shakespeare was part of that process and he did not feel too proud to do it. He was obviously happy on occasions to work with other people or rework somebody else's draft. It seems to me very likely that that is what happened with *Pericles*. You can see exactly the same thing now when you go to the cinema. You see there is a screenplay by two people adapted from an idea by somebody else and it is really quite rare that you have one, and only one, writer. Why? Because people making movies are very concerned about the commercial destination of their product. They are very alarmed about whether or not it is going to work sufficiently well so they do not allow writers to feel that they are working on a masterpiece. They do not allow them to say 'not one of my words is touchable or moveable into a different order'. Film-makers say 'Work for us, provide your treatment, and we will move the pieces around and in the end you will get a credit. We are going to hit the market with what you have done and you will have had a great deal to do with it but you can't claim total ownership of it.'

I do not think the conditions in the Elizabethan theatre were much different. I think either the collectives of actors or, more particularly, the wealthy managers said 'We have got to get this particular play to work and we can't allow these dramatists to get proud or feel a sense of total ownership. We are going to adapt this text, inject speeches into it, possibly remove things from it, chop it about and, if something works in one theatre, we are going to employ a couple of writers to do something very similar for us within days.' Take *The Fair Maid of the West* — there was Part I and Part II within six months because Part I was such a big success.

Then look at Webster and Tourneur (that mystery figure). They were both obviously heavily influenced by Shakespeare and yet they created a sort of separate genre which, in itself, had spin-offs. Both had lots of imitators but frequently it was what was on the top surface, the effects they had created, which was imitated. The other writers were not even getting to the starting point. I think there should be occasions at the Swan when we do something we know is of no great literary value but is still an excellent working theatre text we can put over to an audience so that we can create excitement with it.

None of these texts were written for the classroom. I do not think the playwrights would have believed that this would happen, although I think Tourneur and Webster and especially Jonson would be extremely gratified. I think they would like it. They would probably think maybe all that struggle and kicking and fighting to get people off our patch and preserve some kind of identity in our work finally paid off.

There are a lot of comedies to be done, especially city plays. I once wanted to do a play called *The London Cuckolds* and I talked about it so much that word got around and before I could do it, it was put on at the Royal Court and was a great success. It is in the direct tradition of the Jacobean city comedies yet it was written 150 years after those plays by the contemporaries of Shakespeare. It is debased, outrageous and farcical but there is a direct connection with that earlier genre of work. The city comedies were written for a specific audience, a city audience. You knew there were a certain group of people who you could get into your theatre who had a shared background, shared language, shared vocabulary and you could give them a great entertainment because of all the references you could put in for that particular audience.

But if we are going to put on plays in context then we need also to look at the late mediaeval plays, early Tudor plays and moralities. For instance I think *The Old Wife's Tale* by George Peele is a marvellous, magical play and it is a wonderful contextual play for a great deal of Shakespeare's fantasies.

Then there is Ben Jonson. I feel there is a bounden duty to do more Jonson than has been presented in this country. He is a very great dramatist indeed. All you get are *The Alchemist, Volpone* and *Bartholomew Fair*. I would like to try perhaps even *Sejanus*, and another marvellous play and a staringly obvious one is *Every Man in His Humour*. A lot of people know the title and say 'Ah, that's a play by Ben Jonson, isn't it? And didn't he write one about alchemistry?' But they do not know what the play contains.

Then we must push on beyond the direct Shakespeare period. There is this vast body of Jacobean work that is contradictory and we do not quite know how to tackle it. Clifford Williams did a wonderful production of Marlowe's *The Jew of Malta* where he produced a strange, black comic style and I suppose the *Revenger's*

Tragedy illustrated that there was something vicious and deadly contained in the comedy within that something that was known as 'Jacobean tragedy'. It made many of its effects comically but we do not know enough about it as we have not tested sufficiently how to do the plays.

Looking beyond that, then we should be doing some of the earliest of the Restoration plays because there is obviously a kind of umbilical connection between these plays and the earlier period of drama. We tend to think there was Shakespeare and the Jacobeans and then the theatres were closed down and forty years later Charles II came back and the theatres were reopened and everything was influenced by the French and it was all totally different. Yet it is not totally different. We can find connections and they will sometimes be literary, sometimes practical, sometimes to do with the way we present them.

That is what I think is so exciting about the Swan Theatre. We can see a Tudor play, an Elizabethan play, a Jacobean play and a Restoration play all on the same basic stage, the same simple space that we know was the Shakespearian playhouse format. If it is the same configuration then I think we will see similarities in struc-ture and similarities of moral purpose in the relationship of dramatist to audience.

It is quite extraordinary the enthusiasm that has been unleashed. Directors are genuinely thrilled and excited about the possibility of what they can bring to light for the first time; or rather for the second time, but in a different context. We have the literary and scholarship responsibility. If we do not do the works who is going to do them? If we do not proclaim their existence and celebrate the language in which they were written there is every possibility that by the time we go into the next century the opportunity to proclaim them will have gone.

Preface

Very occasionally one can just happen to be in the right place at the right time. In September 1984 I was in Stratford to review *Hamlet* for *The Scotsman*. Somewhat idly, I attended the press conference held to announce the building of the Swan Theatre; idly, as I was not commissioned to cover it. Afterwards I had a chat with Trevor Nunn and he asked me what I was doing. I had just written a thriller, shortly to be published, and I told him I had worked on the 1983 General Election and had actually been looked after and accommodated by his ex-English teacher, Mr Peter Hewitt. Peter Hewitt had a passion for drama of the Jacobean period, and we had discussed it (between electioneering sessions) and somehow or other the idea formed of my doing a book on Shakespeare's contemporaries rather similar to those I had written on aspects of Shakespeare (*Women in Shakespeare* and *Shakespeare's Players*).

I contacted Harrap to see if they liked the idea, and asked the RSC if they could give me any help I might need, and so I embarked on what has proved to be a most enjoyable task. The RSC in general, and Nicola Russell in particular, have been extremely helpful, from providing accommodation for me to endless photocopying and document-hunting. So I must thank Trevor Nunn for giving me the idea and, indirectly, his ex-schoolmaster, Peter Hewitt. . . .

The next stage was devoted to reading as many plays of the period as possible — not such an easy task. While there are a number of excellent modern omnibus editions of plays put out by various publishing houses, in practice this boils down to a pool of about a dozen which are endlessly recycled, and all these are the most popular ones such as *The Duchess of Malfi* and *Volpone*. It was necessary to comb good secondhand bookshops for old copies of the Revels and Mermaid series to find the complete plays of each of the authors covered in this book.

Then I wanted to find out more about their lives, who they were, what they were like, to flesh them out for those who wanted to see their work, and this proved to be absolutely fascinating. Shakespeare was the exception — not by birth and background, for most of his contemporaries came from a similar one. Marlowe's father was a shoemaker, Jonson's stepfather a bricklayer, Webster's a coachbuilder and so on. (This in itself should nail the view that Shakespeare could not have written his own plays.) But Shakespeare was incredibly circumspect and respectable compared with his working colleagues. Apart from his hasty marriage and the subsequent rapid birth of his daughter, he seems to have led a life of blameless rectitude apart from his affair with the Dark Lady. We do not know what he did during the 'lost years' but it seems unlikely he would have behaved out of character.

He worked very hard — legend has it that when invited out for a carouse with his friends he 'sent out that he was in pain' and did not go. He carefully used his money, buying first into a shareholding in the theatre company and then investing in property both on the South Bank and in Stratford. He retired a comparatively wealthy man, owning one of the biggest houses in Stratford, and a highly respected citizen. We are told that he died after meeting Jonson and Drayton in a pub in Welford-on-Avon, catching cold after a night's drinking. This may or may not be true, although it is likely that if Jonson was anywhere in the area he (Jonson) would be drinking all night.

Compare that with his contemporaries. Both George Peele and Robert Greene died young, diseased and deeply in debt, the latter having to resort to his long-estranged wife for money to ensure a decent burial. Dekker spent long periods in prison for debt.

More and more these playwrights became real people to me. It happened, co-incidentally, that I was working on a news story connected with the work of MI5 about the same time I was reading and researching into Christopher Marlowe. There seems to me to be little doubt, knowing something of how our security services work to-day, that their predecessors might have recruited the brilliant young Cambridge graduate Christopher Marlowe, and then later, finding that for some reason he had become a danger or a threat to them, that they might have engineered his death.

As to Ben Jonson, both I and my family felt that he moved in with us for several weeks, rather as he did upon the unfortunate Drummond of Hawthornden. Jonson inflicted himself on Drummond in 1616, eating and drinking him out of house and home, and throwing parties at his expense. What a marvellous, huge, overwhelming personality — in small doses. . . . A man who had killed another in a duel, had been branded at Tyburn, spent a couple of spells in gaol (one for writing a political play which upset the King) and who, in spite of great success and financial reward, died worth only about £8! Jonson was not the only one to spend time in prison for writing political satires (although he exaggerated greatly his brave stand, being Jonson). Middleton wrote a play so dangerous that it led to the arrest of the whole theatrical company, an enormous fine and a full-scale search to find the author of a piece which had outraged the nobility but was the biggest smash hit of its day.

I have not set out to write a scholarly treatise on the playwrights and their work — the bibliography will show that there are many such for the keen scholar. I have had perforce to be very selective, and others making such a selection might have chosen different plays than those I have picked out, and indeed written about some of the playwrights I have not covered in the book. Also, it is always arguable as to how best to organize a book of this kind, which covers a wide range of subject matter over a fairly lengthy period of time. I trust that readers will see the logic behind the formula I eventually chose.

A brief word about the dating. This is extremely difficult, and often no two authorities will agree. The dates I give are normally those of first performance, in so far as this can be established, although I may occasionally hazard a guess as to when they were written — not necessarily the same thing. (Publication, of course, was something else again!). To complicate matters still further, there were, as I explain in the Table, often divergencies resulting from the old use of the Julian Calendar.

What I have hoped to do is to try to pass on my own enthusiasm for the plays of this period to others and to give an idea of those plays and the lives of those who wrote them. This was the golden age of language, the brilliant flowering of the English drama.

Newlyn 1985   JUDITH COOK

The Fortune Playhouse. Erected 1623. (From a view dating from 1811.)

Chapter 1

Companies, Theatres & Players

The Companies

It is not by chance that the years from 1580 to 1630 (with a peak between 1590 and 1625) produced such a wealth of drama. For the first time drama itself made the leap from the amateur religious and morality plays and groups of strolling players to properly organized and set up theatre companies, playing in custom-built buildings, patronized by aristocracy and royalty. Playwrights were in tremendous demand. Those who ran companies were prepared to advance them money, so that they were enabled to write plays, either on their own or in collaboration with colleagues. There has never been a better time for the would-be playwright.

For most of the sixteenth century actors had been considered as little more than rogues and vagabonds. The 1572 Vagabonds Act forced acting companies on to a professional basis, for it required every company of players to be authorized by one noble and two judicial dignitaries of the realm (this latter restriction was dropped in a later Act in 1598). The Statute says:

> . . . all Fencers, Bearewards, Common Players in Enterludes & Ministrels, not belonging to any Baron of this Realme or towards any other honourable Personage of greater Degree; all Jugglers, Pedlars, Tinkers and Petty Chapmen; which said Fencers, Bearewards, Common Players, Minstrels, Jugglers, Pedlars, Tinkers and Petty Chapmen, shall wander abroad and have not Licence of two Justices of the Peace at the least, whereof one to be of the Quorum when and in what Shire they shall happen to wander . . . shall be taken and adjudged to be deemed Rogues, Vagabonds and Sturdy Beggars.

So it became necessary for companies to find patrons, and the great nobles — and indeed both Queen Elizabeth I and James I — became patrons. Possibly the kudos for a nobleman lending his name to a popular theatre company of his time was somewhat similar to that which accrues to well-known personalities today who become chairmen of football clubs.

This is not the place to try to give a detailed account of the history of the major Elizabethan and Jacobean theatre companies. There are many excellent books on the subject. It is, however, necessary to mention a few details.

The leading theatrical entrepreneur of his day was surely Philip Henslowe. His company was known for most of its life as the Lord Admiral's Men.

It is impossible to think of any playwright of repute of the day, from Greene, Kyd and Marlowe, through Shakespeare, to Dekker, Middleton, Tourneur and Ben Jonson, who did not write for Henslowe at some time. At the same time, he was more than happy to organize bear-baiting to bring in the crowds. It would be rather like finding someone who could run both the Royal Shakespeare Company and Tottenham Hotspur. Henslowe not only had an eye for talent; he was prepared, if reluctantly, actually to advance money to a playwright, or playwrights working in collaboration, to enable them to go away and write plays for his actors. He and his son-in-law, the famous actor Edward Alleyn, ensured that an enormous range of work of all kinds was put on by the Lord Admiral's Men — revenge plays, tragedies, comedies, tragi-comedies, satires and even what we would call drama-documentaries: plays based on actual recent events.

The theatres of that day worked on a 'sharers' system. A group of men, varying from about six to a dozen, would have shares in a particular theatre and theatre company. They would be the most prominent members of the company. They might or might not include a playwright, although we know that Shakespeare was a principal shareholder in his own company for many years. In 1596 (when his company was known as the Lord Chamberlain's Men) the sharers were Burbage, Shakespeare, Kempe, Pope, Bryan, Phillips, Sly and Heminges. Kempe left in 1599 to dance his famous morris dance from London to Norwich. Ben Jonson — so we learn from the *Diary* left by Henslowe — actually borrowed money off Henslowe in order to buy a share in his company, which he then sold back again fairly rapidly. Other sharers would include the person who would now be known as the director or administrator of the theatre — Henslowe in his company, Burbage in Shakespeare's, leading actors and possibly a financial backer. The group would then hire 'hands'. These would include actors for one or more plays, backstage staff and people to help both in the dressing-rooms and probably front-of-house. No doubt a sharer might also have been a person who looked after the costumes and properties, which was an exceedingly responsible job. The costumes in the great companies were lavish, and no doubt needed a good deal of upkeep owing to the conditions in which they were worn.

The sharers also took on 'apprentices'. These were the boys who were trained for the stage, first to take the women's roles in the days before women were acceptable in theatres. If the boys had talent they stayed on and graduated into men's roles. In time they too might become sharers.

There is no doubt that the Lord Admiral's and Lord Chamberlain's (later

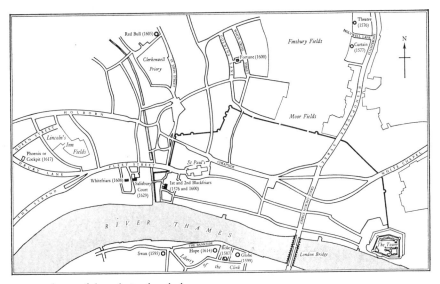

A map of some of the early London playhouses

King's) men were the two leading companies of their time, and Shakespeare's Company was unique in having him as a continuing house playwright for such a long period. While his company put on many plays by other writers, no other company had the benefit of such continuity of talent. Both Shakespeare, and Burbage and his actors, obviously benefited from this. Shakespeare knew exactly for whom he was writing and how best his plays might be cast, and the company were used to putting over his work to the best possible advantage.

Other major companies included those under the patronage of the Earls — Worcester, Sussex, Warwick, Oxford and Essex — and there were also several children's companies such as the Chapel Children and Paul's Children. Much like companies today, they formed and merged with each other, changed their names and patrons, actors and writers were attracted away from one company to join another. We do not know why Shakespeare left Henslowe for Burbage so early; perhaps there was a clash of personalities.

Because of Henslowe's *Diary* we do have some knowledge of what went on inside the companies and how they operated. The sharers provided the backing and finance and took their share of the profits. Hired men received wages, playwrights payments for their 'books', money was handed out for the purchase of cloth, made-up costumes and material for properties. Once companies began to build their own theatres, then a substantial proportion of the 'take' went on the buildings and their upkeep.

The books in which the *Diary* was written were first used by Henslowe's father, John Henslowe, for the entry of accounts for felling and disposal of timber and other matters relating to Ashdown Forest. From 1592 they were used by Philip to note anything he thought of interest. This included notes of loans made to playwrights and actors — including one to get the playwright Thomas Dekker

out of a debtors' prison — inventories of costumes and props, useful medicinal
hints and, when he came to build his own theatre, a detailed list of every item
which went into its building, right down to pounds of nails.

There is no order; the health hints and medicines appearing between items such
as 'sold to Richard Jones a man's gown of peach colour 2 September 1594 to be
paid for by five shillings a week immediately following and beginning as follows
. . . each week received in full payment 30 Nov 1594'. Then 'for back pain
powder of antimony inside a stewed prune'. A 'cure' for blocked ears: 'fry earth-
worms in goosegrease then strain some and drop a little in the ear'.

Some idea of the costumes and properties such a company would have in stock
can be gained from a list of some of the items from an inventory of Henslowe's
taken on 10 March 1598. They include:

Orange tawny satin doublet, laid thick with gold lace
1 Blue taffeta suit
Green coats for Robin Hood
Green hats for Robin Hood and 1 Hobbyhorse
Trumpets and drum and treble viol
1 rock, 1 cave and 1 Hellmouthe
1 tomb of Guido, 1 tomb of Dido, 1 bedstead
8 lances and a pair of stairs for Phaeton.
1 chime of bells and 1 beacon
1 globe, 1 gold sceptre, and the Citie of Rome (sic)
1 golden fleece and 1 bay tree
Old Mahommet's head
1 tree of golden apples
Tamburlaine's bridle and wooden matock
1 head of Seberosie [Cerberus?] and 8 other heads
Sign for Mother Redcap's
Mercury's wings and dragons, 1 chain of dragons
Imperial crowns and ghosts crowns
Cauldron for the Jew
Silver hose with satin and silver panels
French hose of cloth of gold
Tamburlaine's coat with copper lace
Peach colour satin doublet
Black satin doublet layered thick with black and gold lace
Carnation satin doublet, layered with gold lace
Flame-coloured doublet, pinked.

Just from this we can see how grand the costumes were, some made of velvet and
silk, lavishly trimmed with copper or gold lace. Hellmouthe was no doubt used in
several plays, including *Dr Faustus*. *Tamburlaine* was obviously in repertoire, as
was Marlowe's *Jew of Malta*, since he meets his death in the cauldron. Some items
not listed above prove a little puzzling, such as '1 heifer for the play of Phaeton,
the limes dead'. What it does show is a considerable degree of theatrical

sophistication in dressing and setting the stage.

The company system (apart from its refusal to employ women) is one that remained unmatched right up until the subsidized days of our own time. It gave playwrights almost unlimited opportunities to have their works performed, and it enabled them to experiment and grow. It offered actors the chance to learn their craft, and become the first theatrical professionals. It enabled plays to be presented lavishly, and it opened up a whole new world for the audiences which went to see the work of some of the finest playwrights the country has ever produced.

The Theatres

Plays and their players preceded theatres proper by some years. The companies played in inns, in the large private houses of the wealthy, in London in the Inns of Court, and in spaces used for other activities such as bear-baiting. Both inside and out of London, the players were used to setting up and putting on a performance in a different place every night.

The very first theatre proper was called, quite simply, The Theatre. It was built by James Burbage, the father of Richard Burbage who led Shakespeare's company. James was a member of the Earl of Leicester's Company and a carpenter. On 3 March 1576 he signed a 21-year lease for a piece of land just outside Finsbury Fields in north London, a well-known recreation spot for people in the City. The City Fathers were then, and remained, opposed to theatre and all but one of the public theatres were built outside the City boundaries. The Theatre stood on a piece of land between Finsbury Fields and the public road from Bishopsgate to Shoreditch Church.

Burbage made no bones about his wanting the land for a theatre, and his lease contained a clause which said that if he spent £200 or more on the building he could take it down when the lease expired. He was also supposed to be offered an automatic extension of his lease if he wanted it, although the terms had to be renegotiated. Shortly after Burbage built the Theatre, a second theatre, the Curtain, was erected almost next door. The name was not chosen for any theatrical connections; it had been the name of the piece of ground on which the theatre was built.

We do not know quite what connection Burbage had with the Curtain, which was also used by Henslowe, but we are told that Shakespeare's *Henry V* had its first performance there, and it could be that Burbage leased the theatre or used it for some performances while he was waiting for the Globe to be built on the South Bank. Both theatres catered for other entertainments apart from plays — fencing matches, wrestling and some kind of prize-fighting. At first severe restrictions were put on the number of performances which could be given, but after a good deal of lobbying on behalf of the companies by various members of the nobility, players were allowed to perform on every day except Sunday. In times of plague all theatres shut down, sometimes for months at a time.

The new Swan Theatre at Stratford under construction, January 1986 (RSC Press Office)

After these two theatres, a number of others were built. Basically there were two kinds, known as 'private' and 'public'. Private theatres started out as rooms set aside within existing buildings, and the name was retained both for the theatres in which the Children's Companies played and for a more comfortable type of building. It was roofed, probably fairly small, the stage was lit by candles, and you paid more to go in. It was not 'private' in the sense of a club or private house. The public theatres were open to the elements and you took your chance.

Henslowe then pioneered the move to the South Bank with the Rose theatre, about 1592, although he built another theatre, the Fortune, on the north side a few years later. Another north London theatre was the Red Bull at Clerkenwell.

The South Bank proved attractive for many reasons. It was outside the jurisdiction of the City. It had easy access, either by London Bridge or by the host of boats plying for trade across the Thames. There were gardens along the Bankside, bear-baiting was popular and there were several bear pits over there as well. It is a point to remember that Elizabethan and Jacobean audiences were not made up entirely of an élite interested only in intellectual pursuits. Most people actually enjoyed cock-fighting and bear-baiting and did not find anything disgusting in it. After all, another entertainment was to go to public hangings and especially to Tyburn to see people hanged, drawn and quartered — that is, hanged (but cut down living), disembowelled and their bodies quartered.

Following the building of the Rose, another theatre, the Swan, was built there in 1596 by Francis Langley. It was about three-quarters of a mile to the west of London Bridge. Possibly it was the success of Henslowe with the Rose which prompted Burbage to move to the South Bank, but there was also a more pressing reason. In 1595 another lease was drawn up for the land on which the Theatre stood, but it seems Giles Allen refused to ratify it. He had assumed, it is said, that the Burbage family — James and his sons, Richard and Cuthbert — had made a fortune out of the Theatre. This was not so, as in order to lease the land and build it in the first place James had borrowed the large sum of a thousand marks (about £666) from his father-in-law, and the repayments, plus interest, had crippled him.

Unable to come to any agreement with Allen, Burbage promptly dismantled his theatre and had the materials shipped over to the South Bank, The subsequent litigation rumbled on for years. The old Theatre was re-erected in an improved form on the Bankside, and became the most famous theatre of its day, the Globe. It opened in May 1599 and it must have been quite large, as we know that when the Spanish Ambassador saw Middleton's notorious *A Game At Chess* there in 1624 he says that upward of three thousand people attended each performance.

Henslowe seems to have been annoyed at the arrival of Burbage next door to him, and just after the Globe opened he built the Fortune, about a mile north of St Paul's. We have the detailed specifications for it in a document agreed by the builder, Peter Streete, and Henslowe and Alleyn, and from it we know very much what the Globe was like because Streete rebuilt the Globe, and the Fortune followed its specifications. We also know what it cost Henslowe, in everything from hiring a barge and wharfing to the cost of 'various timber', 'deal boards', lime, laths, rails, wages, hundreds of penny nails, a thatcher to thatch the galleries

Detail from Merian's View of London *(in Gottfried's* Neuwe Archontologia Cosmica, *1638) showing the Swan Playhouse. (Guildhall Library)*

and the roof of the stage hut. Many of the nails and such small ironware were bought at the 'sign of the frying pan'. The cost of the actual building was £520, the total cost £1320 and the upkeep between 1602 and 1608 was £120 a year. On 9 December 1621 it was burned down, and Henslowe rebuilt it in brick.

In 1606 Henslowe demolished the Rose, and having bought the Beargarden almost next door to it, built the Hope Theatre on the South Bank. Henslowe had many irons in the fire (he was also a dyer and bleacher), and one of these was bear-baiting. He had tried for years to become 'master of the royal game' without success, and made a strong effort to acquire the title on the accession of James I. The following year it passed to Sir William Steward, but he only held it from July to November 1604 and then Henslowe and Alleyn were given the post jointly. It is difficult to imagine the serious Alleyn in connection with such an enterprise. By 1607 Henslowe was complaining in a petition to James I of the high rate at which they had been forced to buy the post from Steward, and also that they had been told they could not hold bear-baiting events on Sundays 'after divine service, which was the chiefest means and benefit to the place'.

In 1613 the Globe burned down, and before it was rebuilt Henslowe and Alleyn started on the building of the Hope, which was to have a dual purpose, theatre and bear-baiting. In fact it never proved entirely successful. Theatres were built, fell into disuse, were abandoned and were rebuilt. Other well-known theatres of the period include the Blackfriars Theatre (the only public theatre in the City) and the private Cockpit, near Drury Lane. There were a number of private theatres within a line from Westminster to St Paul's. All had to be licensed, and it seems that the Globe and the Fortune also had licensed bars.

As well as bear-baiting and plays the Hope was also the scene of a ridiculous

event in October 1614. John Taylor, the water poet — so called because he had
been a waterman, and for a long time represented their interests — challenged
William Fennor, who called himself 'King James's Rhyming Poet', to a 'flyting
match' or insult competition at the Hope. Taylor paid for a thousand handbills to
be printed advertising the event, and also had the widest possible publicity put out
on both sides of the river in order to bring in the biggest crowd. He thought he
would get his money back from those paying to get in. Everything was made
ready for the great performance, the Hope was packed, Taylor was ready but
there was one tiny snag . . . Fennor did not turn up. The audience was not at all
happy, and Taylor made a very big mistake. He decided, as the match could not
take place, to read them a few of his poems instead.

This was rather like the spectators at the Centre Court at Wimbledon on the
day of the final being informed by one player that the other was not turning up
but not to worry, he would just sing a few songs to while away the time. In a
furious letter in rhyme to Fennor, Taylor described what happened:

> . . . some laughed, some swore, some stared and stamped and cursed,
> And in confused humours all out burst.
> I (as I could) did stand the desperate shock,
> And bid the brunt of many a dangerous knock.
> For now the stinkards in their ireful wrath,
> Bepelted me with loam, with stones and laths,
> One madly sits like bottle-Ale and hisses,
> Another throws a stone and 'cause he misses,
> He yawns and bawls and cries Away, away . . .

He continues in like vein:

> One swears and storms another laughs and smiles
> Another madly would pluck off the tiles,
> Some run to the door to get again their coin
> And some do shift and some again purloin,
> One valiantly stept upon the stage,
> And would tear down the hangings in his rage . . .

In the end it seems the theatre company took matters into their own hands and
went on and began a show. For some time the poet tried to continue reading his
verses while the play was acted at the same time:

> Then came the players, and they played an act,
> Which greatly from my action did detract.
> For 'tis not possible for any one,
> To play against a company alone,
> And such a company (I'll boldly say)
> That better (not the like) e'er played a play.
> In brief, the Play my action did eclipse,
> And in a manner, sealed up both my lips.

The Swan Theatre stage, c.1596: Johannes de Witt's sketch copied by Arend van Buchell

If nothing else, this shows what the audiences were like. Although we know a good deal about the Hope, it is the Swan about which we have the most detailed information, largely because of a drawing made of it in 1596 by a Dutchman, Johannes de Witt. He drew its interior, and although his original was lost, a copy was made by Arend van Buchell which was found in Amsterdam as late as 1888. There are a number of existing sketches of the outside of the Swan — which was not, in fact, a very popular theatre, although we know that the first performance of Middleton's *A Chaste Maid in Cheapside* was given there.

There is much scholarly argument over whether De Witt's drawing is entirely accurate or whether it was altered by the copyist, as some of the details do not fit with what is known of the interior of playhouses of the day, but there is enough agreement for it to be a most important piece of evidence as to the appearance of the inside of one of these theatres. It shows the stage raised on a platform (some stages were as wide as forty feet). Behind is the tiring room (where the actors dressed), with two doors opening out of it to provide stage entrances. Some theatres also had a 'discovery space' recessed between the doors with a curtain in front. This could be used for tableaux, plays within plays and for a variety of other purposes. There is no 'discovery space' in this drawing, but that is not to say there was not one there. Above the tiring house was a balcony which projected on pillars over part of the stage. This was known as the 'heavens', and its main use was to protect the actors from the weather. Level with the 'heavens' is a gallery which could either be used in the play or for musicians. Above the gallery was another floor which was roofed, and was the 'hut' in which the stage technicians worked. Scenery was not 'flown in', in the way we know it now, but it does seem that large stage props were lowered when necessary from the hut. Various effects were also produced there, such as thunder, lightning and gunfire. This floor had a small platform outside on which a trumpeter stood to announce the performance.

Most of the early buildings were made of lath and plaster between timbers on a brick foundation. Only after several theatres had burned down were they constructed entirely of brick. The roofs of the galleries and that of the hut would be thatched. There would be two or three banks of galleries with stairs up to them from the main area inside the theatre. The shape was round or octagonal, Shakespeare's 'wooden O'. The view from the galleries would be rather like that from the circles and galleries today, except that the theatre was more in the round and you would look down on a playing space which projected out into the audience. It cost a penny to get in and stand, and you had to fight for a place to see when it was a popular play. You paid another penny for a place in the gallery, and yet another for a seat. Wealthy people and the nobility could hire 'rooms', like theatre boxes today, for about 6*d*. Some wealthy patrons hired a stool and sat on the stage. Not surprisingly, actors hated this (we will see why when we come to note what the playwright Dekker had to say about this practice) and it was not encouraged.

The inside of the theatre was, we are told, grand. Theatres were sumptuously painted, the hangings were rich, the stage strewn with fresh rushes. It was a definite improvement on an inn yard, and at the end of this chapter we will see what it was like to pay a visit to a play at that time.

The Players

So what do we know about the actors of this time? A fair amount, although the period is dominated by one or two, much in the way Edmund Kean and William Charles Macready were synonymous with the theatre of the early and middle nineteenth century and Sir Henry Irving dominated that century's end. Indeed, nearer our own time, while in the 1930s there were many excellent actors and actresses, Laurence Olivier, John Gielgud and Ralph Richardson towered above the rest.

The earliest known 'star' of the stage was a comedian, Richard Tarlton. He has been described as a 'Charlie Chaplin' figure, and this is perhaps not far off the truth, as the pictures which have come down to us show a little man with bushy hair, squinty eyes and squashed nose, but dressed in large baggy trousers and wearing oversize shoes. He was also a playwright — his play *The Seven Deadly Sins* (first put on in 1585) was very popular — a tumbler, a ballad-maker and a Master of Fencing. He was no fool. He is the first British actor ever to have achieved a national reputation, and he was described by Nashe as a 'king' of players.

He is supposed to have started out in life apprenticed to a water-carrier, then to have become a publican. His first inn was in Colchester, but he moved to London, where he kept the Saba Tavern in Gracechurch Street and ran an ordinary (or common eating-house) in Paternoster Row. It has been suggested that he might have graduated to the theatre after giving comic turns to customers in his own inns. Some time about 1577 he joined the Lord Chamberlain's Players, and when the Queen's troupe was formed in 1583 he was one of its twelve founder members.

He is usually portrayed playing on a penny whistle and with a small drum strung around his neck. He had several speciality acts, including that of a drunk — which is said to have highly amused Queen Elizabeth, and which gave him a licence to say outrageous things — and another which made use of his dog. It is thought that Shakespeare specifically wrote the clown's role in *Two Gentlemen of Verona* to make use of Tarlton and his dog. As a Master of Fence (he won the title after challenging several other Masters in 1587), he taught the craft, and his pupils fought before him, were marked and were approved accordingly. We know that when Tarlton got into a spot of bother in Norwich while on tour he acquitted himself brilliantly. He was also famous for his 'jigs' (perhaps this is where the drum and whistle came in), which were not just dances but a song-and-dance act which was put on after a play had ended. They were often cheeky, satirical and/or risqué in content.

Most of all he was famed for his quick wit and ability to improvise — which was probably a mixed blessing in the context of a company working on a set text.

Richard Tarlton (British Library)   *William Kempe, 1600. (British Library)*

It is difficult for the stand-up comic to make the switch. When working on another book I asked comedian Frankie Howerd if he would talk to me about playing Bottom in Sir Peter Hall's *A Midsummer Night's Dream*. He gently declined, saying it had been a sad experience for him, and that he had never got used to having a set text to speak and being unable to add in his own material.

There remain records of the pleasure he gave to his contemporaries. Nashe said that audiences 'began exceedingly to laugh when he first peeped out his head'; Stow spoke of his 'plentiful . . . extemporal wit'; Spenser has charmingly 'our pleasant Willy . . . with whom all joy and jolly merriment/Is also deaded.' A little more gravely, Sir John Baker notes that 'for the . . . Clown's part he never had his match'.

Tarlton died on 3 September 1588 in the house of 'one Emma Ball of Shoreditch, she being a woman of very bad reputation'. While he was dying he petitioned Sir Francis Walsingham to protect his little son, Philip. This may sound surprising, but it is a sign of the impact of actors at that time and the society in which they mixed that no lesser personage than Sir Philip Sidney had stood as godfather to the child, and that Tarlton felt secure enough to petition such a high-ranking figure as Walsingham. His death was marred by an unseemly wrangle between his mother, his brothers-in-law and his lawyer over the contents of the will and the custody of little Philip.

He lived on in folk memory for a very long time after his death. Many books of jokes attributed to him were published over the years, and he even appeared as a character in plays written by other people. There is no doubt he was loved and remembered by all those who saw him.

The next famous clown, William Kempe, was to be the last in the Tarlton tradition. He too was a comedian in his own right, and like Tarlton was famous for the jigs with which he ended plays. He was also an improviser, and it is said he

Edward Alleyn (By permission of the Governors of Dulwich Picture Gallery)

Richard Burbage (By permission of the Governors of Dulwich Picture Gallery)

and Shakespeare did not get on at all well towards the end of their working relationship, and that Shakespeare was having a jibe at Kempe when in *Hamlet* he
complains about those actors who will insist on speaking more than is set down
for them. In 1599 Kempe left Shakespeare's company to dance a morris dance to
Norwich (known as 'the nine days wonder'), and he seems to have spent the rest
of his professional life in stunts of a similar sort.

He was to be followed by a very different man, Robert Armin, a sensitive actor
who specialized in other kinds of comic roles, not just broad comedy. For him
Shakespeare wrote Feste in *Twelfth Night* and the Fool in *Lear*. He must have been
a considerable actor. It is likely that Armin was part of a trend which was reflected
in all the other companies of the day as well; where the actor who specialized in
comic roles or fools was expected to act his part as one of a team, which did not
allow him to stand outside the role he was playing.

But the two most famous actors of the period were, without doubt, Edward
Alleyn and Richard Burbage. Obviously it did Alleyn little harm when he
married Philip Henslowe's stepdaughter, Joan, but it seems he was an outstand-
ing actor by the time he was sixteen. He was born on 1 September 1566, the son
of a Bishopsgate publican who died when he was four. His mother remarried, one
John Brown, a haberdasher, not long afterwards. Obviously Alleyn fancied
neither innkeeping nor haberdashery, for the first we hear of him is touring in
Leicester with the Earl of Worcester's Company in 1582. The company had got
into trouble, as they appear to have lost their Justices' licence (although they still
had one from the Earl), and, in defiance of the Mayor, played anyway. Afterwards

they apologized to the Mayor and asked him not to tell their patron.

By the end of the 1580s Alleyn was Henslowe's leading man, and he was to play some marvellous roles, not the least being Marlowe's great overreachers — Tamburlaine, Barabbas and Dr Faustus. He was tall, very good-looking in a classic way, had a fine voice and enormous stage presence. He was the kind of actor who, through sheer ability and personality, could make almost any play work, and was described by Nashe as being able to 'make ill matter good'.

His marriage to Joan seems to have been a happy one, and when he was on tour the two corresponded in loving and amusing terms. It was a childless marriage. Alleyn, like Shakespeare, was a careful man, and by the mid-1590s he had invested money in property and had become a man of means. He seems to have been rather like the Victorian actor-managers in some ways — he would try to ensure that any new play had a massive part written into it for himself, no matter what else it contained. While he based himself with his father-in-law, he was not averse, apparently, to putting in guest appearances in other companies when it suited him.

In 1597 he sold his stock in Henslowe's company but retained his shareholding, and he began buying land outside London. He dropped out of regular appearances, but would play by special request from royalty or the City — he was one of the few players who seem to have had City approval. He played a leading part in the pageant put on to welcome James I to London. He played the Genius of the City. (He was later to bait a lion before James at the Tower!)

After joining his father-in-law in 1605 as Master of the Bears (he also became a churchwarden of St Saviour's), he bought land in Dulwich, where he set about establishing a Foundation to ensure his lasting fame. It took him fourteen years to set up almshouses, a Chapel (which was consecrated by the Archbishop of Canterbury) and finally the school and College which still exist today. The consecration of the Chapel on 1 September 1616 prompted the playwright Thomas Dekker — during one of his periodical sentences in prison for debt — to write asking him for assistance, saying

> It best becomes me to sing anything in praise of charity, because albeit, I have felt few hands warm through their complexion, yet imprisonment may make me long for them.
>
> If anything in my Eulogium or praise of you and your noble act be offensive, let it be excused, because I live among Goths and Vandals, where barbarousness is predominant. Accept my will, however, and me ready to do you any service
> THOMAS DEKKER

In June 1623 Joan Alleyn died, and within six months Alleyn had married again. This time he chose a girl young enough to be his daughter, Constance, the daughter of John Donne the poet and Dean of St Paul's, who was younger than his new son-in-law. The relationship between the two men does not appear to have been a happy one, to put it mildly. Constance was refused a dowry, Alleyn refused a loan, he was told not to visit the house, and he was expected to support

Constance's sister too. Constance was refused her mother's rings, childbed linen and her favourite horse.

Alleyn died in 1626 leaving, as he had hoped, a lasting memorial in the form of Dulwich College, a remarkable achievement for an actor. It had cost him, along with the almshouses, £10,000 — a colossal sum for the time. He died worth about six times as much as Shakespeare, who was also considered a warm man. He was respectable and respected, even if he never received the affection accorded to Richard Burbage. He lacked only a knighthood: it was to be nearly three hundred years before an actor was to receive such an honour.

Alleyn seems to have been an actor whose style might be compared to that of Kemble, or possibly Macready. Richard Burbage was altogether more flexible and versatile, and was also known to be a better ensemble player as he did not hog the limelight to such an extent.

He was born about 1567, and with his father already established in the theatre, it is not surprising he went straight into it as a boy player. By the time he was thirteen his brother Cuthbert says he was 'brilliant', presumably in women's roles. He was a man of a different mould to Alleyn in other ways too. He had little interest in building up property and investments outside the theatre; theatre was his life. He also combined the roles of leading actor and what would today be termed director/administrator of his company. He seems to have been very well liked by his actors.

It was said of him: 'He was a delightful Proteus [in *Two Gentlemen of Verona*], so wholly transforming himself into his part and putting off himself with his clothes as he never (not so much as in the tiring house) assumed himself again until the play was done.'

For him Shakespeare wrote his marvellous roles, beginning with Richard III — all the Kings, Hamlet, Othello, Macbeth, King Lear. He had no need to commission hack writers to ensure he had the best part. Also, we know he played leading roles in many plays by Shakespeare's contemporaries. When the company gave Ben Jonson's *Every Man in His Humour* both Burbage and Shakespeare played leading parts.

He was a happily married man with children and he was enormously popular with audiences. He died on 13 March 1618, and the first four lines of an anonymous Elegy sum up what was felt of him:

> The Play now ended, think his grave to be
> The retiring house of his sad Tragedie,
> Where to give his fame this, be not afraid,
> Here lies the best Tragedian ever played.

While these two men overshadowed all the rest, there were plenty of other excellent actors working at the same time. Of some we know a little, like Nathan Field who made the difficult transition from the Children's Companies to the adult stage (he died a bachelor, with a tremendous reputation for womanizing). Some, like Gabriel Spencer, are remembered for other reasons. He seems to have been a good actor but a difficult and unpleasant man, and after numerous fights and duels — in one of which he killed a man — he was in turn killed by Ben Jonson.

The players of the time worked very hard. They appeared in every play — that is, six performances a week — and in a different play every time. We know how remarkable Middleton's *Game at Chess* was because it was played for nine performances in a row: something hitherto unheard of. Actors were expected to be able to sing, dance, fence and mime (there was a series of set gestures for mime) and project themselves out to a noisy and restive audience and hold its attention. There is no doubt that they were true professionals.

So it is a fine day in summer, say, of 1599 and you want to go to a play. You would find out, possibly from handbills, what was on where. Would you fancy *A Chaste Maid in Cheapside* by Master Middleton, at the Swan? *Tamburlaine* by Master Marlowe at the Rose? *Richard III* by Master Shakespeare at the Globe? You would have to cross the River, of course. One hour before the performance was due to commence a flag would be run up the flagpole of the theatre and a trumpeter standing on the platform of the 'hut' would sound a fanfare, as he would each quarter of an hour until the start.

You might walk across London Bridge or, more likely, take a boat after arguing about the fare with the waterman. John Taylor, the water poet, had worked to try to get some kind of licensing system for boatmen, with a set fare and conditions of carriage (rather like today's London taxis). Watermen were notorious for being rude, and Taylor says 'if a railing knave do chance to abuse his fare, either in words or deeds, as indeed we have too many such, should the whole company be scandalized for it?'

Having crossed the river and decided what to see, you would possibly buy some bottle-ale you had filled from the tavern's casks and some food or fruit (you can always throw the latter at the actors if the play is poor . . .). You stroll up to the theatre along the Bankside, possibly through gardens, and join the crowd going in through the door, where you pay your penny for admittance. If that is all you can afford you jostle and push for the best standing place close to the stage. You will be shoved aside by those seeking other people, trying to move you out of their sightlines, or by those selling oranges or posies. Pickpockets would be very active and unless you were very naïve you would hold tightly on to your purse and any other belongings of value. If you had a little more money you would buy a gallery place, or even have a seat, especially if you were escorting a lady. If you remained standing and were a young man you would probably be propositioned by ladies of doubtful reputation trying to make assignations among the audience for after the show.

You would pass the time waiting for the play to begin by having a good look round, perhaps admiring the paintings of moons, suns and stars on 'the heavens' if you were standing by the stage, or the simulated marble effect of the woodwork inside the building. You would note which prominent citizens were sitting with their wives — or is that lady his wife? — in the galleries, and how well they were dressed. If a nobleman and his entourage entered (usually late) it was all part of the entertainment. Who was it, who was with him, how fashionably was he dressed, how did he behave?

Behind the scenes the actors would be making up and donning their elaborate costumes, assisted by dressers. The 'bookman' might be having a last run through with some. The bookman read the whole 'book' to the actors before rehearsals started so that they would know where their individual parts fitted into the scheme of things (there were no such things as complete scripts for actors in those days), and he also acted as prompter during performances. They might be discussing stage business. Some playwrights, like Middleton, gave detailed stage instructions; others left it entirely to the players.

After the last trumpet-call the play would be ready to start, and you would expect to see an actor emerge to give the prologue, followed by the induction in those plays which had one — this often gave a brief résumé of the plot, as there were no programmes or programme notes then. But possibly just as he was about to start a couple of young men would swagger on stage with stools, make a fuss about sitting down and possibly call out to their friends in other parts of the house. Finally, however, the play would get under way.

As an Elizabethan, or later as a Jacobean, you would be used to audiences which talked, became restless, hostile if they did not like the show, and generally moved around. It took a good play and fine actors to hold the attention right through. There do not seem to have been intervals in those days. You might have to stand in some discomfort for a very long time if you chose *Tamburlaine* or *Hamlet*. If you were in the open area of the theatre you might well be showered with rain. Going to the theatre at its most basic required stamina.

It perhaps should be pointed out here that the new Swan Theatre at Stratford is not, nor could it be, an exact replica of the old Swan. The Stratford Swan has had to be fitted into the framework of an existing building, the auditorium of the old Memorial theatre which had been used as a rehearsal room. Happily, it was the right shape. Nor can it be open to the sky as was the original. Open-air productions of classics can be a true nightmare in the British climate, as those who run the Open Air Theatre at Regent's Park and the Minack Theatre in Cornwall know only too well.

Nor would most of today's audiences be happy to stand for about three hours, packed together, and without an interval. . . . So the new theatre has 430 seats. The architect Michael Reardon has designed a Jacobean-type auditorium to fit inside the old building with a raised roof inside which there is something the old Swan certainly would not have had — a rehearsal room. The auditorium, however, does follow the old plan of the Jacobean Theatre with a large apron stage surrounded by tiers of seats on three sides. As it is not open to the sky it will have basic lighting and sound. Compared to the old Swan it will be very comfortable. There do not appear to be any plans to introduce bear-baiting on the nights when there are no plays . . . that would, one feels, be carrying realism a little too far.

To return to the theatre of Shakespeare and Jonson, if you were lucky (and you stood a good chance of being so) you would see a fine play, well acted in the best tradition of the time. The acting style might seem difficult to accept today, for it must — because of the physical nature of the theatre — have been very declamatory, and therefore somewhat static. The daylight too would have made illusion more difficult. There would have been little attempt at realism in costume; the plays of the period were all acted in 'modern dress', with perhaps a trimming or prop to suggest Ancient Rome, medieval Scotland or classical Greece. At the end, if you were happy, you would warmly applaud and then enjoy the jig. If you were making a day of it and could afford it, then you would go on to the tavern or ordinary for a drink and a meal before taking the boat home.

But companies, theatres and players — audiences, too — were dependent on one essential, the playwright. It is to him we now turn.

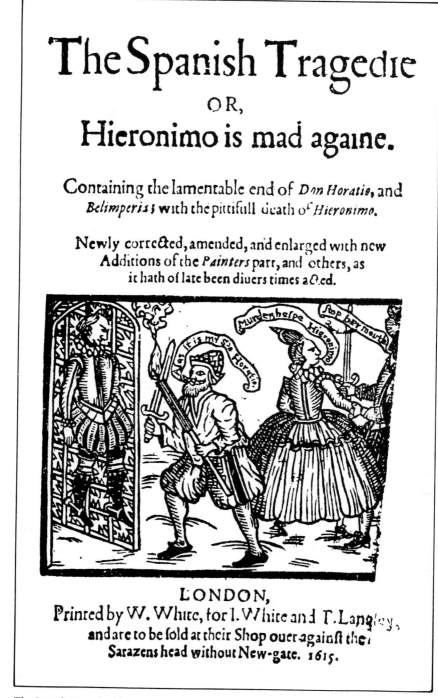

The Spanish Tragedie

OR,

Hieronimo is mad againe.

Containing the lamentable end of *Don Horatio*, and
Belimperia; with the pittifull death of *Hieronimo*.

Newly corre&ed, amended, and enlarged with new
Additions of the *Painters* part, and others, as
it hath of late been diuers times a&ed.

LONDON,
Printed by W. White, for I. White and T. Langley,
and are to be sold at their Shop ouer against the
Sarazens head without New-gate. 1615.

The Spanish Tragedy *title-page*

Chapter 2

Greene, Peele, Chapman & Kyd

Robert Greene

*'. . . no place would please me to abide in
nor no vocation cause me to stay myself in.'*

In September 1592 a man lay dying in a poor lodging-house in the area we know now as the South Bank in London. There were few to mourn him. He had driven away many of those who might have helped him or been of comfort to him by his own behaviour, and one account says that his last deathbed visitor was the sister of a highwayman recently hanged at Tyburn who wanted a name for the child which she claimed was his.

Robert Greene was born in Norwich about 1560. We have no precise date. His parents, he said, 'were respected for their gravity and honest life'. Like many of the Elizabethan and Jacobean playwrights, he was a clever grammar-school boy and he went on to matriculate at St John's College, Cambridge, on 6 November 1575. He then took his Bachelor of Arts, also at Cambridge, before going to Oxford to acquire an MA. He was to remain extremely proud of having attended both universities. He would seem to have been set for a bright future.

After leaving Oxford he went abroad and travelled extensively on the Continent. We know he visited Italy, Spain, Poland and Denmark, and we also know, from his own account, that he threw himself whole-heartedly into wine and women, if not song, and led a dissolute life. He was unable to settle down when he returned to England, and wrote 'At my return I ruffled out in my silks in the habit of a malcontent and seemed so discontent that no place would please me to abide in nor no vocation cause me to stay myself in.' He lived first in London and began to write, his *Mamillia* having been entered on the Stationers' Register as early as 30 October 1580.

By 1586, though, he appears to have been back living in Norwich, possibly with his parents. While there he courted and married a young 'gentleman's daughter' from Lincolnshire, and for a while he seems to have tried to settle down with her in that city. She bore him a daughter, and shortly after Greene left her, having by that time spent all her dowry. The lady — addressed by him later as 'Doll' — returned to her family and friends in Lincolnshire with his child, and Greene settled down for the rest of his short life in London, to be joined later by his friend Thomas Nashe.

'I deserted her', he said of his wife, 'because she tried to reform me.'

Greene has acquired a notorious reputation over the years, which he himself did a good deal to promote (the *Dictionary of National Biography* describes him as being 'singularly vicious'). Yet many of his contemporaries were more charitable.

Chettle described Greene's appearance as being 'of face amiable, of body well proportioned, his attire after the habit of a scholar-like gentleman, only his hair rather long'. He did indeed wear his red hair long, and pulled into a kind of peak which must have looked somewhat bizarre, as Nashe says that he also sported a beard which was long and red and peaked like the spire of a steeple, which 'he cherished continually without cutting, whereat a man might hang a jewel it was so sharp and pendant'. Looking like that he would hardly seem out of place among the punk fashions on the King's Road of the 1980s.

Nashe also said of him that 'while he had little regard for the credit in which he stood with any notorious crimes [criminals], I never knew him tainted' and 'that in a night and a day he would have jacked up a pamphlet as well as in seven years; and glad was the printer that might be so blessed to pay him dear for the very dregs of his wit'.

He wrote prolifically and with exuberance. Pamphlets and romances poured from his pen in abundance, he wrote for the theatre and he turned his talent to social commentaries of the times which, as Dr A. L. Rowse suggests, were the forerunners of today's popular journalism. When it came to writing plays, Greene turned away from the world in which he found himself and wrote gentle romances and sunny comedies.

Yet while he was writing about long-suffering damsels and stout yeomen, his own life was spent among people of a very different kind. Describing himself (thinly disguised as a playmaking poet called Roberto), he says 'his company were lightly the lewdest persons in the land, apt for pilfery, perjury, forgery or any villainy. Of these he knew the casts to cog at cards, cozen at Dice; by these he learnt the legerdemains of nips, foists, coney-catchers, cross-biters, lifts, high lawyers, and all the rabble of that unclean generation of vipers.' Greene certainly seems to have been one of those unfortunate people who programme themselves to self-destruct.

In his capacity of playwright we know he must have been very popular, for Henslowe's *Diary* records that *Friar Bacon and Friar Bungay* and *George a Green, The Pinner of Wakefield*, were performed frequently to audiences which obviously found them highly entertaining. While Greene was prepared to pay his drinks bill by warning people about those who were out to con them, he was not averse to tryng it himself from time to time, and he made himself a talking point by selling his play *Orlando Furioso* to a theatre company for twenty nobles and then, when they had gone off touring round the country with it, selling it again to Henslowe as a new play, for the same amount. Henslowe's Lord Admiral's Men gave it its first performance on 21 February 1591 — the first performance that they were aware of, that is . . .

Towards the end of his life he turned to writing more quick pamphlets on the kind of scandalous topic much loved by some of today's Sunday papers. It obviously brought him in ready money. In *A Notable Discovery of Cosenage, Conie-catchers and Crossbiters* he described the low life of London and all the tricks of the trade, and how to avoid being conned. 'Crossbiting' seems to be a version of what became known in more recent times as the 'badger game'. A whore would take a man to bed with her, and then another man, posing as her husband, would burst in and confront them. The unfortunate client would then be blackmailed into paying out a large sum to placate the angry 'husband' or even to prevent his being physically assaulted. (He might even be co-opted as a spy!) At least in those days nobody could take photographs as well and then send them on to the man's wife (if he had one).

It is apparent that by the end of the summer of 1592 Greene's health was deteriorating rapidly. Various sources say he died of 'dissipation', and we can speculate that this meant either venereal disease or that drink had destroyed him. We know that immediately before his death he was made ill after a supper of 'pickled herrings and Rhenish wine'.

The now notorious pamphlet the *Groatsworth of Wit* and other deathbed repentances were all supposed to have been written after that fatal supper, but it seems more likely that Greene took to public and emotional repentance during his last weeks. Even his facility to dash off a piece of fast prose would have been stretched had he been suffering from acute and terminal food poisoning at the time. In the pamphlet Greene attacked a number of fellow-playwrights, was very rude to Marlowe, turned and rent the actors who had after all performed his own works, but reserved the full force of his venom for the new and up-and-coming talent of William Shakespeare. By this time Shakespeare would have finished *Love's Labour's Lost*, all three parts of *Henry VI*, *The Comedy of Errors* and *The Two Gentlemen of Verona*.

Greene, dying in poverty, turned sourly on those he felt had unfairly been more successful than him, and he saw actors as merely parasites, feeding off the talents of their betters. Shakespeare, as both an actor and a writer, seems to have enraged him most, while Greene, always conscious of his own high academic qualifications, also despised those who had not taken their degrees and were not, therefore, 'university wits'. He wrote:

> for unto none of you, like me, sought these burrs [players] to cleave; those puppets, I mean, that spake from our mouths, those antics garnished in our

colours. Is it not strange that I, to whom they all have been beholding, shall — were ye in that case as I am in now — be both at once of them forsaken? Yea, trust them not: for there is an upstart crow, beautified with our feathers, that with his 'Tiger's heart wrapped in a player's hide', supposes he is as well able to bombast out a blank verse as the best of you and being an absolute Johannes Fac totum, is in his own conceit the only Shake-scene in a country.

In the same pamphlet Greene has his hero, 'Roberto', meet with an actor who is obviously comfortably off and well dressed, with a voice which is 'nothing gracious', who is portrayed by Greene as an arrogant vain fool and who is also described as 'a country Author passing at a Moral', which is again taken to refer to Shakespeare. Greene must by now have been only too aware that he had wasted his life and his talent, and so turned and rent the man who, without having had the benefits of what Greene considered to be an essential academic education, was already held in such high esteem. He was bitterly jealous.

Chettle, making his famous apology after seeing the pamphlet through the printers, says he was unjust to Shakespeare because 'myself have seen his demeanour no less civil than he excellent in the quality he professes, besides divers of worship have reported his uprightness of dealing, which argues his honesty, and his facetious grace in writing that approves his art'. Later, in a play called *Kind Heart's Dream*, he had the ghost of Greene return to apologize in person. It certainly shows how Shakespeare's contemporaries regarded him even in those early days.

The main account of Greene's death comes from Dr Gabriel Harvey, the Cambridge academic. He and Greene disliked each other. Some sources say Greene died at the home of his last mistress, who had borne him the child Fortunatus. Harvey says he died in the lodgings of a poor shoemaker and his wife, who had to look after Greene as best they could. According to Harvey, Greene's only deathbed visitors were two women, one of them a former mistress and 'sister to the rogue known as Cutting Ball who had lately been hanged at Tyburn', who was the mother of his bastard son Fortunatus Greene (who died a year later, in 1593). The lady had arrived demanding recognition for her bastard child.

Also according to Harvey, Greene gave a bond of £10 to his landlord and then wrote to the estranged wife whom he had not seen for six years 'Doll — I charge thee for the love of our youth and by my soul's rest that thou wilt see this man paid, for if he and his wife had not succoured me I had died in the streets — Robert Greene'.

Tradition has it that his landlady covered his body with garlands of bay before he was taken to be buried the next day in the New Churchyard next to Bethlehem Hospital.

He left behind work which was to influence many of the playwrights he so much despised, and, ironically, one of his most accomplished romances, *Pandosto*, furnished the 'upstart crow' with the plot for *The Winter's Tale*.

George Peele

'. . . driven as myself to extreme shifts.'

In many ways the life of George Peele parallels that of his friend and drinking companion, Robert Greene. He, like Greene, seemed to be destined for a successful career and he, also like Greene, came to a sad end.

There are no firm dates for Peele but it is thought he was born some time in 1558, and was on that basis two years older than Greene. It is not certain when he died. His last known work was a tribute to the Earl of Southampton written in 1594, after which he disappears entirely from history. We know that by 1598 he was dead.

Peele's family came to London from Devonshire, and George's father was a city salter and the clerk to Christ's Hospital. Because of this he was given a property belonging to it in which to live. He was obviously of great value in his position as clerk, as he both taught book-keeping and wrote about it and is credited with introducing the Italian system of book-keeping into this country.

Because of his father's connections, young George was a 'free scholar' at Christ's Hospital, and a bright one. In 1571 he entered what was then called Broadgates Hall (now Pembroke College), Oxford, to matriculate, and remained at Oxford, taking his BA in 1577 and his MA in 1579. He was esteemed as both a poet and a playwright while still at university. His first published work, while still at college, was *A Tale of Troy*, and most interestingly (as it makes a link between the Greek dramatists and those of the Elizabethan age) he translated the *Iphigenia* of Euripides and saw to its performance at Christ Church, Oxford. From what one can gather he did work hard, but also managed a lively social life as well.

Towards the end of his university career, however, the social life seems to have taken over, and he ended his stay in debt. The Governors of Christ's Hospital had already contributed £5 to his BA fees (presumably because he could not find the money himself), and shortly after Peele's return to London we see that on 19 September 1579 they bound over his father 'to discharge his house before Michaelmas of his son, George Peele, and all other of his household which have been chargeable to him'. One can only infer that George had brought his rowdy lifestyle home to Christ's Hospital with him, and that this did not go down well with the governing body.

Turned out from his father's house, he embarked on what biographers describe primly as 'a life of dissipation', although it is also obvious that he still worked hard. His first-known play, *The Arraignment of Paris*, was put on in 1581, and he seems then to have also turned to the acting profession, and is said to have been successful at it. He played in Henslowe's Company, the Lord Admiral's Men, for some time, but left in 1589 and joined the Queen's Men. He is also said to have played outside London, and appeared in plays in Bristol and Cambridge. During his time with Henslowe, in 1583, he returned to Oxford to help stage two plays, a comedy called *The Rivals* and *The Tragedy of Dido*.

About this time he married for money, and in this too he was rather like Greene. The lady brought with her a dowry of land and a little property. Peele's plays were quite varied in subject matter and style and he was an accomplished poet, able to write rhyme with ease, so that he earned a steady living turning out verses for literary patrons. Nashe very kindly describes him as 'the Atlas of poetry' — he also said he was 'the chief supporter of pleasaunce now living' — but one example of Peele's ability is quite amusing. In the May of 1591 Elizabeth visited Burghley, and Peele was specially commissioned to write speeches in her honour, 'deftly excusing the absence of the master of the house'.

The one play of Peele's which has come down to us more or less as he seems to have written it is the *Old Wives' Tale*, a comedy we will look at later. He wrote a patriotic play, *The Battle of Alcazar*; a biblical drama, *The Love of King David and Fair Bethsabe* [Bathsheba]; and made an attempt at what was to be a popular entertainment, the historical play, with *Edward I*. There are also a number of lost plays, and he is credited with *The Life and Death of Jack Straw*, *The Hunting of Cupid* (which at one time was in the possession of the Scots poet William Drummond of Hawthornden, who was later to write so feelingly about Ben Jonson) and is also said to have been the author of *The Troublesome Reign of King John*, on which Shakespeare based his play, and possibly to have collaborated with Shakespeare on the first part of *Henry VI*.

Most of his working life was spent living on the Bankside, and we know he had a daughter who lived at least until she was ten. There must have been something a trifle odd about Peele, as he was described by a contemporary as having a strange voice that made him appear 'more woman than man'.

In 1598 Francis Meres wrote in his *Wit's Treasury* that Peele had died of 'a loathsome disease'. In a strange way, he lived on after his death. Such was his notoriety that as late as 1605 he was credited with a compilation of extravagant jokes called *Merry Conceited Jests: of George Peele Gentleman, sometime a Student at Oxford*. In 1607 he appeared in a play, thinly disguised as George Pieboard, a 'peel' being a baker's board used for shoving pies into an oven.

During his orgy of death-bed repentance, Greene had beseeched his friend to mend his ways. After mentioning Marlowe and Nashe, he had written 'and thou, no less deserving than the other two, in some things rarer, in nothing inferior — driven as myself to extreme shifts, a little have I to say to thee: and were it not an idolatrous oath, I would swear by sweet St. George, thou art unworthy better hap, since thou dependest on so mean a stay.'

George Chapman

'. . . a gentleman, Mr George Chapman,
a learned and honest man.'

In the early autumn of 1605 a gentleman who was respected as a poet, playwright, soldier, philosopher and a translator of Homer found himself in a prison cell along with Ben Jonson. The story properly belongs to Jonson, and concerns a play, *Eastward Ho!*, on which the two men had collaborated with Marston, and it will be dealt with more fully in the account of Jonson's life. But it does show that playwriting could be a risky business, and a play which might have the audience rolling in the aisles at its portrayal of recognizable people at the Court of the day might be considered much less funny by those at the receiving end of the joke.

George Chapman seems an unlikely person to have found himself in such a predicament compared with many of his contemporaries. He led a respectable and sedate life, was for some years under the patronage of the young Prince Henry, and his biggest problems seem to have been financial ones. He was to be hag-ridden with debt for most of his life.

He was born in Hitchin in Hertfordshire in about 1560, the son of Thomas and Joan Chapman. He was the grandson of a George Nodes, sergeant to the buckhounds to Henry VIII, and of Margaret Grimeston, through whom he was related to the historian Edward Grimeston. He was one of five surviving children, with an elder brother and three sisters, all of whom lived into adulthood and later married.

Although there is plenty of material available recording details of the wide variety of works he wrote and published, there is much less known about his life. He apparently went up to Oxford, but if he took a degree there is no record of it. He then entered the service of Sir Ralph Sadler, and apparently served him as a soldier in the Low Countries. By 1585 he was living in London, but still in Sadler's service, and seems to have divided his time between soldiering and writing and translation. It was during his time in London in 1585 that he borrowed heavily from a notorious moneylender called John Wolfall. The debt was to haunt him for the next twenty years of his life.

He had been writing poetry since first coming to London, and was also part of the select philosophical circle whose leading members were Sir Walter Raleigh and the mathematician Thomas Harriot. This does not seem to have involved him in the kind of problems such membership was to cause Christopher Marlowe, however. We do not know what drew him to the theatre, but by 1596 he had attached himself to the Lord Admiral's Company and was writing prolifically for Henslowe. There are a number of references to him in Henslowe's *Diary*; we know that in 1596 he wrote a play called *The Blind Beggar of Alexandria*, and in 1599 there is a receipt: 'Received by me, George Chapman, for a Pastoral, ending in a part payment the sum of 40s this 17 July 1599.' Most of Chapman's plays for

George Chapman

Henslowe during these years were pastorals and comedies, and many of them are now lost.

In that same year of 1599 the dreaded John Wolfall seems finally to have caught up with him. Presumably Chapman had failed to meet his promised repayments, and Wolfall had him thrown into the Counter Prison for debt. Whatever caused his money problems, they were not brought about by laziness, for as well as writing plays and poetry, finishing Marlowe's unfinished *Hero and Leander*, and collaborating with other playwrights, in 1598 he had published his translation of the first seven books of the *Iliad*.

He does not seem to have been in prison long, however, although this was not the last he was to hear of this debt. He began on a series of tragedies, set in the French court of the previous century, but by this time (in the early 1600s) he was no longer attached to Henslowe, and appears to have been working as a freelance.

In 1605 came the scandal over *Eastward Ho!* and poor Chapman found himself once again in gaol. That he had excellent contacts is shown by the letters he wrote from prison to the King and the Lord Chamberlain. While they are suitably contrite and flowery (though nothing like as obsequious and full of flannel as those of Ben Jonson, writing at the same time), they are the letters of someone who knows he has a reasonable case to make. But writing plays could still get him into trouble, and in 1609 it appears he was having problems over his play *The Conspiracy and Tragedy of Charles, Duke of Biron*, which had upset the French Ambassador. In 1607 had appeared perhaps his most famous play, also with a French theme — *Bussy d'Ambois*, a sanguinary story that would be used much later by Dumas in *Chicot the Jester* and *The Forty-Five Guardsmen*.

At that time Chapman had as his patron the young Prince Henry, and under that patronage the complete *Iliad* was published. Chapman had been promised a life pension by the King, but the promise died with the young prince in 1612, and Chapman never received it. It seems Prince Charles was much less interested in Chapman and his work, and once again we find him in deep financial trouble. As late as 1608 he was still being pursued over the original debt to Wolfall from 1585, the pursuit having been taken over by Wolfall's son. Chapman had had to approach the Lord Chancellor with a special petition.

Chapman seems more or less to have stopped writing for the theatre after 1612. He did write a dramatic entertainment for his new patron, Somerset, in 1614 on the occasion of the latter's marriage, but turned his attention thereafter to translating. He published first twelve books of the *Odyssey*, then the whole work and, finally, the complete works of Homer.

After their publication he had a quarrel with Ben Jonson, most probably over his scholarship. Jonson wrote a criticism of Chapman's translation in the margin of a copy of *The Whole Works of Homer* which is in the Fitzwilliam Museum. Most people do seem to have fallen out with Jonson at one time or another.

Chapman then fades almost entirely from the scene. His last published work was in 1629, and he died on 12 May 1634, and was buried in the churchyard of St Giles in the Fields in a tomb designed by his friend Inigo Jones. The title of that 1629 publication of his is recorded as *A Justification of a Strange Action of Nero in burying with a Solemn Funeral one of the Cast Hairs of his Mistress Poppaea; Also a just reproof of a Roman smell-feast, being the fifth satire of Juvenal translated.* This shows the recondite themes that could occupy certain working playwrights!

Thomas Kyd

'bitter times and privy broken passions.'

On either 11 or 12 May 1593, and possibly during the night, a young man was bundled out of his lodgings, taken to Bridewell prison and tortured on the rack. The last two weeks of May of that year are lit with a lurid glow which casts a dim light even now, four hundred years later. For the young man on the rack was the writer of the single most popular play to be seen on the stage in London, Thomas Kyd, and he was being tortured to try to make him incriminate the foremost poet and playwright of his time, Christopher Marlowe.

What might have brought Marlowe's own life to its final crisis during that period of time will be dealt with in the chapter on Marlowe, but in those last days of May the lives of Kyd and Marlowe are inextricably linked.

There was nothing in Thomas Kyd's life before this to lead anyone to believe he might suffer such a dreadful fate. He was no famous drunkard, no swaggerer around the taverns, no meddler in Court intrigue, nor was his work, from what we know of it, likely to cause him trouble and land him in prison for its political content (which was the fate of some of his contemporaries). Compared with Greene, Peele, Marlowe himself and those coming later, Ben Jonson, Middleton, Dekker, he was incredibly respectable.

He was born in London in 1558 and christened at the Church of St Mary Woolnoth on 6 November, eleven days before Queen Elizabeth ascended the throne. He was the son of Francis Kyd, like Milton's father a scrivener (or copyist), writer of the Court letter of London and a Freeman of the Company of Scriveners. His mother Anna was the legatee of a publisher.

He went to the Merchant Taylors School in London at the age of seven. It was a new grammar school, and its headmaster, Dr Richard Mulcaster, was a formidable scholar with a real interest in drama. Modern languages as well as classical featured on the curriculum, and Kyd knew some French, Italian and Spanish as well as Greek and Latin. He does not appear to have gone on to either Oxford or Cambridge, although Merchant Taylors school had forty-three scholarship places reserved at St John's, Oxford. It seems most likely that he became a scrivener like his father, and certainly there is a suggestion that this was the case. He also seems to have spent some time as a tutor and as a secretary. His life is obscure except for its last dramatic months.

He attached himself to the Queen's Company soon after it was formed on 10 March 1583. We know that by 15 June the company was touring in Norwich, and that three actors, Bentley, Singer and the famous clown Tarlton, were involved in a brawl there. Possibly Kyd contributed to some of the early and lost plays of that company, such as *The Famous Victories of Henry V*. He is also a strong contender for the author of the early version of *Hamlet*. Writing in 1589, the poet and playwright Nashe satirized Kyd, saying:

> Yet English Seneca, read by candlelight, yields many good sentences, as "Blood is a beggar" and so forth: and if you entreat him fair in a frosty morning, he will afford you whole *Hamlets*, I should say handfuls of tragical speeches . . . the sea exhaled by drops will in continuance be dry, and Seneca, let blood line by line and page by page, at length must needs die for our stage, which makes his famished followers to imitate the Kid in Aesop, who, enamoured with the Fox's newfangles, forsook all hopes of life to leap into a new occupation.

This, coupled with his description of the playwright concerned as a 'noverint' or scrivener, must refer to Kyd.

Earlier, in 1585, Kyd seems to have entered the service of a lord, and it has been suggested that this might be the Earl of Sussex. Presumably it was here he did a certain amount of secretarial work to subsidize his playwriting. Kyd wrote poetry and pamphlets, but very little of his work remains. About 1587 he wrote *The Spanish Tragedy*, and this, the first of what were to be known as the 'Revenge Plays' proper, was the most tremendous success, and was to remain so well into the next century. It seems most violent and bloodthirsty now, but after all, Kyd was writing at a time when bear-baiting was as popular as the theatre, and when people found entertainment in public executions.

The first actual recorded performance of the play appears in Henslowe's *Diary* as 14 March 1592, but it was obviously not its first production. The 1602 Quarto added certain passages; Henslowe records payments to Jonson for additions to the play in 1602, but the printed additions were perhaps written for its 1597 revival. From then on it appeared regularly both in Henslowe's repertoire and in those of another three companies, as well as being performed in Holland and Germany. Kyd had every reason to believe he was set for a successful career.

In 1591 Marlowe and Kyd shared a work-room. There is nothing to lead us to believe the two men did not get on, even if they did not share a similar lifestyle, and presumably they worked together amicably. The alleged reason for Kyd's arrest will also be dealt with in the Marlowe chapter, but basically it came about because the authorities were annoyed at 'malicious libels' concerning foreign refugees, such as the Huguenots and Dutch, which were being posted around London. These were unpleasant, and a present-day analogy would be the 'Wogs Go Home' signs sprayed on walls in inner-city centres. It hardly seems likely that the authorities really thought that a respectable playwright — possibly still in the service of a member of the aristocracy, and with a popular play running in London — would devote his time to writing crude and jingoistic slogans and pasting them up on walls. But it gave those who wanted to use them powers of search, and it was under these powers that they searched Kyd's work-room.

Also under the instructions on the libels sent out by the Privy Council is one saying that those who might be responsible should be taken into custody, and which continues in chilling tone:

> And after you shall have examined the persons, if you shall find them duly to be suspected and they shall refuse to confess the truth, you shall by the authority hereof put them to the torture in Bridewell and by the extremity thereof draw them to discover the knowledge concerning the said libels.
> We pray you herein to use your uttermost travail and endeavour . . .

Somebody had decided to destroy Marlowe, and as part of the plan the innocent and apolitical Kyd was brought in. Marlowe's movements, lodgings and friends over the past few years must have been well known to Walsingham's secret agents, so by a remarkable 'coincidence' Kyd's rooms were searched for proof of his writing what might now be called 'racist' material, and there was found a pamphlet which could be considered blasphemous. This was the perfect reason to arrest Kyd, and those that did so had carte blanche to try to drag from the unfortunate poet what they wanted to know.

Certainly in his 'extremitie' (as he later described it himself) Kyd told his torturers that the pamphlet belonged to Marlowe, and thus set going the sequence of events which was to result in the latter's murder some two weeks later, and before that, within days, in his arrest.

Kyd was in a nightmare position. The ultimate horror for most people is to imagine having to suffer torture, but the ultimate refinement of this is to be tortured for what you truly do not know, by those who are determined to make you reveal the truth. No wonder poor Kyd accused Marlowe of all kinds of blasphemies, from the serious to the ridiculous. We do not know what Marlowe was told when he was arrested six days later, whether he even knew Kyd was in prison or if Kyd had said anything at all. During the weeks that followed, deep in his cell in Bridewell, did Kyd think that somehow Marlowe had said something about him which had resulted in his arrest? Presumably he was told when Marlowe died. He certainly had time to ponder as he lay under the threat of a capital charge, weakened by torture, no doubt in appalling conditions, and all for reasons he could not understand, knowing himself to be innocent.

By 30 May Marlowe was dead. Scholars dispute whether the pathetic letters Kyd wrote to Sir John Puckering, Keeper of the Great Seal of England and effectual head of the Privy Council, were written from prison or after he came out. It would seem more likely they were written from gaol in a frantic attempt to get the charges dropped and the writer released.

In the first Kyd explains why he was arrested.

> When I was first suspected for that libel that concerned the state, amongst those waste and idle papers (which I cared not for) and which unasked I did deliver up, were found some fragments of a disputation touching that opinion, affirmed by Marlowe to be his, and shuffled with some of mine (unknown to me) by some occasion of our writing in one chamber two years since.

There then follows a diatribe against the dead Marlowe.

> . . . that I should love or be familiar friend with one so irreligious were very
> rare.

He did not like slandering the dead but

> thus much have I dared in the greatest cause which is to clear myself of being
> thought an Atheist which some swear he was.

Kyd's second letter to Sir John, possibly trying harder to persuade him, sets out some of the same allegations to be made by the double agent and informer Richard Baines, that Marlowe said St John and Jesus had a homosexual relationship, that St Paul was a 'juggler' (or fraud), that 'things esteemed to be done by divine power might well have been done by observation of men' and so on. Finally, and perhaps frantically, Kyd threw in a little treason for good measure. 'He would persuade with men of quality to go to the King of Scots' and that he, Marlowe, had told Kyd he intended to go too 'if he lived'.

Little of it could have been of any value, and anyway by that time Marlowe had ceased to be any kind of a threat. His fate had been decided earlier when poor Kyd proved, at terrible cost, that he had nothing to tell. He is the least likely figure to have been involved in a political conspiracy, and while one cannot blame those who 'name names' under dreadful duress, it does seem that Kyd truly had nothing to say.

He must have come out of prison a broken man, and he was certainly very poor. On 26 January 1594 — nine months after his arrest — his play *Pompey the Great, his Fair Cornelia's Tragedy* was registered at Stationers' Hall. It was a translation from the French of Robert Garnier, and it was dedicated to the Countess of Sussex. In his dedication Kyd speaks of the afflictions of mind, the misery and the 'bitter times and privy broken passions' of his sad life. Kyd, though out of prison, no doubt remained a marked man.

Before the year was out he was dead. While many of Shakespeare's contemporary playwrights died young, no doubt Kyd's death was hastened by the cruel treatment he had received in Bridewell. Many did not even survive the rack. He was buried on 15 August 1594, just sixteen months after Marlowe. He had never married, and he has left behind no reputation as a womanizer; there was no wife or child to mourn him. His mother, Anna, formally renounced the administration of his estate in the name of her husband, Francis, but this could possibly have been a way of his parents preventing their being pursued by their son's creditors. The other explanation, that they wanted no part in anything to do with their son, is an even less happy one.

At the end of *The Spanish Tragedy*, Hieronimo — who has already fully explained why he embarked on the series of terrible deeds which end the play — is then theatened with torture to make him tell more. Scholars have puzzled over why this should be, as Hieronimo quite obviously has no more to tell. In the event he prevents this from happening, but it is a black irony that six years before he himself was to be tortured for what he did not know, Kyd was to write a character whose fate was to be so similar.

Putative portrait of Christopher Marlowe used by permission of the Master, Fellows and Scholars of Corpus Christi, Cambridge

Chapter 3

Christopher Marlowe

'This word damnation terrifies not me . . .'

On the 30th of May 1593 a young man was killed in a brawl in a tavern in Deptford, allegedly during a quarrel over who paid the bill. Such an event would scarcely have merited any interest at all outside the circle of his own friends and family, even at the time. Certainly it would not have mattered some four hundred years later — except that the man in question was the poet and playwright Christopher Marlowe.

For the next three hundred or so years the story stood, and it was not until this century that the sequence of events was really queried and some startling discoveries were made, not the least being that it would appear that for a substantial part of his life Kit Marlowe was a member of the secret service in the pay of Elizabeth's Spymaster, Francis Walsingham.

We will look at the bizarre events surrounding Marlowe's death at the end of the chapter — events every bit as sinister and disturbing as a modern spy thriller — but before looking at Marlowe's life it is necessary to know something of the background which produced the climate in which he grew up, a climate in which spies and secret agents were to flourish.

Elizabeth had come to the throne in November 1558, just six days after the last Protestant martyrs had been burned at Smithfield. A rhyme of the times says:

Six days after these were burned to death
God sent us our Elizabeth.

She had seen enough of the fires of Smithfield and the tragic procession of men and women burned for their faith, both there and in market squares all over the country. Notes kept at the time by William Cecil show that in 1556 eighty persons were burned, 'whereof many were maidens'. In 1557 'were burned about

London above 64, whereof 20 were women'. Elizabeth stated that she did not want to see any more people suffering in such a manner for their beliefs.

Elizabeth had narrowly escaped death on at least two occasions herself. At fifteen she was accused of planning to marry her widowed step-father, Thomas Seymour, Lord High Admiral. He went to the block, and she fought a bitter battle to keep her own head, it being suggested she would have taken over the throne. Later, Elizabeth's half-sister, Mary Tudor, sent her to the Tower of London, where she entered through the notorious Traitors' Gate. Those going in through it came out in their coffins.

So sure were those attending her that she would never leave the Tower alive that when she stumbled, sat and refused to enter she was physically manhandled to get her to move on, bringing a response from an uneasy Duke of Sussex who reminded the rest that they should 'not go beyond our commission, for she was our late King's daughter and the Prince next in blood . . .' Elizabeth at one time scratched on a window pane:

> Much suspected of me,
> Nothing proved can be,
> Quoth Elizabeth, Prisoner.

So the early years of Elizabeth's reign were marked by comparative tolerance. However, by the time Marlowe was born and was growing up hostilities with Spain had dragged on for years and there had been a succession of plots to put the Catholic Mary Stuart on the throne and depose Elizabeth. Dissident Catholics were involved in plotting both for a Spanish invasion and on behalf of Mary Stuart, with the result that there was growing repression of Catholics and many innocent people were once again to suffer. It was also the kind of paranoid climate in which espionage flourishes.

Marlowe was born into an age not unlike our own, bitterly divided politically and through religion, a time of great change. Our first record of him is his baptism on 26 February 1564, two months to the day before his contemporary, William Shakespeare, was baptised in Stratford. Marlowe was christened in his parish church, St George's, Canterbury. His father, John, was a craftsman shoemaker, and his mother, Anne, came from Dover. His background in fact was rather similar to that of Shakespeare, and it is interesting to speculate that while there are all those who say a 'glover's son' could not have written the works of Shakespeare, nobody seems to deny the authenticity of those of the shoemaker's boy. (It is true, of course, that the work of the 'university wits', Marlowe among them, smacks often of Academe, and as far as we know, Shakespeare never went to university, but the main contention remains.)

His father is described as being a 'noisy, self assertive, improvident and arrogant fellow', endlessly engaged in lawsuits and usually in debt. Marlowe had three surviving sisters, two of whom were said to be not very respectable and one was described as a 'scold, common swearer and blasphemer of the name of God'. Two brothers had died in infancy.

Like Shakespeare, Marlowe went to his local grammar school, King's School,

Canterbury, which still exists. No doubt he studied a similar curriculum. The playwright John Lyly had preceded him at King's, and Lyly's father William, High Master of St Paul's, had produced a standard work on Latin grammar used in the schools. Just before his fifteenth birthday, Marlowe was elected a Queen's Scholar, and he remained at King's for another two years before going up to Cambridge to read for his degree.

Here the story takes on immediately topical overtones. Cambridge had once been considered an inferior university to Oxford, but this was no longer the case. It had embraced the Reformation with enthusiasm and was known as a hotbed of new ideas and new learning. It was an exciting place to be. It was also used as a recruiting ground for English spies.

Christopher Marlowe went up to Corpus Christi College in December 1580 on a scholarship, the Archbishop Parker Scholarship. According to Dr A. L. Rowse, the first thing we know about his arrival is a charge of one penny entered in the Buttery books for a drink after his arrival there during the second week in December. He shared a room with three other students on the ground floor, on the right-hand side of the staircase in the north-west corner of the old court.

It is now generally accepted that Marlowe was homosexual. While this was not uncommon in his day and age, any more than it is now, the practice of homosexuality was in theory a capital offence, although such punishments were rare. Whether he was aware of his proclivities before going to Cambridge we do not know. But it is interesting, as just as with Blunt, Burgess and other notorious modern spies, it did make him vulnerable to outside pressures.

From the first Marlowe's seems to have been a questing and adventurous mind. He had a fine intellect. He was a true Renaissance Man, accepting nothing without questioning it, always seeking new ideas and reading avidly. To acquire his BA, he would study rhetoric, logic and philosophy, and he seems to have been a brilliant student. At Cambridge he would see plenty of drama, both student productions and plays by travelling players. Robert Greene, the playwright, had taken his degree at Cambridge in 1580.

But there are some very odd aspects of Marlowe's time at Cambridge. He missed seven weeks of his second academic year, half a term in 1582–3 for which there is no explanation. In 1584 he took his degree and then settled down, apparently, for another three years to take his MA, and then go into Holy Orders. He spent most of his time in Cambridge, but again there are unexplained gaps when he appears to have been away. He went down for good at the end of the Lent term 1587 and applied for his MA in the usual way, but this was withheld.

He finally received it after an almost unprecedented intervention by the Privy Council of Queen Elizabeth. A statement says:

> Whereas it was reported that Christopher Marley was determined to have gone beyond the seas to Rheims, and there to remain, their Lordships thought good to certify that he had no such intent; but that in all his actions he had behaved himself orderly and discreetly, whereby he had done her Majesty good service and deserved to be rewarded for his faithful dealing.

Their lordships' request was, therefore,

> that rumour thereof should be allayed by all possible means, and that he
> should be furthered in the degree he was to take this next Commencement.
> Because it was not her Majesty's pleasure that anyone employed, as he had
> been, in matters touching the benefit of his country should be defamed by
> those that are ignorant in the affairs he went about.

So what had he been doing? Well, we do not know for sure, but at that time in
Cambridge Catholic students did drift away to the English seminary at Rheims.
(It had been founded originally in Douai by a Dr Allen, but was later moved to
Rheims.) Allen, and the members of his college, did not only support Philip II of
Spain in his proposed invasion of England but also the deposition of Elizabeth in
favour of Mary Stuart. Allen's seminary was a nest of traitors, a hotbed of
intrigue, a powerhouse for plots.

Francis Walsingham, in charge of the secret service, was a Cambridge man
known to have recruited undergraduates into the service. What better method to
find out what was happening in Rheims than to send a bright undergraduate over
there, posing as a disaffected Catholic student? From what we know of Marlowe
he would have enjoyed the intellectual game of chess involved in espionage, and
he would have revelled in the excitement. Above all, it would have amused him.
With his arrogance and natural feeling of superiority, he would have been drawn,
one feels, quite easily into Walsingham's net.

But just as today, those who once enter this shadowy world — however entic-
ing and exciting it might seem at the outset — are caught for life. There is no
going back. If you try to put it behind you, then you will remain at risk from the
opposing side and a risk to your own, because of what you know. Once there is
no more use for you, then yours is a precarious existence. It is not too far-fetched
to say that Marlowe took the first steps on the road to the Deptford Tavern while
he was still at university.

However, spying or not, he had already embarked on his literary career. He
translated works from Ovid and wrote the *Tragedy of Dido*, adapted from Virgil.
In 1587 the first part of his major work, *Tamburlaine*, was performed. We will
look at his plays separately, but it must be said here that it was immediately obvious that Marlowe's was a very great talent indeed — his 'mighty line' was born
during his Cambridge years, and by the time he had decided against taking Holy
Orders he had become the pioneer playwright of his age. Like all the other poet-
playwrights of his generation, and for the next forty years, he made for London.

He arrived on a theatrical scene brimming over with talent and excitement.
There was never a better time in the history of the English theatre to be a
playwright than in the closing years of the sixteenth century. When he arrived in
London people were flocking to the playhouses, where the most popular works
were those of Greene, Kyd and their colleagues.

At what point he first became involved with Philip Henslowe and his Lord
Admiral's Men we do not know, but he obviously appealed to a clever entrepreneur like Henslowe. However the two met, it was Henslowe who put on the

first part of *Tamburlaine*, and found he had on his hands the Elizabethan equivalent of a real hit. It was unlike anything that had been seen on the stage before, and its influence and the effect of that first production were to remain well into the next century. Whatever we may now feel about the dramatic content of *Tamburlaine*, there is no doubt that Marlowe had broken through a barrier. He was a true pioneer.

Marlowe's association with Henslowe was to remain for the rest of his life, and here he was also extremely fortunate, as in Edward Alleyn he had one of the two greatest actors of the day to portray his leading roles. (The other was Richard Burbage.)

We know too that early on in his dramatic and literary career, Marlowe had acquired a patron — Thomas Walsingham, cousin to Francis. Did he get to know him when both were employed by Walsingham? We know Francis employed his younger cousin on espionage work. Did Francis use his influence to arrange matters for Marlowe?

We know very little of how Marlowe lived. As he was immediately successful he did not have to struggle to make his way. He seemed to live among his fellow-writers, although we do not know how close he was to any of them in terms of friendship. He was considered to be both irreverent and boisterous, with a penchant for low life. He seems very like some of our contemporary writers, especially the late Colin MacInnes, who shared many of his faults and virtues. Kit Marlowe was contentious, arrogant, difficult and fiery-tempered, but also, it seems, had great charm.

On 28 September 1589 he was involved in a fight with one William Bradley in Hog Lane, in the suburb of St Giles-without-Cripplegate. Many theatrical people lived in the area — including Shakespeare — and it was also the home of a certain Robert Poley of whom we shall hear more. Bradley was the son of an innkeeper who kept the Bishop Inn on the corner of Gray's Inn Road and High Holborn. It seems the two men fell out and began to fight a duel. Bradley had also quarrelled with the poet Thomas Watson, who tried to separate Marlowe and Bradley. Bradley then turned on Watson, driving him into a ditch at the point of his rapier and dagger, where Watson in self-defence ran him through. Bradley died almost at once.

Watson and Marlowe were immediately arrested and put in Newgate prison. After thirteen days Marlowe was allowed out and bound over to appear, with Watson, at the Old Bailey Assizes on 3 December 1589. They duly appeared and Marlowe received a pardon and was immediately released, whereas poor Watson — who had intervened on his behalf and killed Bradley in self-defence — had to wait another five months in a stinking Newgate cell before he received his.

Scholars disagree as to the order in which Marlowe wrote his plays (apart from *Tamburlaine*, which was published in 1590). It seems that *The Jew of Malta* came next and was offered to the Earl of Pembroke's Men, not, as with the others, to Henslowe. The links between the two were, however, very close, and Shakespeare's earliest efforts, *Henry VI Part I* and *Titus Andronicus*, appear in the lists of both companies. It seems impossible to believe that Marlowe and

Shakespeare did not at least know each other.

We do know, of course, that the three last plays were written between 1590 and 1593, and while the most severe disagreement has been over the order of *Edward II* and *Dr Faustus*, the majority opinion now is that *Faustus* came last.

In 1592 Marlowe seems to have been in trouble again, and we find him being bound over to keep the peace on 9 May, in the sum of £20, by Sir Owen Hopton, JP for Middlesex. The charge would seem to be similar to that known today as 'threatening behaviour' towards a constable, Allen Nicholls of Holwell Street, and his assistant constable.

It was also in 1592 that Robert Greene attacked his fellow-playwrights from his deathbed in *A Groatsworth of Wit*. He had had a snipe at Marlowe before, in 1588, when he warned theatres against 'daring God out of heaven with that Atheist, Tamburlaine' and 'such mad and scoffing poets that have prophetical spirits as bred of Merlin's race'. Greene's notorious pamphlet is famous mainly for its attack on Shakespeare, the 'upstart crow', but he was also vitriolic about Marlowe, accusing him of atheism, of pursuing Machiavellian policies and, apparently in the first version, of homosexuality. It was widely said of Marlowe that he considered that 'all that loved not tobacco and boys were fools'.

It is very interesting that the playwright Chettle, who had seen to the publication of the pamphlet, almost immediately proffered a handsome and public apology to Shakespeare of the most generous kind. But of Marlowe he said merely that he had cut from the final, printed tract the charge which 'had it been true, yet to publish it had been intolerable' (a reference to his homosexuality) and that he himself had no wish to be acquainted anyway with this 'play maker'.

By the end of September 1592 both Robert Greene and Thomas Watson (he of the fight with Bradley) were dead and Marlowe had only eight months more to live. While we do not know his relations with his fellow playwrights, we do know that from the time of his first arrival in London he had been part of a select circle whose leading lights were Sir Walter Raleigh and Thomas Harriot. The latter was a distinguished astronomer and mathematician. It seems the circle was a matter of concern to the government, and those who belonged to it were considered — wrongly — a band of dangerous atheists and possible malcontents.

In fact they seem far more likely to have been deists who questioned the conventional view not only of Christianity but other world faiths. They were also interested in a wide range of other subjects as well. But it seems that from one of these meetings, either in 1591 or earlier, Marlowe brought away a paper which had been read there. There is a division of opinion as to whether he wrote the paper or whether it was written by somebody else, the balance coming down on the side of those who do not think Marlowe actually wrote it, although he might have agreed with some of the views expressed in it.

1592 and 1593 were plague years. Thousands of people were dying, and in 1593 the people looked for a scapegoat and found it in the form of immigrants, those people who had fled from Europe in successive waves following religious persecution on the Continent. Protest took the form of 'libels' pinned on walls, and again there are overtones of today and the National Front literature. A typical example warned Belgian, French and Dutch nationals living in London to beware, for they would receive 'many a sore stripe'. After various other physical threats, they were given until 9 July to get out of the country.

The authorities acted swiftly and instituted a search for the culprits. Whether it was also used as a cover to investigate other things we do not know, but we do know that the rooms of Thomas Kyd were searched, and that among his papers was found the fragment of the document that Marlowe had had in his possession from a meeting of the Raleigh-Harriot circle. Kyd was immediately arrested for blasphemy on 12 May. As we know, he was tortured to make him say to whom the paper had belonged, and he said it had nothing to do with him; it had belonged to Marlowe, and was left there by him before he had ceased to share the room.

No time was wasted, and a warrant was immediately issued for the arrest of Marlowe on 18 May 1593. Marlowe was known to be staying at the home of his patron, Thomas Walsingham, in Kent. The warrant for his arrest said he must be fetched from Walsingham's house, and that 'in case of need' those arresting him should 'require aid'.

Marlowe presumably knew nothing of Kyd's arrest. The unfortunate Kyd, put on the rack, had dredged up anything he could think of to brand Marlowe as an atheist, but none of it was exactly devastating. Far more sinister was the evidence of a known and unpleasant informer, Richard Baines, who also gave evidence to Francis Walsingham of Marlowe's apparently serious blasphemies. Marlowe was brought to London, and duly appeared before 'their Lordships' on 20 May and was then treated quite leniently. There was no imprisonment and no rack for Marlowe. He was merely asked to report daily to their Lordships until told otherwise. He was then released without further condition.

On 30 May Kit Marlowe spent the day in a tavern belonging to Eleanor Bull at Deptford. It seems to have been a pleasant place, with a garden. With him were three other men, Robert Poley, Ingram Frizer or Frezer, and Nicholas Skeres. It seems the men spent the day there amicably, had a late lunch, walked in the garden in the afternoon, supped again in a private room, and then somehow a quarrel took place during the course of which Marlowe died.

The first rumour was that Marlowe 'was in love with a woman who played him false'. His rival was 'Francis Ingram', and Marlowe had plotted to meet his stolen lady love for an illicit assignation at a Deptford tavern. Ingram came upon them, fought a duel and killed Marlowe.

In 1597 Thomas Beard, accusing Marlowe of blasphemy in a pamphlet entitled *God's Judgement*, said

in London streets as he [Marlowe] proposed to stab one on whom he had a grudge with his dagger, the other party, perceiving so avoided the stroke, that withall catching hold of his wrist, he stabbed his own dagger into his own head, in such sort that notwithstanding all the means of surgery that could be wrought, he shortly afterwards died thereof.

Beard said he blasphemed to his last gasp.

A later version, from 1600, by William Vaughan, says:

In Deptford, a little village about three miles from London, as he meant to stab with his poniard one named Ingrams that had invited him thither to a feast, and was then playing at the tables, he quickly perceived it, so avoiding the thrust that withall drawing out his dagger for his defence, he stabbed this Marlowe into the eye in such sort that his braines coming out at dagger point he shortly died.

It was at this time that we hear that the argument was over 'the reckoning' — in other words, the bill.

It was Dr J. L. Hotson in 1925 who put on record what really did happen in Deptford on that day in May 1593. By this time there were some truly mad theories around, including one (published in 1892) that Marlowe killed Frezer, then took the pseudonym Shakespeare, writing the early plays until he was in turn murdered by Ben Jonson in 1598, who then wrote the rest of Shakespeare's plays as well as his own. . . .

Hotson went back to the documents of the time. He discovered a Queen's Pardon to 'Ingram Frizar' dated 28 June 1593 for homicide in self-defence. It stated that the 'same Ingram slew the aforesaid Christopher in self defence and not feloniously or of malice aforethought so that in no other wise could he avoid his own death'.

The Coroner's Inquest says that there were some sixteen witnesses at Eleanor Bull's tavern to the fact that the four men both arrived and spent the day together. They dined first about 'the tenth hour before noon' in a private room and then passed the time together 'in quiet sort'. The afternoon had been passed walking, sitting and talking in the garden. They had returned, in company, to the room at about the sixth hour and there supped. Here the account becomes very strange.

According to the coroner's report of 1 June, Marlowe was lying down on a bed in the room while Ingram was sitting with his back to him and the bed, between Poley and Skeres. Suddenly there was a quarrel over the reckoning, and Marlowe leapt up from the bed, snatched Ingram's own dagger from behind his back and stabbed him twice. Ingram was unable to move, as he was closely confined by sitting between his two friends. Marlowe is supposed to have made two wounds, however, on the *front* of Ingram's head, both about two inches long and a quarter of an inch deep. Ingram at first could do nothing 'and could no way take flight'. Then, fearing he would be slain and unable to move because of his companions, he was somehow able to struggle with Marlowe, get hold of the dagger (value 12 pence), turn the blade and stab Marlowe with a mortal wound over the right eye of which he immediately died. This was witnessed by Poley and Skeres. Nobody questioned that Marlowe should have jumped up and attacked a man from behind, a man who (according to his account) could not move but sat facing firmly forward and away from him . . . yet Marlowe merely cut him on the front of his head.

All three men were to feature later. Robert Poley was a known Walsingham secret agent. He had been Walsingham's double agent during the Babington plot, and was so successful that Anthony Babington trusted him completely, even after his arrest. He wrote to him from prison 'Farewell, Robin, if as I take thee true to me . . .' He was regularly employed as a spy.

In March 1595 Skeres was arrested by Sir Richard Martin 'in very dangerous company' at the house of one Williamson, servant to the Earl of Essex. He was imprisoned in the Counter prison to await examination. He seems to have disappeared into imprisonment, and we know that in 1601 he was removed from Newgate to Bridewell.

Both Skeres and Ingram Frizer had been involved in 1589 with a fraud concerning some land. Frizer seems to have bought and sold property on a number of occasions at a considerable profit to himself. Ingram Frizer was accused of fraud by a certain Anne Woodleff and her son, Drew. Drew was bound to Thomas Walsingham as an employee in the sum of £200. Skeres was also named by the Woodleffs. So there is a connection again between Skeres, Frizer and the Walsinghams. It seems a remarkable coincidence, therefore, that all three of Marlowe's companions on that fateful day had Walsingham connections.

Why was Marlowe killed? Looking at the evidence today, it certainly looks like a political murder; the coroner's account alone making a nonsense of what was supposed to have happened. None of it rings true. Had Marlowe become too much of a liability? Was he no longer an asset, with his membership of radical and 'atheist' circles, his caustic wit and irreverence, his homosexuality? Did his old employers suspect that perhaps Marlowe, with his arrogance and subtle mind, had been carried away with his game of chess and played the double agent? It does seem that by the May of 1593 Marlowe, in spite of his fame as a playwright and recognition as a major poet, had become a luxury it was felt the State could no longer afford.

Probably the best self-portrait we have of Marlowe is in Dr Faustus, who feared not 'damnation'. Perhaps, though, Robert Greene should after all have the last prophetic word, for he wrote to Marlowe:

> I know the least of my demerits merit this miserable death, but wilful striving against known truth, exceedeth all the terrors of my soul. Defer not, with me, till this last point of extremity; for little knowest thou how in the end thou shalt be visited.

Etched by E. Bocourt

Thomas Middleton

Chapter 4

Middleton, Dekker, Marston & Tourneur

Thomas Middleton

'Facetious Middleton, thy witty Muse
Hath pleased all that books or men peruse.'

Toward the end of the first week in August 1624 a gentleman called John Chamberlain wrote to a friend. In his letter he said 'I doubt not but you have heard of our famous play of Gondomar by all sorts of people — old and young, rich and poor, masters and servants, papists, wise men and fools . . .' He continues in similar vein, then writing 'Lady Smith would persuade me to take her to see it but I could not sit so long for we must have been there before one o'clock at farthest to find any room.' The play brought about what must be one of our earliest recorded traffic jams as carriages and people blocked the streets around the Globe theatre on the Bankside, and it ran for an unprecedented nine performances in succession, grossing about £1500 at the box office. This was a truly colossal sum at the time. The play was *A Game at Chess*, and it was to make its author, Thomas Middleton, a wanted man.

Middleton was born in London in 1580 and was christened at St Lawrence's Church, Old Jewry, on 14 April. Shakespeare and Marlowe were in their teens, Ben Jonson about six years old. He was born at exactly the right time for a would-be playwright, as both he and the Jacobean theatre reached their peak together. Thomas was the child of a prosperous merchant, William Middleton, a bricklayer — unlike Ben Jonson, his father's occupation does not seem to have made Middleton paranoid about bricks and bricklaying. By the time he was five, however, his father had died, and as he was a wealthy man he left considerable property and bequests to his wife and children.

Possibly Middleton's extremely lifelike portrayals of women, second only to those of Shakespeare, came about because he was a fatherless child and was influenced by a strong mother and an older sister. Anne Middleton married again, only seven months after her husband's death, but it seems to have been a disaster and the couple did not remain together long. She married Thomas Harvey, a grocer, who had lost all his own money backing Raleigh and Grenville's unlucky expedition to Renoake Island. No doubt Anne Middleton was lonely and missed a father for her two small children, and was an easy prey, therefore, to an impoverished man on the lookout for an attractive and wealthy widow. Middleton's early comedies are much concerned with this kind of situation. So Harvey married Anne and then spent most of his time trying to get his hands on the money left to his newly acquired bride and stepchildren. Middleton's early years were spent in a constant atmosphere of litigation as his mother stood her ground and would not give in.

We know he went up to Oxford and matriculated in 1598, but he does not appear to have taken a degree there. There is a suggestion that he may have spent some time at Gray's Inn, as there is a record of a Thomas Middleton being there about that time, but there is no proof it was the playwright. All we know about his time in Oxford is that he once had to rush home to take his sister Avice's side in the continuing row with his stepfather.

We do know that by 1600 he was totally immersed in the theatre, and we hear that 'he remaineth here in London daily accompanying the players'. By then he was writing for Henslowe, both on his own and as a collaborator with others, and we note that in 1601 Henslowe advanced £5 to four playwrights, Middleton, Dekker, Munday and Webster, for a play called *Caesar's Fall*, in which it seems Middleton also acted when it was performed on 22 May. Seven days after this Henslowe paid the four dramatists an advance of £3 for another play, *The Two Harpies*.

In 1603 Middleton married. His wife is a more interesting figure than many of the other playwrights' wives, and it is obvious that he did not choose her for her money. It was likely she was an intelligent, well-educated and lively girl. Her name was Magdalen, the daughter of Edward Morbeck, a clerk of Chancery, and granddaughter to a famous musician and composer, John Morbeck. Her uncle, Dr Roger Morbeck, was an author and physician, Provost of Oriel College, Oxford. She also had strong links with the theatre, as her brother, Thomas, was an actor.

It seems to have been a good marriage, although she brought her husband none of the land and property some theatre wives seem to have had as dowries. The couple were obviously hard up, and Thomas was sued for debt three times between 1610 and 1612. There was a single surviving child, a son Edward, born in 1604.

Middleton was a very hard-working dramatist, and his work shows a wide range, the most comprehensive in subject matter outside Shakespeare. The plays were popular and regularly performed, and he also had a strong influence on the

A Game at Chess *title-page (British Library)*

type of play we would now call the drama-documentary, a play based on a real-life incident which he generally worked on with other writers, possibly to get the production on stage as quickly as possible while the original events were still fresh in the minds of those in the audience. In 1620 he was appointed Chronologer to the City of London at a salary of £6 13s. 4d. per annum, which was soon raised to £10. The job was certainly no sinecure if undertaken properly. First there was a kind of reporter's side which consisted of keeping a journal of events in the City, then he also had to be prepared to write speeches for the Mayor or leading aldermen, and lastly he had to devise entertainments for civic banquets when requested. Middleton seems to have worked conscientiously in the post — unlike his successor Ben Jonson, who found it useful for the money, and proceeded to do as little as possible.

It was *A Game at Chess*, however, which really brought Middleton before the public eye, other than as a witty and hardworking writer. It is the one well-documented incident in his life. The play appeared at a sensitive time. Six thousand English troops had been sent to Flanders on an abortive mission. Prince Charles and the Duke of Buckingham had paid a prolonged visit to Spain on the pretext of the Prince bringing home a royal, Spanish bride. They returned without one, and James I's attempts at political intrigue were widely mocked. Anti-Spanish feeling in England ran high, manifesting itself in the kind of jingoism which periodically hits the English.

Middleton set the row between England and Spain in the context of a game of chess, where moves are made and pieces taken as in the real game, but all as part of the plot of the play. It is a very clever piece of work. The white pieces were, of course, the English. The black pieces, who come from the country of 'Gondomar', are the Spanish. The characters on both sides were, to say the least, pretty thinly disguised. The forces of good (White) led by the White Knight (Prince Charles) and the White Duke (Buckingham) are presented in a very ambivalent manner, and the history of James I's inept political intriguing was treated with biting satire. (Middleton has both White and Black 'Dukes' as chess pieces.)

On the other hand, the people represented by some of the Black pieces could in no way be in doubt. This was especially true of the Spanish Ambassador, an astute politician. Just to make sure everybody recognized him, it is reported that the players managed to get hold of one of his cast-off suits for the actor playing the role, and that he was also carried around in a litter (the poor man had a fistula in real life). This litter was said to be the actual one used by the Ambassador, but was no doubt an excellent replica. Middleton appears to have updated his play while he was writing it. Current events were added as they took place, and it seems that the treacherous White King's Pawn was based on Lionel Cranfield, Earl of Middlesex and Lord Treasurer, who was impeached in the April of 1624.

News of jammed streets and queues to get into the theatre for a remarkable new play soon got about, although its production had been carefully timed for when the King and Court were out of London for the summer. It would be rather like putting on a play today which featured not only the Prime Minister but her entire

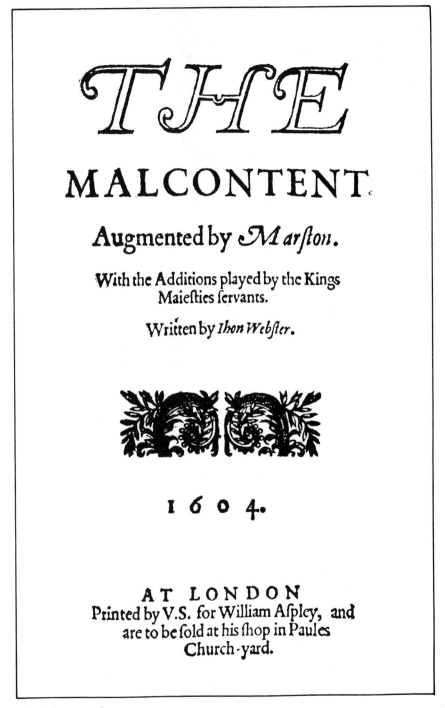

THE

MALCONTENT.

Augmented by *Marston*.

With the Additions played by the Kings
Maiesties seruants.

Written by *Ihon Webster*.

1 6 0 4.

AT LONDON
Printed by V.S. for William Aspley, and
are to be sold at his shop in Paules
Church-yard.

The Malcontent *title-page*

Cabinet, most of the Opposition leaders and with the Falklands war thrown in for good measure. King James was told about it by the enraged Spanish Ambassador, who complained of this 'very scandalous comedy acted publicly by the King's own players' in which he himself was represented on the stage, 'in a rude and dishonourable fashion'. He added that 'there was such merriment, hub-bub and applause that even if I had been many leagues away it would not have been possible for me not to take notice of it' and 'there were more than 3000 persons there on the day the audience was smallest . . .' On 12 August James wrote, via his secretary, an indignant letter to the Privy Council asking whatever the Master of the Revels had been about to sanction such a play, and requiring the Council to summon the company immediately and to punish Middleton.

On 21 August the Council replied in a letter to James that they had summoned the players before them. The players, said the Council, had 'produced a book, being an original and perfect copy thereof (or so they affirmed) as seen and allowed by Sir Henry Herbert, Knight, Master of the Revels, under his own hand and subscribed by him in the last page of the said book'. The players were discharged with 'a round and sharp reproof' on the grounds that they had por-trayed the monarchy on stage, and were forbidden to act in anything at all until the King's pleasure was known. To ensure that they complied with this, they were bound over in the sum of £300. It was made clear to the unfortunate Sir Henry too that he was hardly the most popular man at Court.

But how about Middleton, due to be punished by royal decree? Well, he quite simply refused to obey the summons to appear before the Council. The Council told the King that the author was, as supposed, 'one Middleton, who, shifting out of the way and not attending the Board as was expected, we have given war-rant for the apprehending of him'. Arthur Scargill's refusal in 1984 to take notice of a court summons during the coal strike, thus putting himself in contempt, is no new thing. Middleton did it three and a half centuries earlier. Finally, after scour-ing London for him without success, the Council issued a warrant on 27 August for the arrest of his twenty-year-old son, Edward, on the assumption that this would bring Middleton in. It did. On 30 August he gave himself up, and his indemnity was formally accepted. A tradition preserved in a manuscript note by a contemporary hand in Dyson's copy of the play says 'Middleton was committed to prison where he lay for some time and at last got out upon a Petition to the King'.

In the end the furore died down. The players returned to the stage and Middleton to his joint employments as City Chronologer and playwright. He only lived another three years. His home was in Newington Butts, and here he died and was buried in the parish church on 4 July 1627. The next year his wife Magdalen applied to the civic authorities for financial assistance, and was given twenty nobles.

Thomas Dekker

'. . . it can be no great glory to be an Ordinary Poet.'

It seems rather sad that the few facts we know of the life of Thomas Dekker, one of the liveliest writers of his time, all seem to be connected with his financial problems. Yet though we know little about his personal life, we do have from him one of the best accounts of what it was like to be part of Jacobean London in general and the theatre scene in particular.

We know so little of him that even the date and place of his birth are in doubt, but it is generally thought to have been about 1570 and in London. We know nothing of his schooling or whether or not he went to university. Some early biographical notes say he then spent his early years 'in vagabondage', but it seems much more likely that this meant he was a strolling player (who would be considered little better than a vagabond), and it makes much more sense because by the mid-1590s he was writing plays in London.

By 1597 he was writing for Henslowe, and there are numerous entries in Henslowe's *Diary*. We note that on 8 January 1597 twenty shillings was lent to 'Mr Dikker' — Henslowe's spelling is always creative, and sometimes a name is spelt differently on every occasion it appears — to buy a 'book' off him. This could have been an outline plot and was unlikely to have been a whole play at that price, for four weeks later another entry notes that he paid 'Mr Dickers' £4 for a book of his called *Fayeton* [*Phaeton*]. On 18 January 1598 Mr Dickers had £3 from Henslowe 'to be repaid the end of one month next ensuing and I say lent'.

In February we read 'Lent unto Thomas Dowton for the company to buy a suit for Phaeton and two rebates and one farthingale, the 16 of January 1598 the sum of £3 I say lent.' This is followed by 'Lent unto Thomas Dowton the 28 January 1598 to buy a white satin doublet for Phaeton, forty shillings, I say lent.' But what of the author? 'Lent unto the company the 4 February 1598 to discharge Mr. Dikker out of the Counter in the Poultry, the sum of forty shillings.' The Counter was the debtors' prison, and Dekker was to get to know it very well indeed, for it seems he spent three years in it from 1613 to 1616.

It is suggested he married in the mid-1590s, but if he did we know nothing about her, nor if there were any children. He was a hard-working and prolific playwright, often collaborating with colleagues, as we note from Henslowe. 'Lent unto William Bornes the 10 August 1599 to lend unto Beng. Jonson and Thomas Dikkers in earnest of their book and which they will be writing called *Page of Plymouth*, the sum . . .' It is blank as is the price of another — 'Lent unto Jonson, Dickers and other gentlemen for a play Robert the II, King of Scotland.' No trace of these plays remains.

While his must have been a hard and debt-ridden life, there is so much good humour in Dekker's writings that we can only feel he must have been a most attractive character, and much of the man himself and his way of life is evoked by a prose pamphlet he wrote, *The Gull's Horn Book* (1609). While it throws light on the life and behaviour of the times, it also has overtones of those who inhabit the arts world today.

Take, for instance, his chapter on how to behave in 'the ordinary'. The ordinary was an eating-house which offered a substantial meal at a set time every day, and where all kinds of people mixed together. The poet/playwright who wanted to make the maximum impact possible should arrive there, he says, about 11.30, 'for then you shall find most of your fashion mongers planted in the room waiting for their meat'.

> If you be a Poet and come into the ordinary, though it can be no great glory to be an Ordinary Poet, order yourself thus. Observe no man; doff not your cap to that gentleman today at dinner to whom, not two nights since, you were beholden for supper; but, after a turn or two in the room take occasion, pulling off your gloves, to have some Epigram or Satire or Sonnet fastened to one of them. Marry, if you chance to get into your hands any witty thing of another man's that is somewhat better. I would counsel you then, if demand be made who composed it, you may say: "Faith, a learned Gentleman, a very worthy friend." And this seeming to lay it on another man will be counted either modesty in you or as a sign that you are not ambitious of praise, or else you will not take it upon you for fear of the sharpness it carries with it.

Obviously, another place in which you would spend a good deal of time would be the tavern, whether you were a 'rank coxcomb', or 'a country gentleman who brings his wife up to learn the fashion, see the tombs in Westminster, the lions in the Tower or take physic', or even 'a young farmer, who many times makes his wife in the country believe he hath suits in law, because he will come up for his lechery.'

Naturally, you must look the part.

> Having therefore thrust yourself into a case most in fashion — how coarse soever the stuff be, 'tis no matter so it be in fashion — your office is . . . to inquire out those taverns which are best customed, where masters are oftenest drunk (for that confirms their taste and that they choose wholesome wines) and which stand furthest from the Counters . . .

Next you attach yourself to whoever appears to have the most money to spend and find out where his interest lies — fencing, riding, dancing perhaps? Does he love dogs? You are addicted to them.

> The use of this familiarity is this. If you want money five or six days together you may still pay the reckoning with this most gentleman-like language: 'Boy, fetch me money from the bar' and keep yourself most providentially from a hungry melancholy in your chamber.

To really cut a dash you should not only inquire what is on the menu but insist on seeing the kitchen, letting it be known you are on friendly terms with the kitchen wench. When the food arrives you should discuss its various qualities in a knowledgeable way.

> For your drink, let not your physician confine you to any one particular liquor; for it is requisite that a gentleman should not always be plodding in one art, but rather a general scholar — that is to have a lick at all sorts and then away . . . your discourse at table must be such as that which you utter at the ordinary; your behaviour the same but somewhat more careless; for where your expense is great, let your modesty be less and though you shall be mad in a tavern, the largeness of the items will bear your incivility. You may, without prick to your conscience, set the want of your wit against the superfluity and sauciness of the reckoning.

When chatting with those new to the town you should ask loudly which famous gallants are sitting in another chamber and send them up a bottle of wine. Better still, employ somebody to go around saying how witty you are, what a gamester too, and which citizens' wives you can have at any time to sup with you, how much you spend on entertainment and, indeed, what a splendid fellow you are altogether. 'But in such a deluge of drink, take heed that no man counterfeit himself drunk to free his purse from the danger of the shot . . . it had wont to be the quality of cockneys.'

Finally, however 'the terrible reckoning, like an indictment, bids you hold up your hand' and pay. Leave as you entered. Kiss the hostess warmly, accept a last drink on the house from the cellarman and bid the whole assembly good-night.

Lastly, a brief look at how Dekker sees the average playgoer, the Jacobean equivalent of the person who sits behind you in the theatre today, comments noisily on the action throughout, misses half of it, asks his or her companion questions about what is going on and then passes noisy sweets back and forward along the row before leaving for the interval with the maximum fuss, returning ten minutes after the performance has recommenced.

Just think of the scope in Dekker's day, when you could actually sit on stage!

> Present not yourself on the stage, especially at a new play, until the quaking Prologue hath, by rubbing, got colour into his cheeks and is ready to give the trumpets their cue that he is upon point to enter; for then it is time, as though you were one of the properties, or that you dropped out of the hangings, to creep from behind the arras with your tripos or three-footed stool in one hand and a tester [sixpence] mounted between forefinger and thumb in the other . . . By sitting on stage you may, without travelling for it, at the very next door ask whose play it is; and, if you know not the author you may rail against him and, peradventure behaving yourself so that you will enforce the author to know you.

He continues:

> It shall crown you with rich commendation to laugh aloud in the midst of the most serious and saddest scenes of the terriblest tragedy; and to let the

clapper, your tongue, be tossed so high that all the house may ring of it.

Now, sir, if the writer be a fellow that hath either epigrammed you or hath had a flirt at your mistress or hath brought your feather or your red beard or your little legs on stage, you shall disgrace him worse than by tossing him in a blanket or giving him a bastinado in a tavern if, in the middle of his play, you rise with a screwed and discontented face from your stool to be gone; no matter whether the scene be good or no; the better it is, the worse you do distaste it; and being on your feet, sneak not away like a coward; but salute all your acquaintances that are spread either on the rushes or on stools behind you and draw what troop you can from the stage after you . . . the poet [playwright] cries, perhaps: 'A Pox go with you!' but care not for that. There is no music without frets.

Marry, if either the company or indisposition of the weather bind you to sit it out, my counsel is then that you turn plain ape; take up a rush and tickle the earnest ears of your fellow gallants to make other fools fall a-laughing; mew at passionate speeches; blare at merry; find fault with the music; whew at the children's action; whistle at the songs; and, above all, curse the sharers that, whereas the same day you had bestowed forty shillings on an embroidered felt and feather Scotch fashion for your mistress in the court or your punk in the city, within two hours after you encounter with the very same block on the stage, when the haberdasher swore to you the impress was but extant that morning.

It certainly shows what the playwright had to put up with! One can only take delight in such a humorist. He continued writing well into the 1630s, referring in a tract in 1638 to his more than 'three score years'. Did he live to see the Civil War? We do not know. He disappears into the dark from whence he came, having illuminated for us so wittily the kind of life he led.

John Marston

'Who winks and shuts his apprehension up.'

While much of the detail of the lives of Middleton and Dekker is lacking, their presence through their work and through their effect on their contemporaries makes them seem very real. Much more shadowy are their contemporaries Marston and Tourneur.

Marston is a man who seems to have achieved totally unwanted notoriety from the time when he first put pen to paper. His early works were considered indecent, he became involved in a public slanging match with Ben Jonson, and he possibly later went to prison with him for writing a play which offended the King.

The Marston family came from Shropshire, but John was born in the city of

Coventry about 1576. (He was, oddly enough, baptised in Wardlington, Oxfordshire, on 7 October.) His mother is said to have been the daughter of an Italian surgeon. We do not know where he went to school but the family moved to London when his father, also called John, became a lecturer at the Middle Temple. The playwright matriculated, at the age of sixteen, at Brazenose College, Oxford, in the February about 1592. He then trained for the law. We do not know what attracted him to the theatre — in 1599 his disappointed father bequeathed some law books to his son, 'whom I hoped would have profited by them in the study of the law, but man proposeth and God disposeth', but his first works were published in 1598, and it was not as a man of the theatre that he fell foul of the authorities.

His early works were *The Metamorphosis of Pigmalion's Image* and *The Scourge of Villainy*. Marston had fully intended these two rather turgid poetic tracts to put across a strong view on contemporary morals but it seems he was misconstrued. Perhaps he was carried away by the salacious bits. Anyway, in 1599 both books were ordered to be publicly burned by no less a person than the Archbishop of Canterbury, as they were considered to be indecent and licentious. If theatre audiences then flocked to see his plays on the off-chance that they would be somewhat risqué, they would be in for a disappointment. His best-known play is probably the tragi-comedy *The Malcontent*. This was published in 1604, with additions by Webster, and written a year or two earlier.

He married a clergyman's daughter if Ben Jonson is to be believed, for he said of Marston 'that he wrote his father-in-law's preachings and his father-in-law his comedies'. For during the early years of the seventeenth century Marston was locked in a literary duel with Ben Jonson which came to be known as the Poets' War, and which is dealt with in detail in the chapter on Jonson. In brief, he had started out as an admirer of Jonson and, according to Marston, he had written a character into one of his plays which he intended as a flattering portrait of the other playwright. The choleric Jonson did not see it like that, and the subsequent enormous and public row rumbled on for a long time and split the theatre scene to its roots. We have a laconic comment by Jonson that he beat Marston 'and took his pistol from him'.

Marston seemed destined to find himself in trouble he did not seek. In 1605 he was involved in the scandal over the play *Eastward Ho!* which he wrote with Jonson (they seem to have made up their quarrel) and George Chapman. Tradition has it he went to prison with Jonson and Chapman for his part in the affair, but there is no proof of this, and one source suggests he ran away once the other two playwrights were seen to be heading for trouble. His tragedies tend to be dull, but his part in *Eastward Ho!* and other comedies make him notable.

By 1607 Marston had obviously had enough of the theatre and he abandoned playwriting altogether and (presumably thankfully) took Holy Orders. We know that in 1616 he had a living at Christchurch in Hampshire which he finally resigned as late as 13 September 1631. In 1633 his collected plays were published by William Shares, and he died on 26 June 1634 in the parish of Aldermanbury in London. He is buried in the Temple Church beside his father.

Cyril Tourneur

'O, that marrowless age
Would stuff the hollow bones with damn'd desires.'

It has been said about Tourneur that the only certain thing we know about him is the date of his death. There is considerable disagreement about exactly which plays he did write, and scholars and critics are quite passionately divided over the most famous of these, *The Revenger's Tragedy*. One strong band of partisans favours Middleton, and will delve into the text in minutest detail to prove their point, while a smaller but no less positive group ascribes the play to Webster. Yet there is something about this play which sets it apart from the works of either of these two other writers, and since a decision has to be made, I have come down on the side of those who, in spite of everything, think Tourneur wrote it as tradition says.

Tourneur was born about 1575 and was probably the son of the Sir Richard Tourneur who spent his life in the service of the Cecils, since Cyril Tourneur too was to be given a position through that family's patronage. There is also more than a strong suggestion that Tourneur, like Marlowe, was recruited into the secret service of his day, and again the close connections with the Cecils make this a distinct possibility.

His first play, *Transformed Metamorphosis*, was printed by Valentine Sims at the sign of the White Swan in 1600. The date of the *Atheist's Tragedy* is variously given as 1600 and 1603, and the disputed *Revenger's Tragedy* as 1607. A play of his called *The Noblemen* was licensed to Edward Blount on 15 February 1612 and acted at Court by the King's Men on 23 February of that year. Also in 1612, he collaborated with Webster and Heywood in *Three Elegies* on Prince Henry's death.

One reason for the doubts over Tourneur's authorship of various plays is that his manuscripts were the victims of the person who is loosely described as 'Warburton's cook'. Again and again when reading about plays of this period you read that a certain play disappeared altogether because the script was burned 'by Warburton's cook', or a play title is mentioned as 'one of the manuscripts burned by Warburton's cook'. So who was Warburton's cook?

John Warburton lived from 1682 to 1759 and was an indefatigable collector of almost everything, but certainly he was fascinated by old manuscripts. He managed to get hold of the original 'books' of a number of plays by famous Elizabethan and Jacobean playwrights — from early Jonson through Middleton to later writers. Many were very rare editions indeed, and have now become lost plays.

Unfortunately, Warburton was not very careful with anything in his collection once he had acquired it. He lived riotously, and drank hard, continually running out of money. In July 1720 he sold one batch of valuable manuscripts to the

Earl of Oxford in order to have more money for drink, but at a later date most of his collection of rare Elizabethan and Jacobean plays were, through his own carelessness and the ignorance of Betsy Baker, his servant, 'unluckily burned or put under pye bottoms'. A list of some fifty-five lost plays exists in his own hand-writing. Many were unique, their loss irreplaceable, and among these are works by Tourneur.

In 1613 Tourneur seems to have been involved in undercover work for the government, for there is a note of a grant of 41 shillings paid on 23 December upon the signing of a warrant 'for his pains in carrying letters for his Majesty's service to Brussels'. After that he seems to have lived in the Low Countries for some years, as he received an annuity of £60 from the Governor of the United Provinces.

In 1625 Cecil appointed him Secretary to the Council of War, and later that year Tourneur, in the capacity of Secretary to the Lord Marshal, accompanied the Cadiz Expedition, sailing on the flagship, *Royal Anne*. In December 1625 he was one of the 160 desperately sick men landed in Ireland while the vessel itself returned to England. Tourneur died in Ireland on 28 February 1626, leaving a widow. All we know of her is that she was called Katherine, and that he left her destitute.

Francis Beaumont (By permission of Lord Sackville; photograph: Courtauld Institute of Art)

Chapter 5

Beaumont and Fletcher, Webster, Ford &Massinger

Francis Beaumont and John Fletcher

*'. . . both bachelors; they lay together; had one
wench in the house between them.'*
James Aubrey

Beaumont and Fletcher are almost always spoken of together, like Morecambe
and Wise or Gilbert and Sullivan. But their partnership was in fact relatively
brief, while Fletcher wrote far more than Beaumont, continued writing after his
partner's death, and also left a body of work of his own and written in collaboration with other playwrights, including possibly Shakespeare.

Both men came from very different backgrounds than those of most of their
contemporaries. They were not the sons of artisans but of gentlemen. Francis
Beaumont was born at Grace-Dieu in Leicestershire in 1583 or 1584, the youngest
son of a judge, Sir Francis Beaumont, Justice of the Common Pleas. He was
entered at Pembroke College, Oxford (then Broadgates Hall) about 1596 or
1597, but appears to have left suddenly a year later when his father died. On 3
November 1600 he was entered as a member of the Inner Temple, and it seems to
have been assumed that he would follow his father into the law as a profession,
but there is no evidence that he ever pursued any legal studies. We do know that
he and his brother John soon became friends of both Ben Jonson and Drayton.

Remarkably (in view of his expressed views on most of his contemporaries)
Jonson seems to have rated Beaumont very highly, and according to Dryden 'Ben
Jonson, while he lived, submitted all his writings to his [Beaumont's] censure,

John Fletcher (By permission of Lord Sackville; photograph: Courtauld Institute of Art)

and 'tis thought used his judgement in correcting, if not contriving all his plots.' Whether or not this latter statement is true, it certainly suggests both respect and friendship between the two men.

Beaumont was unlikely to have found himself short of money. The eldest Beaumont brother, Sir Henry, died in 1605, leaving a substantial estate to be shared between John and Francis.

John Fletcher too sounds as if he should have had reasonable financial stability, but this was not the case. His father, first Senior Fellow of Bene't (later Corpus Christi) College, Cambridge, then became vicar of Rye, where John was born in 1579. He then rose rapidly, becoming Chaplain to the Queen and, after holding two previous bishoprics, Bishop of London. But he died in 1596, leaving nine surviving children and a mountain of debt. Fletcher went up to Corpus Christi College, Cambridge, in 1591.

The partnership between the two men began about 1606. There has been much speculation as to the nature of the friendship and just how intimate it was. James Aubrey in his *Brief Lives* voiced a general supposition, although Aubrey's scandalous writings are not reliable. He was the first of the gossip columnists, one might say, although no gossip columnist today could possibly get away with the kind of things Aubrey wrote — both he and his newspaper would be in court for libel until they were bankrupt.

James Aubrey said: 'Mr. Francis Beaumont was the son of Judge Beaumont. There was a wonderful consimility of fancy between him and Mr. John Fletcher which caused that dearness of friendship between them . . . They lived together on the Bankside, not far from the Playhouse, both bachelors; lay together; had one Wench in the house between them, which they did so admire: the same clothes and cloak between them.' Of their working relationship, he said 'I have heard Dr. John Earles, since Bishop of Sarum, who knew them say that Mr. Beaumont's main business was to lop the overflowings of Mr. Fletcher's luxuriant and flowing wit.'

Possibly the two men did have a homosexual relationship; certainly they seem to have been inseparable between 1606 and 1613, when Beaumont married. After the marriage the working relationship ceased entirely. Beaumont married Ursula, heiress to a Henry Sly of Sundridge in Kent, and there were two daughters of the marriage, the younger, Frances, being born posthumously. Beaumont died on 6 March 1616, and we do not know the cause of his death. He was buried in Westminster Abbey, next to Chapman and Spenser. Although he himself had money, and he also married it, it does not seem to have remained in his immediate family, for we are told that his eldest daughter, Elizabeth, married a Scots colonel and fell on hard times, and that his younger, Frances, ended up having to go into service.

Although we know of Fletcher's work after Beaumont's death we know virtually nothing about the rest of his life. He may have married in 1613; somebody called John Fletcher was married in that year at St Saviour's, Southwark. Fletcher continued writing until his death in 1625. 1625 was an appalling year for the plague, more than 35,000 people dying in London and its surrounding suburbs alone. All the theatres closed, and some companies went bankrupt.

We know that Fletcher died of the plague. Aubrey says:

> John Fletcher, invited to go with a Knight into Norfolk or Suffolk in the
> Plague time of 1625, stayed to make himself a suit of clothes, and while it
> was making fell sick of the Plague and died. This I had from his tailor, who
> is now a very old man, and the clerk of St. Mary Overy's in Southwark.
> Mr. Fletcher had an issue in his arm. The clerk (who was wont to bring him
> ivy leaves to dress it) when he came, found the spots upon him. Death
> stopped his journey and laid him low here.

John Webster

> *'Webster was much possessed by death*
> *And saw the skull beneath the skin,*
> *And breastless creatures underground*
> *Leaned backward with a lipless grin.'*
> T. S. Eliot

Webster's work is indeed much possessed by death, and possibly one reason for this is that he was born in an area where death was ever present. He was within earshot of the bell which rang before the executions of Newgate prisoners, in a parish whose vicar had been burned at the stake.

He was the son of a wealthy coachmaker who lived at the corner of Cow Lane and Hosier Lane, West Smithfield, in the parish of St Sepulchre-without-Newgate. His father had married a much younger woman, Sarah Peniall, when she was sixteen, and John was born at his grandparents' house when his mother was just seventeen years and one month old. His father was obviously extremely well off, as we know that in 1597 he had to pay £12 in taxes, which was a very big sum indeed at that time.

The vicar who had suffered was John Rogers, vicar of St Sepulchre, who was the first Marian martyr and who had been burned in front of his wife and eleven children on 4 February 1555. His death was an ever-present reminder to those living nearby of the ruthlessness of religious and political persecution. The Websters leased their coach-yard from St Bartholomew's, and it adjoined the home of the wealthy, beautiful and clever Penelope Rich — Spenser's 'Stella', who was to become notorious as the mistress of Charles Blount, Earl of Devonshire. It was also close to Newgate prison itself, and every night before the execution of prisoners, either locally or at Tyburn, the Great Bell of St Sepulchre's would toll for those due to die the next day.

We have no record of where Webster went to school, but it is thought to have been at Merchant Taylors. It does seem almost certain, however, that he is the John Webster who was entered at the Middle Temple on 1 August 1598. His

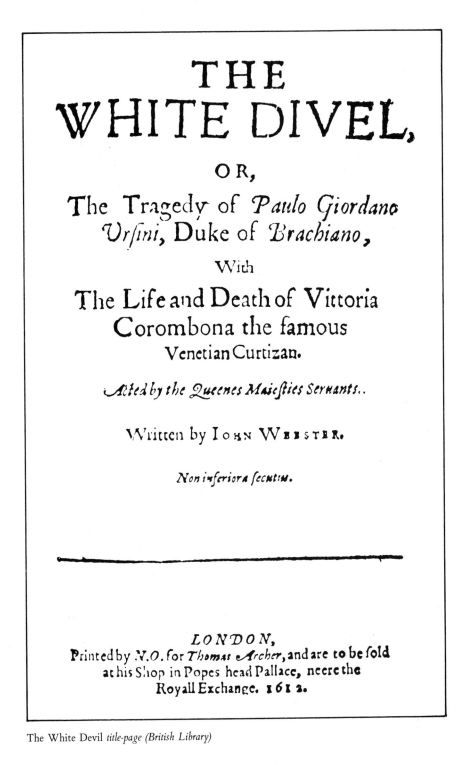

THE
WHITE DIVEL,

OR,

The Tragedy of *Paulo Giordano*
Ursini, Duke of *Brachiano*,

With

The Life and Death of Vittoria
Corombona the famous
Venetian Curtizan.

Acted by the Queenes Maiesties Seruants..

Written by IOHN WEBSTER.

Non inferiora secutus.

LONDON,
Printed by N.O. for *Thomas Archer*, and are to be sold
at his Shop in Popes head Pallace, neere the
Royall Exchange. 1612.

The White Devil *title-page (British Library)*

close association with two other Temple playwrights, Ford and Marston, make this even more likely, as is the fact that he is much preoccupied with legal matters and trial scenes in his plays.

If the body of his work which has come down to us is all he wrote, then he could not have earned his living from the theatre. He first appears writing for Henslowe in 1602 (he was advanced money, as was Henslowe's custom), and collaborated with Dekker, Drayton and Middleton on a play called *Caesar's Fall*, and later on *Christmas Comes But Once a Year* — an unlikely subject for this particular playwright. Miss M. C. Bradbrooke, former Mistress of Girton and noted Elizabethan and Jacobean scholar (to whom we are indebted for most of what we do know about Webster's life), suggests that John remained firmly within the family firm while writing for pleasure. It would seem likely that his father and brother looked after the practical side of the firm while he dealt with legal and administrative matters.

This does seem a very likely explanation, for just as Jonson never lost his 'bricklayer' image, Webster came in for much snide comment on his connection with coachbuilding; notably in Henry Fitzjeffery's poem:

But h'st! with him Crabbed Websterio
The Playwright, cartwright: whether? either? ho!
No further. Look as ye'd be look't into:
Sit as ye would be read: Lord! who would know him?
Was ever man so mangl'd with a poem?
See how he draws his mouth awry of late,
How he scrubs: wrings his wrists: scratches his pate,
A midwife! Help! By his Brain's coitus,
Some Centaur strange: some huge Bucephalus,
Or Pallas (sure) engendered in his brain,
Strike Vulcan with thy hammer once again.

And he continues, in even nastier vein, concluding: 'But what care I, it will be so obscure/ That none shall understand him (I am sure).'

This does suggest not only that Webster's work was hard going for its audiences at the time (as we know it was) but also that writing was a painful and difficult business for him, and that his work emerged but slowly.

The White Devil was printed in 1612; it was put on by the Red Bull Theatre Company (which was not the best choice, as it was a company which tended to specialize in plays which suited a rough-and-ready audience). It was not a notable success, although Webster obviously rated the young actor Richard Perkins very highly, as he mentions him in his postscript — 'in particular I must remember the well-approved industry of my friend Master Perkins, and confess the worth of his action did crown both the beginning and end'. It was the first time any actor received such an honour.

The Duchess of Malfi, however — which was probably first acted in the winter of 1613/14 — was immediately popular, and has remained in repertoires almost ever since. (It was not published till 1623, however, when the independence in its dedication — to Lord Berkeley — was striking.) It was first presented by the King's Men at the Blackfriars Theatre, with William Osler (who died on 12 December 1614) as Antonio. It was so popular that the son of John Heminges (who had originally put on the play), was to write in 1633 in an elegy for the amputation of his duelling finger:

> It had been drawn and we in state approach,
> But Webster's brother would not lend a coach,
> He swore that all were hired to convey
> The Malfi duchess sadly on her way.

By 1615 Webster had contributed some thirty-two Characters to the sixth edition of the late Sir Thomas Overbury's collection, *Characters Drawn to the Life of Several Persons of Quality*. In 1624 it seems he dabbled a little in politics when he wrote the Lord Mayor's Pageant for the installation of John Gore as Lord Mayor in the October of that year. His pageant is described as 'a politically daring climax providing his judgement upon the government of the day'.

We know very little else about him. We are not even sure if he married. We know he was dead by 1634, as he is bracketed with Fletcher as a dead playwright. What else of this apparently very serious man who wrote such dark works and who found it a painful business? Only the unlikely comment of his friend Heywood that he was a plain man and remained 'but Jack at all times'.

John Ford and Philip Massinger

'. . . to cast an eye of favour on my downtrod poverty.'

The common bond between these two playwrights is that neither ever appears to have made a good living out of writing for the theatre, and both spent their lives being hard up. Of John Ford we know very little. He was born at Ilsington in Devon in 1586 into a family of Devonshire gentry, and baptised on 17 April. He was related to Lord Chief Justice Popham. It is thought he went to Exeter College, Oxford, and then at sixteen he was admitted to the Middle Temple. His early years there seem to have been disrupted and stormy, for we know he was rusticated for two years for failing to pay his Buttery bills.

In 1610 his father died, leaving him the grand inheritance of £10. One supposes Ford did sort out his affairs with the Middle Temple, for he was still there in 1617, and presumably practised law although he was not called to the Bar. Between that date and 1620 he published a number of pamphlets, but did not write for the theatre.

In fact, unlike Webster — who earned a decent living at another occupation, and wrote through choice — it looks as if Ford was a pretty unsuccessful lawyer who turned to the theatre as an extra means of making some money. He wrote for a long while only in collaboration with others, which could not have been very remunerative, and he was forty before he had a play published in his name alone.

He seemed to spend his life battling with financial problems, and we know little else about him except that four of his plays disappeared at the hands of Warburton's notorious cook. By 1639 he was dead.

One contemporary description reads:

Deep in a dump John Ford was got
With folded arms and melancholy hat.

Massinger too was on the face of it born into comfortable circumstances. His father was a Fellow of Merton in 1572, and early accounts of his life describe him as a 'servant' or 'retainer' of the Earl of Pembroke. He obviously held a very high place within the Earl's household, managed the Earl's business affairs in London; a letter from Henry, Earl of Pembroke, refers to him in a treaty of marriage between the Pembroke and Burghley families, another describes him as the bearer of letters from Pembroke to the Queen. He went on to become the first MP for Weymouth, in 1588, and then for Shaftesbury in 1601. He was also Examiner to the Council of the Welsh Marches.

Massinger was born in Salisbury and baptized in St Thomas's church there on 24 November 1583. On 14 May he was entered at St Alban's Hall, Oxford, and described as 'the son of a gentleman'. He spent three or four years there, where he is described as taking much more interest in romances, poetry and drama than in serious study — a criticism which has been levelled at many writers and actors ever since. His father died when he was about nineteen or twenty, and — surprisingly, in view of his career — seems to have left his family without any means at all. It is interesting to see that playwrights from the artisan background like Shakespeare, Marlowe, Middleton and indeed even Jonson (who ran through his money when he had it), seem to have made a far better living financially from writing than did their contemporaries who had been born into comparative wealth.

Like many others, the young Massinger gravitated first to Henslowe, who was obviously always on the lookout for new talent. During his early years he wrote in collaboration with others. He worked with Field and Fletcher, and possibly also with Tourneur on *The Second Maid's Tragedy*. Fairly early on in his career he appears to have approached his father's old master, the Earl of Pembroke, pleading for patronage and asking him 'to cast an eye/Of favour on my downtrod poverty'. He told the Earl that if he received patronage it would be possible to devote himself to better work than he was able to do while having to struggle so hard. We know that in 1613 he was in prison for debt.

In 1616 he joined the company of the King's Men, leaving them briefly in 1623, to return after Fletcher's death in 1625. His political views inclined to what was known as the popular party, and, like Middleton and Jonson, he wrote some plays which were not popular with the Court. In *Think What you List* and *The Emperor of the East* he only thinly concealed criticism of James I's favourites and other political figures, and on 11 January 1630 Sir Henry Herbert (he who had already been in deep trouble over *A Game at Chess*) refused a licence to an un-

Philip Massinger

named Massinger play because 'it did contain dangerous matter such as the depos-
ing of the King of Portugal by Philip II and there being a peace sworn between the
Kings of Spain and England' — this is believed to be an early version (called
Believe as You List) of *Think What you List*.

We know he married, but not when he did so. Presumably he and his wife —
and family, if he had any — lived poorly. In the dedication of his first play in 1623
he apologizes for writing for the theatre at all, saying that 'my misfortunes having cast me on this course' he therefore published his play 'to the world'.

He wrote fifteen plays on his own, borrowing the plots for several from the
work of Cervantes. To the present-day playgoer his plays seem full of stock
characters more akin to Victorian melodrama than to the plays of his own day,
particularly his villains. Sir Giles Overreach, the rumbustious villain of *A New
Way to Pay Old Debts*, is described as 'a cruel extortioner', and he would fit easily
into a play such as Boucicault's *Streets of London*. Even the innocent young
daughter from the same play who against her will is supposed to snare a lord by
trying to get him to make her pregnant (and thus enforce marriage) has
similarities with her Victorian counterparts, although it is unlikely in the extreme
that mid-nineteenth-century audiences would have had the 'ruin' of a damsel
explained to them in such forthright terms.

Hazlitt said of him 'his impassioned characters are like drunkards or madmen,
their conduct is extreme and outrageous, their motives unaccountable and weak'.
He continued that Massinger shows 'a peculiarly corrupt tone of thought even in
his heroines when they are intended as models of virtue. Their morality lies entirely in their obedience to outward observance not to inner principle. Purity is
not to be found in his world and his obscenity seems purposeless.' Massinger may
have provided prototypes for nineteenth-century melodrama but he saw human
nature with more honest eyes.

There is a suggestion, but no proof, that Massinger became converted to
Roman Catholicism at some stage in his life. His death is something of a mystery.
He lived at the Bankside, near the Globe Theatre, and apparently was in good
health even the day before his death. It is said that 'he went to bed well and was
dead before morning'. Whereupon his body, 'being accompanied by comedians',
was buried about the middle of the churchyard belonging to St Saviour's church.
His burial entry reads: '1638 March 18th. Philip Massinger, stranger, in the
church — 2*l*.' The word 'stranger' means he was not a parishioner (which would
be accounted for if he had become a Catholic), and possibly this was why there
was such as large fee for the burial — 2*l*, or £2. Tradition says he was buried in the
same grave as his friend John Fletcher. If Fletcher was, as we are told, a plague
victim, then he was very fortunate to have received separate and Christian burial
and not to have been thrown into the plague pits with the rest of the victims of the
great plague of 1625. There was plague in 1637/8 as well, and while it was not so
severe it lasted for a long time; the theatres were closed for fifteen months.
Possibly it struck Massinger too, and this was kept quiet so that he could be
properly buried, accompanied by 'comedians' — which would mean actors.

After his death his widow went to live in Cardiff, possibly with her family. All we know of her is that she received a pension thereafter from the Earl of Pembroke.

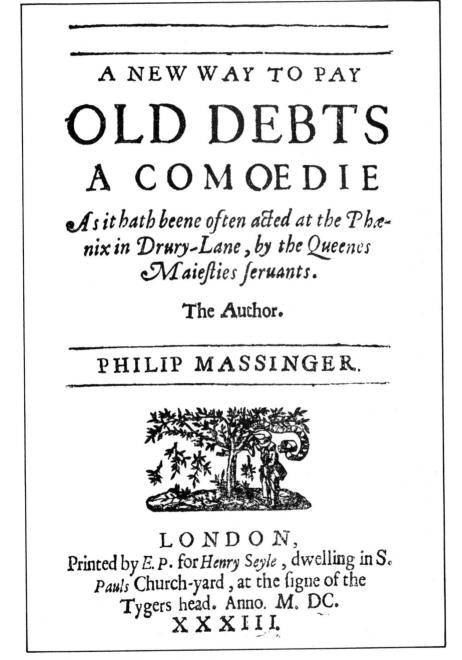

A New Way to Pay Old Debts *title-page*

Ben Jonson (National Portrait Gallery)

Chapter 6

Ben Jonson

'For as thou couldst all characters impart
So none could render thine, which still escapes
Like Proteus, in variety of shapes — '
                                Edmund Waller

In the summer of 1618 a large, portly gentleman in his mid-forties set off on a walking tour to Scotland. He had no reason to travel on foot as he was not short of money, so he obviously did it by choice. He arrived in Edinburgh towards the end of the summer, where he was received with honour by civic dignitaries — which was only right for a man who two years before had had his major works published in Folio form, and who was about to receive an honorary Oxford degree.

He was still in Scotland when Christmas came, settled in with the Scots poet William Drummond of Hawthornden. Of Drummond, his guest said 'He was too good and simple and that often a man's modesty made a fool of his wit.' At least, nobody could have accused Ben Jonson of that. . . . His fellow-playwright, Thomas Dekker, describes his appearence as being distinctly unhandsome, with a face like a 'bruised, rotten russet apple, or a badly pock-marked brass warming pan'.

We will learn later what Drummond thought of his expensive guest as he waded through Drummond's ale and wine and threw parties at the Scots poet's expense.

We know more about Ben Jonson than any other poet/playwright of his time. This is not only because he lived a good deal longer than any of his contemporaries but also because he wrote at length about himself and his views and thoughts. He was well recorded (especially by the unfortunate Drummond), for his Falstaffian lifestyle was such that he made an impact on his times it was not possible to ignore. While most of his fellow-playwrights remain shadowy figures — Shakespeare, most of all, flits in and out of the theatrical scene of his day like a wraith — Jonson's contentious nature, his brawling and roystering and battles with the law (including three terms of imprisonment) have ensured that irrespective of his remarkable body of work he is known as one of the most colourful characters of an age when there were plenty of them about.

Jonson was the kind of man, obviously, who would have been wonderful company in the public bar, or the life and soul of the supper party, but an appalling long-term house guest.

He is thought to have been born in London in the summer of 1572, after the death of his father. He told Drummond, on the famous visit, that his grandfather came to Carlisle, he thought from Annandale, that he served King Henry VIII and was a 'gentleman' but his son (i.e., Jonson's father) lost 'his estate' under Mary Tudor and, 'having been cast into prison and forfeited', came out and went into the Church. So, says Drummond, Jonson was 'a Minister's Son'. His father died during his mother's pregnancy, and Ben was a posthumous child, born a month afterwards.

We do not know how true this account is. Jonson felt desperate about his humble beginnings all his life, and never ceased to take offence at the mere mention of them, for shortly after his father's death, his mother married a master-bricklayer from Westminster. He grew up in Westminster and went to Westminster School, which even then was one of the best schools in London. He seems to have been a formidable scholar while he was there, and remained proud of his knowledge of classical languages all his life, feeling able to patronize Shakespeare for having 'small Latin and less Greek'. Later, when he was to criticize a variety of foreign poets to Drummond — especially Petrarch's sonnets, 'which he said were like that Tyrant's bed where some who were too short were racked and others too long cut short . . .' — Drummond was to write, acidly, that anyway 'all this was to no purpose for he neither doeth understand French or Italian'.

Like Shakespeare, Jonson left school without going on to university, most likely because he needed to earn his keep. He seems to have been apprenticed as a bricklayer to his stepfather, and became a master-bricklayer. Not surprisingly, he ran away from this as soon as he could, and made off to fight in the wars in the Low Country. He was never to forget his beginnings in the bricklaying trade, and even had he managed to do so, his less charitable contemporaries were continually to remind him.

In the Low Countries, he told Drummond, he did great things, including challenging a crack swordsman from the other side to face-to-face combat in front of the opposing armies, where he killed him and took from him his armour.

He returned from the wars penniless in 1592 and married a woman called Anne Lewis, of whom we know even less than we do of Anne Hathaway. Jonson described her as 'a shrew but honest'. They had several children. A daughter, Mary, died at the age of six months and was possibly the first child, as in her moving epitaph her father describes her as being the child of her parents' youth. He asks the gentle earth to cover her lightly.

He was even more devastated by the death of his son, who died at the age of seven of the plague in 1601. Even in an age where every family could expect to lose several children in infancy, his verse on his son's death is deeply touching,

Euery

MAN IN

HIS

HVMOVR.

A Comœdie.

Acted in the yeere 1598. By the then
Lord Chamberlaine his
Seruants.

The Author B. I.

I u v e n.

Haud tamen inuidens vati, quem pulpita pafcunt.

LONDON,

Printed by WILLIAM STANSBY.

M. D C. XVI.

Every Man in his Humour *title-page*

moving us across the centuries.

Here we see the real person behind the bombast: the man who had such a confident notion of his own worth as a writer could say

> Rest in soft peace, and asked, say here doth lie
> Ben Jonson, his best piece of poetry.

Little Benjamin was obviously a much loved and wanted child.

It seems that Jonson and his wife drifted apart, and by 1618 Jonson was telling Drummond that he had not bedded with her for some five years. He also told Drummond other strange stories about his family life — that in his youth he was 'given to venery', that he thought going to bed with a maid nothing to the enjoyment of 'the wantoness of a wife' and that at one time a man 'made his own wife to court him' and he enjoyed her two years before he knew of it, and that while married he had lain with another woman 'diverse times', who allowed him all privileges 'except the last act which she would not agree unto'. Anne Jonson obviously had a lot to put up with.

He also told Drummond about the death of his son. Jonson was staying at the time at Sir Robert Cotton's house in the country. During the night he saw in a vision

> his eldest son [then a child and at London] appear unto him with a mark of a bloody cross on his forehead as if he had been cut with a sword, at which amazed he prayed unto God, and in the morning he came to Mr. Cambden's Chamber to tell him, who persuaded him it was but an apprehension of his fantasy at which he could not be dejected. In the mean time come letters from his wife of the death of the boy in the plague.

It is not certain how Jonson made a living to support his wife and family after his return from the Low Countries, though it seems pretty well accepted that he became an actor — but not a very good one, unlike the competent Shakespeare. He did not first tread the boards in the great London theatres but travelled the roads with a band of players. Later, during the War of the Poets, Dekker said of him 'thou hast forgot how thou amblest (in leather pilch) by a play wagon, in the highway, and took mad Ieronimoe's part to get service among the Mimics'. This would mean Jonson played Hieronimo in Kyd's very popular *Spanish Tragedy*.

By 1597 he had attached himself to Henslowe's company. His relationship with that famous impresario was to be sporadic; Jonson would spend his working life going from company to company, having rows, reconciliations and fits of pique. We know from Henslowe's *Diary* that on 28 July 1597 he lent Jonson £4 'to be repaid on demand' and that on 2 December 1597 it says: 'Lent unto Benjamin Jonson upon a booke which he was to write for us before Crysmas next after the date hereof which he showed the plotte unto the companie, I have lente him in readie money the sum of . . . [the amount is blank]'. On another occasion Henslowe notes he paid Jonson one pound for the plot of a play which was never delivered. It is obvious that Henslowe gave playwrights advances, much in the way today's publishers advance authors on their royalties.

Initially he seems to have collaborated with other playwrights — not at all unusual at the time — on several plays which are now lost. He wrote *The Page of Plymouth*, for instance, with Dekker, and it is a pity it is lost, for it was obviously one of the earliest 'drama documentaries' based on a real-life murder for which Ulalia Page and her lover, George Strangwidge, were executed in Barnstaple in 1589.

One lost play is *The Isle of Dogs*, where he appears to have collaborated with Nashe. We know virtually nothing about this play except that it landed Jonson in prison (Nashe having legged it to Great Yarmouth), and that it was some kind of satire. Imprisoned with Jonson — for reasons we do not know — was one of Henslowe's actors, Gabriel Spencer. Presumably Jonson's imprisonment came some time between the July and December of 1597, when Henslowe lent him money.

1598 was a crucial year for Jonson. The first major play of which he was the sole author was performed, and he also went to prison again, during which time he became converted to Roman Catholicism for a period of twelve years.

Jonson had continued writing with other playwrights, two other missing plays being *Robert II of Scotland* and *Richard Crookback*. There had been a play about Richard III before Shakespeare's, but one can only surmise how popular Jonson's would have been at a time when Shakespeare's play had been drawing enthusiastic audiences for several years. Henslowe gave Jonson an advance for it, but that is about all we know.

But in 1598 Jonson wrote *Every Man in His Humour*. Scholars disagree over which event came first, the production of the play or Jonson's imprisonment. We know that Jonson went to prison in the September of that year, and we also know it was for killing that same Gabriel Spencer with whom he had been imprisoned the previous year.

Henslowe, writing to his actor son-in-law Alleyn — who was away on tour somewhere — notes sourly that he has hard and heavy news to tell. 'Since you were with me, I have lost one of my company which hurteth me a great deal, that is Gabriel, for he is slain in Hog's Fields by the hands of Beng. Jonson, Bricklayer, therefore I would fain have a little of your counsel.'

The 'Bricklayer's' story to Drummond was that he fought a duel with Spencer: 'he had killed his adversary, which had hurt him on the arm and whose sword was ten inches longer than his, for the which he was imprisoned and almost at the Gallows. Then took he his religion by trust of a Priest who visited him in Prison, thereafter he was 12 years a Papist.'

Jonson had pleaded 'clergy' to avoid the death penalty. To do this he had to be able to read what was known as the 'neck verse', the first verse of Psalm 51, which criminals who were pleading benefit of clergy had to read out in Latin to prove they were literate. It followed that pretenders to learning could not be sent to the gallows. Some people learned it off by heart just in case.

The Middlesex Sessions Rolls note that Benj. Jonson killed Gabriel Spencer on 22 September 1598 in the Fields by Shoreditch with a three shilling rapier, that he was tried at the Old Bailey, convicted on his own confession of felonious homicide and was branded with a Tyburn T on his left thumb.

So to *Every Man in His Humour*. This is particularly interesting, as it brings Shakespeare on to the scene, for it was performed by his company with Shakespeare himself taking one of the parts — as we know from the list of actors prefixed to the play in the Folio of Jonson's work in 1616. Shakespeare's name is shown opposite that of one of the leading roles, that of Mr Knowell. This does not necessarily mean that he played that part, as sometimes such cast lists gave the actors' names in the order of their importance as shareholders or for other reasons — and Shakespeare was the resident playwright — but it is certain he did take part. While some sources say it was performed before Jonson went to prison, others say it was put on after he came out, and there is a tradition that Shakespeare's company had rejected it but that after Jonson came out of prison Shakespeare himself read it, liked it and persuaded the company to put it on. Whatever happened, the play was a success, and established Jonson as a successful dramatist and a poet of note.

Plays followed thick and fast from Jonson, but the next major event in Jonson's working life was his involvement in what became known as the War of the Poets or the Theatre War.

Some time in 1599 Marston resurrected an old play called *Histriomastix*. At that time Marston rather admired Jonson, so he gave one of the characters in the play, called Chrisoganus, some of the characteristics and habits of Jonson. He was to say later that he intended this as a compliment.

Not only did Jonson not take it as such, he was enraged. The sequel to *Every Man in His Humour* was *Every Man out of His Humour*. This was playing, and Jonson added various words and sentences to the part of Carlo Buffone to suggest Marston, and rubbed it in by having a character called Clove refer to Buffone in a disparaging way. Buffone is described as being 'a public, scurrilous and profane jester' who could scent out a good dinner three miles off.

Marston struck back. His next play *Jack Drum's Entertainment* in 1600 portrayed Jonson much more recognizably, and this time with malice aforethought, in the character of Brabant senior. Those who knew Jonson must have smiled at the description of his sounding when talking like a large drum being beaten in a small room.

While the character showed some of Jonson's likeable traits, he was also portrayed as being extremely pompous, and pontificating on the proper way to write comedies in words which Jonson had used. It was a fairly insulting parody.

Not to be outdone, Jonson produced *Cynthia's Revels*. This ridiculed Marston in the role of Hedon, and then for no apparent reason added a swingeing attack on Dekker, who appears to have done nothing whatsoever to incur Jonson's wrath. It seems that both Marston and Dekker were easily recognizable to the audiences of the day.

So this time Marston and Dekker collaborated on a send-up of Jonson in the bombastic character of Lampatho Doria in their play *What You Will*. Jonson was struggling to finish his next work, *The Poetaster*, which contains portraits of Marston and Dekker, thinly disguised as two terrible hacks called Crispinus and

Demetrius. The two appear in a Roman gallery of fame in which Demetrius/ Dekker comes at the bottom of the heap. Marston and Dekker just got their play out first, but Jonson's *Poetaster* seems to have won this round.

There is some proof that even Shakespeare had been dragged in by this time. An anonymous play written in 1600–1 called *The Return from Parnassus* has the character of Will Kempe say 'O that Ben Jonson is a pestilent fellow, he brought up *Horace* giving the poets a pill, but our fellow Shakespeare hath given him a purge that made him betray his credit.' The purge can be read as the character of the bragging Ajax in *Troilus and Cressida*. In his preface to *Poetaster* — spoken by Envy — Jonson takes a number of swipes at his critics and their 'spy-like suggestions' and 'petty whisperings', but in his 'Apologetical Dialogue' at the end he describes those with better natures who had been drawn into the quarrel and ends by saying that he, Jonson, was fed up with the whole thing and was to turn his attention to writing tragedies.

That very nearly was that. But it was to be Dekker who had the last word. He wrote a play *Satiromastix* — which was presented a few weeks after *Poetaster* — in which he included one of Jonson's own characters, a Captain Tucca. To compound the insult Dekker says it would have been impossible to invent such a swaggerer, leaving his audience in no doubt as to his meaning. *Satiromastix* was staged by Shakespeare's company, presumably with his blessing as a senior member of it.

After which Jonson indeed faded away from the public scene for a year or two and wrote both tragedies and comedies. But even though he made it up with Marston later (they were to collaborate on a play which got them both into trouble, *Eastward Ho!*) the memory of the Poets' War still rankled as long after as 1618, when Jonson visited Drummond.

Concerning his contemporaries, Jonson told Drummond that 'Daniel was jealous of him, Drayton feared him and esteemed him not, that Francis Beaumont loved too much himself and his own verse and that he beat Marston and took his pistol from him.' He continued in this vein that 'Sir W. Alexander was not half kind to him and neglected him because a friend to Drayton, that Markham was not of the number of the Faithful [i.e., a sort of bookseller's hack] and but a base fellow and that such were Day and Middleton, that Chapman and Fletcher loved him and Overbury was first his friend, then turned to mortal enemy.'

In spite of having apparently made it up with Marston years before, he told Drummond that 'Marston wrote his father-in-law's preachings and his father-in-law his [Marston's] comedies.' Shakespeare, he said, had 'in a play brought on a number of men saying they had suffered a shipwreck in Bohemia where there is no sea by some 100 miles'.

It was in 1605 that Jonson was, as one might say today, in the headlines again. Along with Marston and Chapman, he wrote a very funny play, *Eastward Ho!* We will look at the play again when discussing Jacobean comedies, but the story needs to be told now. It was written for a company called The Children of Her Majesty's Revels. There are several plots and sub-plots, but it was the passages which sent up the Scots which caused an enormous amount of offence at the

Court of a Scots king who had only been on the throne for two years, and who had filled the Court with Scots favourites and place-seekers. A satire at the expense of these same Scots was not, therefore, a wise move.

It particularly offended Sir James Murray, who complained in no uncertain terms to the King, who ordered the arrest of the playwrights. Certainly Jonson and Chapman were put in prison, but there is no documentary proof that Marston suffered the same fate, although Jonson states categorically that he did.

Jonson gave his version of the affair to Drummond. He was reported, says Jonson,

> by Sir James Murray to the King for writing something against the Scots in a play Eastward Ho and voluntarily imprisoned himself with Chapman and Marston, who had written it amongst them. The report was that they should have then had their ears cut and noses. After their delivery he banqueted his friends, there was Camden, Selden and others. At the midst of the feast his old mother drank to him and showed him a paper, which she had (if the sentence had taken execution) to have mixed in the prison among his drink, which was full of lusty strong poison and that she was no churl, she told she minded first to have drunk of it herself.

So here we have a splendid picture. Jonson, hearing of Chapman and Marston's imprisonment, rushing to give himself up and be 'voluntarily' imprisoned, his dear old mother prepared to give him poison rather than see him suffer a terrible punishment, and finally his triumphant release where he throws a party for everybody. Note too that the suggestion is that Jonson had little part in the writing of the play, it being written by Chapman and Marston 'among themselves'. Great stuff. . . .

There the matter rested until 1901, when letters from Chapman and Jonson to various members of the nobility were found in a collection of seventeenth-century manuscripts owned by a Mr T. A. White of New York. These were letters written by the two men while in prison in 1605. There is certainly no confirmation that Jonson went there of his own free will, or that Marston was there with them. So far from playing the swaggerer while in gaol, Jonson wrote obsequious letters pleading with a variety of titled people to get him out.

A typical letter is that addressed to 'The Most Nobly-Virtuous and Thrice-Honoured Earl of Salisbury'. After some general preamble Jonson writes:

> I am here my most honoured Lord, unexamined or unheard, committed to a vile prison and with me a gentleman (whose name may perhaps have come to your Lordship), one Mr. George Chapman, a learned and honest man. The cause (would I could name some worthier, though I wish we had known none worthy our imprisonment), is (the word irks me that our fortune have necessitated us to so despised a course), a play, my Lord.

There is much more in this vein. In conclusion Jonson writes:

> But lest in being too diligent for my excuse I may incur the suspicion of

being guilty, I become a most humble suitor to your Lordship that with the honourable Lord Chamberlain (to whom I have in like manner petitioned), you will be pleased to be the grateful means of our coming to answer; or if in your wisdoms it shall be thought unnecessary, that your Lordships will be the most honoured cause of our liberty, where freeing us from one prison you shall remove us to another; which is eternally to bind us and our muses, to the thankful honouring of you and yours to posterity; as your own virtues have by many descents of ancestors ennobled you to time.

Your Honour's most devoted in heart as words — Ben Jonson.

Whether it was the deluge of letters from Jonson or the more restrained correspondence of Chapman we do not know, but it does not seem that the men remained in prison for long, and by the beginning of October 1605 they had been freed.

Whether or not Jonson did throw a party of his own we have only his word on which to rely, but on 9 October he certainly attended one. It was given by Robert Catesby, one of the conspirators in the Gunpowder Plot which had been timed to take place not quite four weeks later. One feels only Jonson could have gone straight from prison to such a party.

Jonson was working hard, and the next ten years were probably the most comfortable of his life. Shakespeare's company had put on *Volpone* in 1605, but Jonson, ever the rolling stone, did not offer them another play until 1610, and then he gave them one of the greatest comic plays in the English language, *The Alchemist*. It is ironic that Jonson, whose lasting fame as a playwright is founded so firmly on his great comedies, should spend his working lifetime desperately wanting to be taken seriously as a writer of tragedies.

Between 1609 and 1616 Jonson also steadily composed masques, many in conjunction with the great designer Inigo Jones, although it seems the two never did agree very well on the staging of Jonson's work. The masques were very popular with the Court, and in 1616 he was granted a pension of a hundred marks by King James, making him in effect the country's first Poet Laureate.

1616 was an important date for Jonson in two other respects. First, his great friend William Shakespeare died on 23 April and later Jonson had a number of his own works published in a First Folio edition.

There are those who say that Jonson was ambivalent in his feelings towards Shakespeare, but there seems little real proof; rather the reverse. Certainly he included Shakespeare in his usual run of impertinent comments, and criticized him for his apparent lack of knowledge of classical languages and his abysmal geography, but he also said that Shakespeare was a man he loved 'this side of idolatry'.

Shakespeare made his will on 25 March 1616 and described himself as being 'in perfect health and memory, God be praised'. We do not know, therefore, exactly what illness brought about his death. Half a century later, a Stratford vicar noted: 'Shakespeare, Drayton and Ben Jonson had a merry meeting and, it seems, drank too hard for Shakespeare died of a fever there contracted.' Local tradition gives the

*Ralph Cotterill (Mooncalf), Richard Moon (Jordan Knockem) and Lila Kaye (Ursula) in the 1969
RSC production of* Bartholomew Fair. *(Photo: Reg Wilson)*

Bell at Welford-on-Avon as the venue for this last carouse. Shakespeare was never
noted as a drinker and reveller, and one wonders if he went on foot and was
soaked to the skin as he trudged along the long, winding, muddy, riverside foot-
path from Stratford to Welford some three miles away, and if he contracted
pneumonia. We do not know if Jonson stayed at New Place with the
Shakespeares or in a local hostelry. Drayton usually stayed at near-by Clifford
Chambers, and although Jonson rarely had a good word to say for Drayton,
presumably he buried his feelings in a social evening with his old friend William.

When Shakespeare's works finally came to be collected in the First Folio in
1623 Jonson wrote one of the most generous tributes ever made by one writer
about another. Describing how Shakespeare had surpassed the 'sporting Kyd or
Marlowe's mighty line', he rightly recognized his greater rival was 'not of an
age, but for all time!' What more could be said than that?

Possibly it was Shakespeare's death which prompted Jonson into collecting
together his own works so that they could be properly edited by himself and he
could oversee their publication, rather than being left to the mercies of
posthumous editors, however well-meaning. Publishing his works in this way
brought him widespread criticism for his arrogance, but it was a most sensible
measure. However, still determined to be considered primarily as a tragedian,

Jonson missed out some of his best work, including *Bartholomew Fair*.

In 1618 he paid his famous visit to William Drummond. We have already noted some of the remarks he made to that poet. Goodness only knows what Drummond really made of it all; he seems to have been a rather quiet and studious soul, and one imagines that he did not have any idea what he was letting himself in for when he extended his invitation to Jonson to drop in. Presumably some of the more scurrilous gossip retailed by Jonson was to entertain the large numbers of guests who availed themselves of Drummond's hospitality in order to meet the great sophisticated playwright and man about town from London.

The gossip included the story of 'Sir Henry Wotton' caught in the act of seducing one of his maids who 'before his Majesty's going into England, being disguised at Leith on a Sunday when all the rest were at church, being interrupted of his occupation by another wench who came in at the door, cried out "Pox on thee for thou hast hindered the procreation of a child" and thus betrayed himself.'

Some of the stories scarcely reflect well on Jonson himself. One was how Sir Walter Raleigh had sent him as a governor to his son to France in 1613.

> This Youth being knavishly inclined, among other pastimes (as the getting of the favour of Damsels on a cod piece) caused him [Jonson] to be drunken and dead drunk so that he knew not where he was, thereafter laid him on a cart which he made to be drawn by Pioneers through the streets, at every corner showing his governor stretched out and telling them that there was a more lively image of the Crucifix than any they had, at which sport young Raleigh's mother delighted much (saying his father young was so inclined) although the father abhorred.

Jonson said he could tell horoscopes but did not trust them, and this reminded him of an incident where he had cozened a lady who had an appointment with an old astrologer in the suburbs. When she kept it she found Jonson there 'disguised in a long gown and a white beard at the light of a dim burning candle up a little Cabinet reached by a ladder'.

After Jonson had been reconciled with the Church 'and stopped being a Recusant, at his first communion in token of true reconciliation he drank out all the full cup of wine'.

Several times, Drummond reported, Jonson told him he had had to sell his books 'out of necessity'. This would not have come easily to Jonson, who set much store by his library, as we know when he lost many of his books in a fire in 1623. Nor will it surprise anyone to know, after the kind of heavy night in which our hero so often indulged, to learn that 'he hath consumed a whole night in lying looking to his Great Toe, about which he has seen Tartars and Turks, Romans and Carthaginians fight in his imagination . . .'

Of Drummond's own verses Jonson said 'that they were all good, especially my Epitaph on the Prince, save they smelled too much of the schools and were not after the fancy of the time'.

One wonders if Drummond got a word in edgeways. As Jonson stomps off into the mist towards England, we can imagine Drummond standing there almost entirely surrounded by empty bottles and filled with an overwhelming sense of relief. He expressed his own feelings as follows:

> He is a great lover and praiser of himself, a contemner and scorner of others, given rather to lose a friend than a jest, jealous of every word and action of those about him (especially after a drink which is one of the elements in which he liveth), a dissembler of ill parts which reign in him, a bragger of some good that he wanteth, thinketh nothing well but what either he himself or some of his friends and countrymen hath said and done. He is passionately kind and angry, careless either to gain or keep, vindictive but if he be well answered, at himself. . . . Interpreteth best sayings and deeds often to the worst, oppressed with fantasy, which hath ever mastered his reason, a general disease in many poets.

Presumably Jonson did not feel he had outstayed his welcome in any way, for on 10 May 1619 he wrote to Drummond suggesting he might do a little research for him on a project on which he was engaged, and sending his regards to a formidable list of people he had met while staying with him. We do not know what Drummond replied, but looking at it from nearly four centuries later, we can only be grateful that he recorded the meeting in such detail.

From then until he died in 1637 Jonson seems to have lived a life in more straitened circumstances. He received his honorary Oxford degree in 1619, and we know that at that time he lectured in rhetoric at Gresham College in London. From 1616 to 1625 he wrote nothing at all for the stage, confining himself to masques and poetry. Financial necessity alone drew him back to the theatre, although his later plays were very different from those by which he had made his name; more vehicles for expressing his own opinions and attacking those with which he did not agree than carefully constructed pieces in their own right. Not surprisingly, he was endlessly in disagreement with those he criticized in such a way.

In 1628 he was appointed City Chronologer, and he also suffered a stroke which was to leave him partly paralysed. He did only a little more writing for the Court, partly because his work seems to have gone out of fashion and also because he remained on bad terms with Inigo Jones.

The last years of his life seem rather sad. That he died poor is shown by the fact that the entire value of his estate came to only £8 8s. 10d., little enough compared with what Shakespeare left, or Alleyn, who could leave sufficient money to endow Dulwich College. Jonson seems to have had no surviving children, and most of his best friends, dearest enemies and working colleagues were dead. In those last years he did have the support of a group of admiring younger men, known as the 'Tribe of Ben', and it is interesting to note that they regarded him first and foremost as a poet, not a playwright.

Although he died poor he was buried in style, and his grave remains in Poets' Corner in Westminster Abbey. There is a theory that the stone-carver made a mistake and his epitaph should have read *orare* (i.e., *orate*, pray for) Ben Jonson. But it seems much more fitting that it should rightly be, as it is:

O Rare Ben Jonson.

Rather than say farewell to such a marvellous personality on this sad note, perhaps we should end with a few lines of verse by a fellow-playwright, Francis Beaumont, recalling nights on the town with Ben:

Methinks the little wit I had is lost
Since I saw you, for wit is like a rest
Held up at tennis, which men do the best
With the best gamesters; what things have we seen
Done at the Mermaid! heard words that have been
So nimble and so full of subtle flame
As if that every one from whence they came
Had meant to put his whole wit in a jest
And had resolved to live a fool, the rest
Of his dull life.

Eric Porter (as the Jew) in the 1965 RSC production of The Jew of Malta. *(Tom Holte Theatre Photographic Collection)*

Chapter 7

The Plays of Christopher Marlowe

'I am become Death — Shatterer of Worlds.'
Bhagavad-Gita

What is primarily under consideration in this section of the book is plays as theatre. That might sound pretty obvious, but it is not so, because the majority of works on the subject of Elizabethan and Jacobean plays, heavily academic or not, are about the plays as texts, the plays as writing and only rarely with plays as theatre or in performance.

For this reason there are considerable problems in discussing the works of Marlowe, for it is not by chance that only *Dr Faustus* is regularly performed — there are considerable problems today in putting on *Tamburlaine*, *Edward II* and *The Jew of Malta*.

There is no doubt at all that Marlowe revolutionized the theatre of his time. Before Marlowe, we have the gentle romances of Greene, some fairly good comedies, some rather second-rate tragedies — though this does not include Kyd's *Spanish Tragedy* — and a large number of plays which are either almost forgotten or which have disappeared without trace. Marlowe pioneered the grand spectacle, the powerful show and, of course, the kind of writing for the theatre which had hitherto been unknown. Truly, as Ben Jonson says, he has a 'mighty line'.

What makes the plays difficult for modern audiences is that, *Faustus* apart, they remain episodic. There is little drama in the true sense in *Tamburlaine*. Elizabethan audiences would have loved it for its sheer spectacle, its power and its violence. At a period of time so close to the morality plays, where evil men had to be seen to be properly punished, it did not even have a 'moral' as such. Tamburlaine claws his way to power, conquers half the known world, but he does not develop as a character and although he dies at the end he is not 'punished' for his crimes in the accepted sense of the word. Tamburlaine was the first of Marlowe's great over-reachers, and it was obviously a part much loved by its interpreter, Edward Alleyn.

As we know, the two parts of *Tamburlaine* were written separately. But by the time Marlowe had been in London a little while, both were put on by Henslowe, and they created an enormous success for their 23-year-old author. In *Tamburlaine* Marlowe did not break the earlier theatrical tradition altogether, for most plays of the time were of an episodic nature. The deep intricacies of plot and the development of character was to come later — although not much later — with the plays of Shakespeare.

The two parts of *Tamburlaine* cover a simple story based on fact. The fourteenth-century historical character Timur was the son of a Mongol chief. His career mirrors those of Attila the Hun and Genghis Khan. He fought his way (laying waste as he went) across Russia, the Middle East, Turkey and India. When the citizens of Baghdad stood in his way he razed the city to the ground and killed the inhabitants. He died at the age of sixty-nine, just as he was about to invade China. Within a relatively short space his empire had disappeared. He was lame, and was in fact known as Timur the Lame, from a wound he had received in battle.

Marlowe makes his Tamburlaine the son of a Scythian shepherd, and he has no physical defects — in fact the reverse. He is amazingly handsome as well as strong and agile. Tamburlaine brings in a new order, an order of conquest, violence, male pride and ruthlessness. At the beginning this is welcomed, but it soon becomes apparent that once this particular genie has been let out of the bottle, then there is no going back. The catalogue of wars, killings, torture, slavery and devastation grows ever greater until Tamburlaine finally meets the only enemy he is unable to conquer — death.

Nowadays we might well liken Tamburlaine to a Fascist dictator, which is probably another reason why he does not appeal to modern audiences in the way he did to Elizabethans. Hitler is too near to Tamburlaine for comfort. The difficulty now, even when there is a magnificent production of the play such as that which opened the new National Theatre, is that it fails to hold the attention for the whole of its length because the scenes of carnage, humiliation and disaster eventually become repetitious and the senses are bludgeoned.

Not only was Tamburlaine Marlowe's first overreacher, he was also a man without religion. The famous lines in which he says:

Is it not passing brave to be a king,
And ride in triumph through Persepolis?

are greeted by his listener with 'To be a king is half to be a god!' to which Tamburlaine replies, significantly 'A god is not so glorious as a king.'

That his audiences relished the cruelty is apparent from accounts of the time, not least the fact that one of the phrases in the play became a catch-phrase. This is the famous scene where Tamburlaine is pulled on to the stage in a chariot hauled by kings 'with bits in their mouths'. He whips them and shouts: 'Holla, ye

Ian McKellen (Faustus) and Emrys James (Mephistopheles) in the 1974 RSC production of Dr Faustus. *(Photo: Joe Cocks Studio)*

pampered jades of Asia!' Audiences loved that, and the phrase turns up again and again elsewhere, and was to be 'sent up' later by Ben Jonson. The idea of people who were being so ill-treated being described as 'pampered' would raise few laughs now — one hopes.

We know that when Alleyn played the part he had a magnificent suit of clothes with red velvet breeches (it appears in Henslowe's lists), and that there was a splendid saddle for Tamburlaine. We also know that at one of the earliest per-formances real bullets were used, and in one scene, the execution of the Governor of Babylon in the second part of the play, a bullet went astray and killed a member of the audience. The rest, however, stayed on and enjoyed it. . . .

Perhaps the best explanation of why the play was so popular is that given by Dr A. L. Rowse:

> The Elizabethan audience was given, in full measure, what it relished. There was the appeal to the war-atmosphere, when the time itself stood on tiptoe, expecting (and accomplishing) great deeds. There was the contem-porary value set upon individual heroic achievements, as with Drake or Philip Sidney or Grenville, the belief in energy and initiative, in a man carv-ing out his way for himself and expecting to enjoy his reward. Without any doubt, members of the Elizabethan audience saw themselves in the part of Tamburlaine as its creator did. In addition there was pageantry, there was colour as at the tournament or tilt, there was the clashing of armies; above all, there was the fury of torrential speech, the glory of language released at this molten, brazen moment into poetry that was never to be forgotten.

One of the most striking points about Marlowe's plays is that they all exist around one character who dominates the entire action. (In 1951 Sir Donald Wolfit was a Tamburlaine in the grand manner!) Most of those who surround that character are merely ciphers put there either to further the action or as a foil to the central figure — no wonder they were popular with a great actor like Alleyn, who we know preferred stalking the stage and dominating it to what we might term the more 'ensemble' approach of Burbage.

The Jew of Malta, Marlowe's next play, was written about 1589, and again we are shown a character of all-consuming evil, although in a different style to that of Tamburlaine. Marlowe opens his play very boldly with a real-life personage as prologue, none other than Machiavelli himself, wrongly considered by the English audiences to be the epitome of evil and intrigue. We first meet the Jew counting out his money in his home — 'infinite wealth in a small room' — and we learn that like Shakespeare's Shylock still to come, he had been very badly treated by the Christians of Malta, and is therefore out to seek his revenge. Jews were both distrusted and disliked, and a Jew as a villain would be both popular and topical.

Unlike *Tamburlaine*, there is some humour of a black and grisly kind in *The Jew*, not least when he and a Turkish slave called Ithamore try to cap each other with the nasty deeds they have done — 'As for myself', says Barabas,

> I walk abroad a' nights,
> And kill sick people groaning under walls;
> Sometimes I go about and poison wells . . .

And poison wells he does, or rather the food for a whole nunnery, and ends by committing treason on a grand scale when he first betrays Malta to the Turks and then also proposes to the Christians that he betrays the Turks to them. In between whiles he has killed his own daughter, Abigail, for going over to the Christians. He meets his end by being boiled in a cauldron, and this was obviously the high spot of the play as he disappeared into it with fearful screams.

Rather like the second part of *Tamburlaine*, *The Jew of Malta* falls off, but whereas *Tamburlaine* remained grand, if repetitious, the *Jew of Malta* tails off into a string of what we would consider today to be crude and rather sick jokes. It was, however, like *Tamburlaine*, immensely popular, and revived time after time. It attracted enormous popularity in the year after Marlowe's death when the Queen's physician, Dr Lopez, a Jew, was hanged — wrongly, as many now feel — for supposedly plotting to poison the Queen. It was a pity Marlowe did not live to see his play become the most topical piece of the year.

It certainly influenced Shakespeare directly, and from Marlowe's idea grew his play's far greater rival, *The Merchant of Venice*. Shylock, like Barabas, has been badly treated by a Christian community; Shylock, like Barabas, seeks to revenge himself, and like him is caught in his own trap. Shylock, however, is a human being, and while it was fashionable for years to play him as an outright villain those days have long since gone. The baiting of Shylock in the first half of the play causes real unease and dislike in a world which has since experienced the Holocaust. If it makes us uncomfortable now to see Shylock on stage, how much more so would it be to see Barabas, who is a villain because he is a Jew?

It now seems generally agreed that *Edward II* came before *Dr Faustus*, and it certainly seems appropriate that this should be so in terms of Marlowe's brief life. As did Shakespeare with his history plays, Marlowe turned to Holinshed's *Chronicles* as a source. It seems quite likely that at least the first and second parts of Shakespeare's *Henry VI* were then being played on stage, and by Henslowe's company for whom Marlowe was also writing. Possibly in this case Marlowe was influenced by his then unknown contemporary. As in the Shakespeare history plays, real-life events are telescoped and edited to suit the drama — which is necessary, for the action of the play is supposed to cover twenty-three years.

Again we have a protagonist surrounded by lesser characters, but this is not so marked as in the first two plays, and the protagonist himself is very different. We would probably describe him now as an anti-hero. The two parts into which the play naturally falls are equally disparate too, for it is almost as if the characters have become different people. The play must have caused something of a *cause célèbre* in its day, for it dealt with the obsessive love of Edward for two favourites. In the first, it is his total infatuation with Piers Gaveston, who has been banished but returns on Edward's insistence. We are shown a king without kingship, dallying with his favourite, squandering his wealth and totally neglecting his

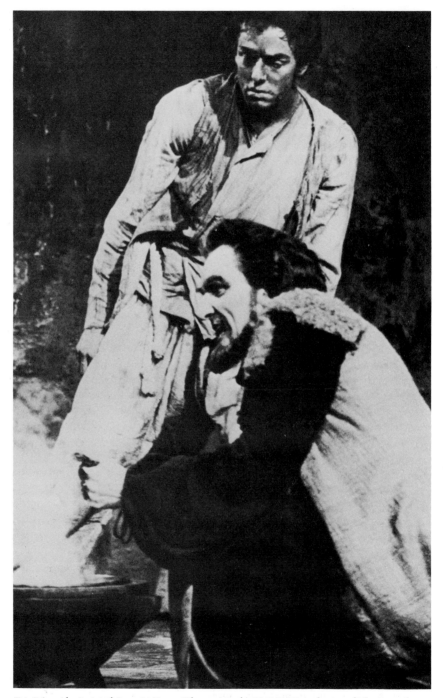

Eric Porter (the Jew) and Peter McEnery (Ithamore) in the 1965 RSC production of The Jew of
Malta. *(Shakespeare Centre Library, Stratford-upon-Avon)*

kingdom and his wife Isabella, who counts as nothing beside Gaveston. This is set against a background of continual wars between Edward and his barons, during which Isabella leaves the country.

Isabella, Edward's queen, is merely a long-suffering woman in the first half of the play, and it is specifically stated that there is no love between her and Edward's opponent, Mortimer. In fact she seems typical of Marlowe's lifeless women. Zenocrate in *Tamburlaine* seems to exist only to show us that Tamburlaine had a certain amount of human feeling towards her when she was alive, that she could bear him four sons necessary for the continuance of the plot, and that her death should provide the excuse for extravagant language from Tamburlaine and a magnificent funeral scene.

In the second half of the play Gaveston has been killed but the King has a new favourite, Spenser. Isabella has now totally changed character to become a two-dimensional villainess who with Mortimer returns, bringing with her civil war in an attempt to regain the throne. Edward is forced into abdication, followed by a gruesome and what was probably considered to be an apposite death, and Mortimer is then put to death on the orders of Edward II's son, while Isabella is incarcerated in the Tower.

Edward II is not often performed today, although there was a notable production in 1970 by the then Prospect Theatre Company with Ian McKellen as Edward, and it is not too difficult to see why. It suffers from many of the same problems as the three parts of *Henry VI*, but without the fascinating smaller characters which Shakespeare invented. We have to accept in Marlowe's world that the Edward who has been shown as so unsympathetic in the first half of the play becomes sympathetic to us in the second in spite of his proclivities and his weaknesses, but there is no logical link to show us how this comes about. Equally, Isabella is almost impossible to play, for either she is a simple, wronged and innocent woman or she is a scheming villainess, but she could hardly change overnight from one to the other.

So far as we know, *Edward II* was nothing like as popular as Marlowe's first two plays. For years after his death props for *Tamburlaine* and *The Jew* (including 'the cauldron for the boiling of the Jew') appeared in Henslowe's inventories of properties, but *Edward II* is seldom referred to. We also know that Alleyn did not play the part when the play was first performed. Presumably he was not attracted to it after the all-conquering Tamburlaine and the devilish Jew. No doubt too Elizabethan audiences felt as uncomfortable with the portrayal of homosexuality on stage as we do about the baiting of the Jew of Malta today.

But the play of Marlowe's which has had by far the most lasting popularity is without any doubt at all *Dr Faustus*. The legend of Faust was not new when Marlowe took it over. We do not know how far it goes back, but the story is one that is integral to the condition of man — that he will do anything, literally anything, even sell his own soul, for forbidden knowledge. The English translation of the Faust legend *The Damnable Life and Deserved Death of Doctor Faustus* came out in 1592, and it must have caught Marlowe by the throat.

Here is the ultimate overreacher, not a man of war and conquest but a seeker after knowledge, a man who wanted power over his immediate universe. Certainly he would have wealth, the most beautiful women in the world, all the obvious things, but far more he wanted knowledge. He wanted to raise spirits, converse with the dead, push his intellect to its uttermost. Faustus despised man and did not need God. There are such obvious analogies here between Marlowe and his creation: Marlowe the freethinker, the amoral pagan, the brilliant intellect, the outsider and (so it would seem) the secret-service agent caught up in a web of politics. What is more, the play could be presented as a continuation of the tradition of the morality plays, for Faustus, of course, must meet his appointed end and go to Hell.

While again Faustus dominates almost all the other characters in the play, the action is far more compulsive than that of any of the others, for as in a Greek tragedy, we know that Faustus has fixed himself on a wheel right at the very beginning of the play from which there is no climbing off. Also, unlike the other plays, there is a foil for Faustus in Mephistopheles.

Another departure is the scenes of broad, but not cruel, comedy in *Faustus* which have led some people to believe that Marlowe had a collaborator. It seems far more likely that Marlowe, fully aware of his splendid inevitable story, could relax and allow his sardonic humour some scope in this his last play. The basic plot is, of course, of the simplest. The scholar Faust desires wealth, power and above all knowledge; Mephistopheles is sent from Hell to offer him a bargain — Faustus's soul at the end of his life in exchange for everything he wants in this world. Faustus agrees, has his desires and is claimed finally by Mephistopheles.

At the end he does show fear of what is to come, and in his last soliloquy Marlowe gives him marvellous language:

O, I'll leap up to my God; Who pulls me down?
See, see, where Christ's blood streams in the firmament!
One drop would save my soul, half a drop . . .

After appropriate thunder and lightning devils enter and lead Faustus off to hell. But one is left, inescapably, feeling that if Faustus had his time once more he would do it all again.

In the deeply religious and superstitious times in which it was written the play was sensational. We know that Henslowe produced it with all the effects he could muster: thunder, lightning, gunfire, dozens of devils, a gaping Hell-mouth into which Faustus disappeared, great stuff. No doubt the more credulous believed that the stage Faustus just might conjure spirits or raise the dead.

Alleyn, when he played the part, used to wear a surplice and have a cross around his neck . . . just in case. We know from accounts of performances that many in the audience were both shocked and terrified by 'the visible apparition of the Devil on the stage', and we are told that in Exeter

certain players acting upon the stage the tragical story of Dr Faustus the Conjurer, as a certain number of devils kept every one his circle there, and as Faustus was busy in his magical invocations, on a sudden they were all dashed, every one harkening the other in the ear, for they were all persuaded there was one devil too many among them. And so after a little pause desired the people to pardon them, they could go no further in this matter; the people also understanding the thing as it was, every man hastened to be first out of doors. The players, as I heard it, contrary to their custom, spending the night in reading and in prayer got them out of town the next morning.

Many actors have trodden in the footsteps of Alleyn, including in recent years Richard Burton in the cinema and Ian McKellen.

We come back again to the fact that Faust grips because he, like Shakespeare's great heroes and villains, is for all time. In the twentieth century above all man has shown that his thirst for knowledge has subsumed everything else, and in his desire to push his curiosity to the ultimate he has unleashed demons far more appalling than any that could have been dreamed up by the audiences who watched Marlowe's play, or even by their creator. Scientific man has combined two myths; he is the Dr Faustus who has unlocked Pandora's box.

So much of Marlowe is in Faustus's line 'this word damnation terrifies not me'. So much of man is in it too. When Dr Robert Oppenheimer saw the explosion of the first atomic bomb at Los Alamos — the project to which he had given everything and for which he had sacrificed everything — he looked at the fiery glow and the mushroom cloud and quoted from the *Bhagavad-Gita* 'I am become Death — Shatterer of Worlds.' But he was to live to regret it.

THE

CHANGELING:

As it was Acted (with great Applaufe)
at the Privat houfe in D ʀ ᴜ ʀ ʏ ꝑ L ᴀ ɴ ᴇ,
and *Salisbury Court.*

Written by { *THOMAS MIDLETON,* and *WILLIAM ROWLEY.* } Gent'.

Never Printed before.

L O N D O N,
Printed for Hᴜᴍᴘʜʀᴇʏ Mᴏsᴇʟᴇʏ, and are to
be fold at his fhop at the fign of the *Princes-Arms*
in St *Pauls* Church-yard, 1 6 5 3.

The Changeling *title-page (British Library)*

Chapter 8

Bloody Revenge & Tragedy

'Remember, man, as you pass by
As you are now, so once was I.
As I am now, so shalt thou be
Cut off by death — and follow me.'
Epitaph in Laugharne Churchyard, Dyfed

With the possible exception of Ben Jonson, it would never have occurred to any of the Elizabethan and Jacobean playwrights — including Shakespeare — that their texts would become set books in schools and universities. They wrote only for performance. It is easy to forget this when faced with the mountains of academic works on the play texts.

So when scholars talk of uneven texts and poor writing, this is in the context of how the plays stand up today to close examination by academics and students. It is probably one reason why so many of them are not actually put on the stage any more. Obviously out of the many plays written during the period there are bound to be some very bad ones, and some were definitely hack work, but it is not fair to damn them all because they are not Shakespeare. While the best of all possible worlds would be a marvellous piece of writing which also works perfectly on stage, many of today's plays show very clearly that it is quite possible for a play to be enjoyable — indeed, to be a gripping piece of theatre — with a text which would not stand up at all to the kind of scrutiny given to late sixteenth- and early seventeenth-century plays.

One way of considering the 'hack' dramas of the period is to draw an analogy with the early days of the cinema and the types of films which became popular — cowboy and Indian movies, great romances, musicals and horror films. The best of them became true classics. Turning to tragedies, if we find the end of some of the sixteenth- and seventeenth-century plays hard to take, with their heaps of corpses, just think for a moment how popular horror movies in general, and Hammer Films in particular, remain today. Such films are similarly drenched in blood, usually feature a series of deaths, and end in violent fashion. Yet we suspend belief. At its most basic there are real similarities. We must bear in mind too that while members of the audience no doubt revelled in the horrors and fears (much in the way cinema audiences were horribly gripped by Hitchcock's *Psycho*), these were people who might well have spent the previous Saturday watching half a dozen people hanged at Tyburn and were planning, the following afternoon, to lay a few bets on a contest between some dogs and a chained bear. Also death was an ever-present unwanted guest, and going to the theatre itself could be a risk. Tens of thousands of people died each time the plague visited London on a grand scale, and then the theatres would close.

One rather unfair criticism made of the tragedies is that they are unbelievable in plot and make far too much use of coincidence, but this can be levelled at many later classics. Emily Brontë's *Wuthering Heights* does not bear close examination as to the reality of its characters, and its time scale makes no sense, yet it remains one of the most enthralling pieces of fiction ever written. Dickens in his popular novels stretched the long arm of coincidence almost until it broke, but it does not make him any the poorer for that — such is the pace of the stories, and the richness of the characters, that much can be forgiven him. Throughout Shakespeare we have to believe that young men did not recognize the girls with whom they were in love, when the girls were dressed as boys, or that Desdemona would not have had the common sense to explain to Othello how she came to lose her handkerchief.

Although commentators often put the plays into neat compartments, it is actually rather more difficult than it would appear. There are what is popularly known as 'the revenge plays' and there are 'tragedies', yet very often the themes overlap, with revenge a strong theme in the tragedies even when it is not the underlying motive for the whole play.

The playwrights — and remember they were pioneering the stage play — were influenced in their tragic writings by two past authors, the Roman Seneca and the more recent Machiavelli. Seneca lived in the first century A.D. and wrote turgid and heavy blood-spattered tragedies in which were contained little crisp moralizing homilies. They seem to have been written more for public recitation than for dramatic performance. It is from Seneca that the revenge theme comes. His plays tended to follow a five-part pattern. There was an 'exposition' where somebody — often the ghost of someone murdered before the action starts — explains the events leading up to the play and what will probably happen. Then comes the 'anticipation', where those setting out to avenge the murdered man's death explain how they are going to set about it. This is generally followed by some kind of 'confrontation' between the revenger and the proposed victim, where both sides conceal their feelings and intentions. The 'partial execution' is when the avenger suffers some temporary setback or delay, and it all ends with the 'completion', the triumph of vengeance. The audiences of the time we are discussing would in general go along with the view of Church and State on private vengeance — 'Vengeance is mine, saith the Lord' — but secretly would probably have a fair amount of sympathy with the person who took the law into their own hands, especially if they could not find justice any other way.

Seneca went in for a great deal of blood-curdling description of tortures and executions, and the writers we are discussing went further in that they often portrayed such events on the stage. Gallons of animal blood and red dye were sold to theatre companies to simulate the blood in death scenes. Seneca also made full use of the supernatural — ghosts, spirits and strange unexplained happenings — and this too was enthusiastically incorporated into the work of his successors. Again, where would the makers of horror films be without their Frankensteins, Draculas, Werewolves and Things from the Black Lagoon?

Next came Machiavelli. He was seen as a far more sinister figure in England than his writings show him to be. *The Prince* was extremely popular, but it is not actually the carte blanche for political double-dealing and cynicism that its reputation makes it out to be. It was a book about the reality of power politics, and a rather sad book at that, for Machiavelli was trying to explain what went on in the corridors of power. It was not an assassin's or villain's guidebook with useful chapters on a million ways to murder or how best to double-cross your opponents. But his name became synonymous with death and intrigue, with the smiling villain who plots and murders while presenting a fair face to the world. Here he was no doubt assisted by the stories which reached England of happy Italian families like the Borgias, and it was one reason why many of the tragedies are set in Italy, as it was generally assumed they all behaved like that over there. If the setting was not Italy, then Spain would do. It was nearly as bad with its Inquisition and Papists .

In the later years there was material much nearer home too. While the great peak of Elizabeth's reign had passed before her death, it was all to seem like a Golden Age in comparison with that of James I. Weak, effete, vain, extravagant, corrupt and with homosexual tendencies which led him into misjudged favouritism and made him many enemies, James ruled a Court rotten with graft and corruption. His young male favourites had almost unlimited licence and he quite literally 'sold' honours. The going price of a knighthood was £30, and he created 838 new knights. For £1905 you could buy the new rank of Knight Baronet. James created three dukes, a marquess, 32 earls, 19 viscounts and 56 barons, mostly for cash down which brought him in about £120,000 all told. He surrounded himself with sycophants telling him only what he wanted to hear, while they trod on each other in their haste to claw their way up the ladder. It is not surprising that the later tragedies reflect the darkness of the times in which they were written, and that the plots for some are based on real-life events.

Let us begin then with two classic revenge plays. Kyd's *Spanish Tragedy* (probably written in 1587) was the first true English play in this style, and it was to set the pattern for many that came after. Although it was to become fashionable for writers like Jonson, Dekker and Middleton to deride Kyd's piece, the play remained a firm favourite for years and years. The plot, put simply, sounds somewhat ludicrous. *The Spanish Tragedy* is a play within a play within a play, for it opens with two characters discussing what has happened and what is to come. These are the spirit of Revenge and the ghost of Andrea, who has recently died in the war between Spain and Portugal which ended in a victory for Spain in 1580. Andrea complains that Revenge keeps on going to sleep, but Revenge replies that he has planned out the course of events we are about to see. Both commentators — who are of course invisible to the characters in the play — comment on the action throughout and chart its course, so that the characters become puppets in a play of revenge.

The man who is to become the avenger is Hieronimo (or Jeronimo in some texts), Marshal of Spain. During the battle in which Andrea has died, Hieronimo's son Horatio has taken prisoner a young man called Balthazar, the son of the Portuguese Viceroy. He promptly falls in love with the beautiful niece of the King of Spain, Belimperia. (Andrea, as he tells us in his opening speech, had also fancied the lady.) Belimperia's brother Lorenzo is rather keen on a match between the two, but unknown to him, Belimperia and Horatio have fallen in love and plan to marry. When Lorenzo finds this out he tells Balthazar, and the two then murder the unfortunate Horatio, leaving his body hanging in a garden to be found by his father Hieronimo.

Hieronimo becomes unhinged with grief, but he is not so mad that he cannot work out a revenge for his son's death. He persuades Lorenzo, Balthazar and Belimperia to appear with him in a play to be presented at Court for the entertainment of the King. During the play he stabs Lorenzo and kills him, Belimperia stabs Balthazar and then turns the knife on herself and dies. King and Court are horrified, and seize Hieronimo, who bites out his tongue so that he cannot be made to say any more (although there is no logic in this, as before he does so he explains his motives fully and at length!)

To get away with *The Spanish Tragedy* today you would have to perform it with the most tremendous gusto and treat the blood and death much in the way the French do in their theatre of Grand Guignol. There is little or no attempt to round out the characters and make them believable people. There are no surprises. The plot unfolds inevitably once the series of actions has been set in motion. Those involved in the events remain unchanged by them; they do not grow or alter in the way Shakespeare's characters do. It ends predictably, if bloodily, and it is unlikely that today's audiences would be emotionally moved, as it would not be possible to identify with either the people in the play or the events in which they are caught up. It would not seem like a real tragedy.

If Kyd, as is thought, did write the first version of *Hamlet* it was no doubt very similar in both style and content. Apart from the most obvious differences between Shakespeare's *Hamlet* and Kyd's *Spanish Tragedy* — the subtlety and complexity of the characters and the magnificence of the language — the basic premise is very different. In Shakespeare's *Hamlet* we too start with a ghost crying for revenge (it seems likely that the ghost wrapped in a white sheet crying 'Hamlet, Revenge' so often mentioned in works of the time refers to the earlier Kyd version); we have a son told by the ghost to avenge his murder — that is, the murder of Hamlet's own father; the wicked uncle and the adulterous queen; and indeed even the play within the play, which is meant to trick the King into revealing his wickedness. All of it is there, but Hamlet is no Elizabethan or Jacobean avenger. If he was we would not have the play as we know it, for Hamlet is unable to make up his mind on a straightforward revenge killing; that is his dilemma. If he had been, then possibly Shakespeare's *Hamlet* would have gone the way of Kyd's.

Tourneur's *Revenger's Tragedy* is very different in style to Kyd's play and a much subtler piece of work, written about 1606 or 1607 (published 1607). The framework again is that of the 'classic' revenge play, and many of the characters are not only thinly drawn but are given names of virtues and vices out of the old morality plays — Castiza (chastity), Vindice (revenge), Lussurioso (lust) and so on. There is an explanation, a set series of events, and eventually a masque in which people are killed, with the 'revenger' himself dying at the very end of the play.

At the opening we meet the revenger, Vindice. There is no ghost but death is present, for he is fondling the skull of his dead mistress, Gloriana, poisoned by the old Duke because she would not go to bed with him. Vindice explains this to us, and while he is speaking a slow procession passes behind him and he tells us who they are — the old evil Duke, his lustful son Lussurioso, his bastard son Spurio, his wife the second Duchess, her three sons . . . All are corrupt. In fact, in this play virtually everybody has his or her price. Vindice, who for some time will keep us informed of what he is about, tells us he is about to disguise himself in order to be revenged, as Malvolio would say, on the whole pack of them.

The play proper starts with the Duke having to condemn his youngest stepson to prison for raping the virtuous wife of the good Lord Antonio, after which the lady kills herself. Enter Vindice in disguise, and he sets about his task with ingenuity and enthusiasm.

The two brothers of the imprisoned man (who is quite unrepentant) want to rescue him from prison. Vindice will assist them — and betray them. They are both, anyway, double-crossing each other. Lussurioso wants a virtuous girl for his bed, and he has his eye on Castiza. Vindice will arrange it, although she is his own sister, and he will persuade his mother into prostituting her dowerless daughter by pointing out the wealth and luxury this will bring. The old Duke wants a woman too — he shall have one. But it is the skull of Gloriana, wigged, painted and hidden behind a veil on a dummy's body, and when the old Duke kisses her he falls to the ground poisoned. Finally there is a masque before Lussurioso and his friends, during which Vindice and his brother kill them. The carnage is finally stopped by Lord Antonio, who has taken charge of matters, but he decides that Vindice must die for what he has done, in spite of Vindice's protests that he did what he did all for the best. As Antonio shrewdly remarks: 'You that would murder him would murder me . . .'

In the play everyone is in the business of deceit, deceiving first others and then themselves. Vindice alone stands outside this for about two-thirds of the action, but finally he too deceives himself completely by believing that any means, however evil, can justify the end, and that it is possible to wallow in evil and commit murder and somehow remain unaffected and untainted — a lesson which is learned by Beatrice-Joanna in Middleton's play *The Changeling*.

Ian Richardson (Vendice) in the RSC's 1967 production of The Revenger's Tragedy. *(The first production for the company by Trevor Nunn.) (Tom Holte Theatre Photographic Collection)*

Tourneur's vision of the world is one of inherent evil in which no light shines, but it contains some wonderful language and imagery, most of which is given to Vindice. He describes his view of the world when he says:

Now 'tis full sea a-bed over the world.
There's juggling of all sides, some that were maids
E'en at sunset are now perhaps i' th' toll book.
This woman in immodest thin apparel
Lets in her friend by water; here a dame
Cunning nails leather hinges to a door
To avoid proclamation.
Now cuckolds are a-coining, apace, apace, apace, apace!
And careful sisters spin that thread i' th' night
That does maintain them and their bawds i' th' day.

When persuading his mother, Gratiana, to force his sister into Lussurioso's bed he describes the life in store:

O think upon the pleasure of the palace,
Securéd ease and state, the stirring meats
Ready to move out of the dishes
That e'en now quicken when they're eaten!
Banquets abroad by torch-light, music, sports,

Ian Richardson (Vendice) and Clare Kelly (Gratiana) in the 1967 RSC production of The
Revenger's Tragedy. *(Shakespeare Centre Library – photo: Gordon Goode)*

> Bare-headed vassals, that had ne'er the fortune
> To keep on their own hats, but let horns wear 'em.
> Nine coaches waiting — hurry, hurry, hurry.

To which the realistic Castiza responds: 'Ay, to the devil.'

However ridiculous the plot might sound, told baldly in this way, the fact
remains that when it is well acted and imaginatively directed — as in Trevor
Nunn's version for the Royal Shakespeare Theatre in 1969 — the *Revenger's
Tragedy* by its atmosphere of claustrophobia and its sheer theatricality works on
stage. And that, after all, is what it is all about.

It is only possible, in a book of this scope, to give a flavour of the plays, but one
of their most striking aspects is that many of them feature very strong women

once they move out of the format of the straight 'revenge' play. The place of women in the society of the time and the comparisons between the roles will be looked at later, but it is impossible to consider the tragedies without making this point. They range from the ruthlessly ambitious and cynical Evadne — a very twentieth-century woman — in *The Maid's Tragedy* through the cynicism of Livia in *Women Beware Women*, the beautiful evil of Vittoria in *The White Devil* to the amorality of Beatrice-Joanna in *The Changeling* and the one great tragic female character outside Shakespeare, the Duchess of Malfi in the play of that name. It is almost beyond comprehension that they could have been adequately played by boy actors.

Both of Webster's two great tragedies are grim to a degree. Full to the brim with violence, intrigue, murder and treason, death is the unseen character which haunts the action throughout, and there is little to show a ray of hope in either play. But his plots are not drawn purely from his imagination, nor are they revenge plays, although revenge plays its part. They are based on two real-life stories.

The background to *The White Devil* (published in 1612) is this. There was, of course, no foreign news service as we understand it in the sixteenth century, but many merchant venturing houses and banking houses had offices in different parts of Europe, and those who ran them wrote regularly to their head offices, providing information on what was going on locally. They were the forerunners of the Press Association and Reuters.

One of these was the banking house of Fugger, and in the early part of 1586 its Venetian 'manager' sent in the report of a gory story. Over Christmas 1585 there had been serious disturbances in Padua, which with its university had something of a reputation for student unrest. It seemed that a band of armed men led by Ludovico Orsini, a member of the great Orsini family, invaded the palace of a young widow, Vittoria, Duchess of Accoramboni. Her husband had died the previous November after taking the waters at Lake Garda for his health. He had died somewhat mysteriously. Orsini's men broke into the palace at two in the morning and slaughtered Vittoria and her brother while they were kneeling at Mass. News of the outrage soon got out, and the students took to the streets demanding justice. The government, which was in Venice, reacted by sending troops armed with cannons, and after much fighting took the palace from Orsini. Three of his men were torn to pieces by the mob outside. The rest were hanged. Orsini, who said he had committed the crime 'at the command of great personages', was sentenced to death by garotte, but as he was a nobleman he was granted both the right to death in private and that of paying the executioner fifty crowns to make it quick.

When the full story came out it transpired that Bracciano and Vittoria had been lovers long before they married, from the time she was twenty-three. He is said to have been responsible for the death of Vittoria's first husband (although some sources say her brother did this task), and for the death of his wife Isabella, who was a member of the equally powerful Medici family. Vittoria's first husband had been nephew to a cardinal who was later to become Pope, so it can be seen that the two had made themselves some pretty powerful enemies. Before his death Orsini had implied that he was acting on behalf of the Duke of Florence, head of the Medici clan. It was like an up-market Mafia feud, complete with killings.

It would be hard to make a play about these people more dramatic than it was in reality, but Webster altered some events and personalities to suit his purpose. Most of Webster's characters, unlike Shakespeare's, do not alter or grow. The good remain good, the evil, evil. They are as they are. They are either caught up in events or they provoke them but they remain, basically, the same. The 'white devil' of the play is Vittoria, but it might just as easily have been called 'the White Devils', for the most wicked and interesting example of true evil in the play is Vittoria's brother, Flamineo. The sub-title is *The Tragedy of Brachiano with the Life and Death of Vittoria*, though one cannot say whether or not this throws any light on Jacobean priorities.

History is somewhat ambivalent as to how deeply implicated the real-life Vittoria was in the family murders, but there were other examples of such women to hand should Webster seek them. Lucrezia Borgia too might not have been as black as she has been painted, but the Borgias — who had slaughtered their way to the top, and had produced a Pope with a grown-up family, including the notorious Lucrezia and Cesare — were discussed with awe throughout Europe.

In Webster's play Vittoria (aided and in some cases egged on by Flamineo) sets about getting her own way, which is the death of Isabella and her own husband Camillo. The character of Isabella, who was considered a wanton in real life, becomes chaste and holy. The deaths of both are shown in dumb show, with Isabella's being particularly exotic. She kisses the lips of a poisoned picture.

Vittoria is brought to trial for the suspected murder of her husband, but her accusers are aware from the outset that the evidence against her is purely circumstantial. They feel, however, that at the least they will have succeeded in branding her publicly as an immoral woman. Vittoria is aware the trial is prejudged anyway, but come what may she will fight to the last breath. The result is a compulsive piece of theatre, as most trial scenes are. Vittoria conducts her own defence brilliantly, and the most to which she can be sentenced is a kind of house arrest at a House of Convertites, a kind of prison for penitent prostitutes. She is later rescued by Bracciano, but it is interesting that conventional male morality takes over here and Bracciano himself becomes somewhat doubtful as to Vittoria's morals (although so far as we are aware from the play he is her seducer).

The plot follows then roughly the course of the real history, but the ending, with its intrigues and double-dealing, is far more subtle, and the spate of deaths with which the play finishes is chilling rather than tragic. Vittoria meets death bravely. Like Shakespeare's Richard III and Macbeth, she is, whatever her faults, immensely courageous. When struck down by Ludovico (made by Webster a secret admirer of the late Isabella) she taunts him, saying:

'Twas a manly blow;
The next thou giv'st, murder some sucking infant;
And then thou wilt be famous.

As she and her brother Flamineo are dying, both catch glimpses of the black void to which they are bound. Vittoria says:

> My soul like a ship in a black storm,
> Is driven, I know not whither.

And Flamineo:

> I recover like a spent taper, for a flash,
> And instantly go out.

The imagery throughout the play is remarkable, and it is even more so in Webster's next play, *The Duchess of Malfi*, which he wrote in 1614. For this play he went further back for his source. The real Duchess of Amalfi was born in 1477. Her father, the Marchese di Gerace, son of Ferrante I of Naples, died young of mushroom poisoning — or something. Her brother could well be termed a precocious high-flyer. By the time he was twenty he had inherited his father's title and wealth, married the grand-daughter of Pope Innocent VIII, made his name as a soldier, been left a widower and become Cardinal of Aragon.

The Duchess started early too, marrying a much older man when she was only twelve years old. He died of gout some years later, leaving her to administer a large and impoverished estate. To assist her she employed Frederico Bologna, who had run the household of the last King of Aragon. In 1504 he joined the Duchess, and they soon fell in love and were secretly married. When her brother discovered the misalliance he had her put to death. Those are the bare bones of a story which was first published in Bandello's *Novelle* in 1554, was translated into English (with much embellishment), and was put out by William Painter in 1567.

Webster's play opens with the Duchess and Frederico confessing their love for each other, and it is obvious that theirs is a genuine and true affection, the one good and worthy emotion in an evil world. Somewhat unbelievably, their marriage is kept secret long enough for them to have three children. The high-flying Cardinal becomes two brothers in the play, both equally evil. These are Ferdinand, Duke of Calabria, and the Cardinal. Both feel sullied by their sister's marriage with a low-born man, both also feel mixed motives apart from wanting their sister's wealth. The inference is that Ferdinand's feeling for his sister is incestuous. The Cardinal is a sadist.

To assist them to bring about the destruction of the Duchess and her family the brothers employ the wicked Bosola. The Duchess is imprisoned with insane people, possibly tortured, and is finally strangled along with her maidservant and her children. Bosola, having first wallowed in murder, becomes appalled by what he has done and turns against Ferdinand and the Cardinal. Webster moves into horror-film territory towards the end, making Ferdinand develop lycanthropia — he believes he has become a wolf.

However absurd it might sound, the Duchess of Malfi remains a great play. Like the *White Devil*, it is full of marvellous imagery. The character of the Duchess is a fine one, growing and becoming great because of her imprisonment,

Judi Dench (Duchess of Malfi) and Richard Pasco (Antonio) in the 1971 RSC production of The Duchess of Malfi *(Photo: Joe Cocks Studio)*

refined by suffering. She has resigned herself to death, and in a scene of supreme courage she faces her murderer, who asks if she is not frightened at the prospect. No, she replies, in her penultimate speech, nor would the manner of death prove any more or less terrifying:

What would it pleasure me to have my throat cut with
Diamonds? or to be smothered with cassia?
Or to be shot to death with pearls?
I know death hath ten thousand several doors
For men to take their exits; and 'tis found
They go on such strange, geometric hinges,
You may open them both ways . . .

She had begged her executioner to give 'my little boy some syrup for his cold' yet
reminded him that she was 'Duchess of Malfi still', and at last she tells him to pull
the cord tight round her neck and 'pull down heaven upon me' before asking him
to tell her brothers so that 'when I am laid out, they then may feed in quiet'.

The brave and noble end of the Duchess is contrasted later with that of her
brothers. The play tails off somewhat after her death, leaving Bosola as much the
most interesting character. While Ferdinand meets a madman's end, the Cardinal
is in full control of his senses, and suffers a premonition of what is to come when,
wandering in his garden and staring into his fishpond, he sees 'a Thing, armed
with a rake, that seems to strike at me'.

Finally Antonio is killed himself by mistake — 'Such a mistake as I have often
seen/In a play' — and leaves his son and a friend to pick up the pieces. The son
will inherit the Duchess's fortune, and as to the brothers:

These wretched eminent things
Leave no more fame behind them, than should one
Fall in a frost, and leave his print in snow;
As soon as the sun shines, it ever melts. . . .

One cannot conclude this brief account of the Websterian world better than by
quoting a celebrated passage from Rupert Brooke's study, published
posthumously in 1916, a poet on a poet:

The end of the matter is that Webster was a great writer; and the way in
which one uses great writers is two-fold. There is the exhilarating way of
reading their writing; and there is the essence of the whole man, or of the
man's whole work, which you carry away and permanently keep with you.
This essence generally presents itself more or less in the form of a view of the
universe, recognizable rather by its emotional than by its logical content.
The world called Webster is a peculiar one. It is inhabited by people driven,
like animals, and perhaps like men, only by their instincts, but more blindly
and ruinously. Life there seems to flow into its forms and shapes with an
irregular, abnormal, and horrible volume. This is ultimately the most
sickly, distressing feature of Webster's characters, their foul and indestruc-
tible vitality. It fills one with the repulsion one feels at the unending soulless
energy that heaves and pulses through the lowest forms of life. They kill,
love, torture one another blindly and without ceasing. A play of Webster's
is full of the feverish and ghastly turmoil of a nest of maggots. Maggots are
what the inhabitants of this universe most suggest and resemble. The sight

of their fever is only alleviated by the permanent calm, unfriendly summits
and darknesses of the background of death and gloom. For that is equally
a part of Webster's universe. Human beings are writhing grubs in an
immense night. And the night is without stars or moon. But it has sometimes a certain quietude in its darkness; but not very much.

The Maid's Tragedy probably had its first performance before *The White Devil*,
for it is generally dated as having been written by Beaumont and Fletcher in 1610
or 1611, although it was not registered at Stationers' Hall until 1619. It is a much
slighter piece than the last two plays, and although the writing is very stylish, it
has nothing of the power and dark imagination of Webster. It is worth looking at
because it is different again in tone and subject matter. It also contains a splendid
character in Evadne, but its plot looks pretty silly in cold print.

The setting is Rhodes. Melantius, a gallant soldier, has just come home from
the wars and he is expecting a wedding — that of his best friend Amintor, who is
betrothed to the sweet but extremely wet Aspatia. So he is not surprised to arrive
in the middle of wedding preparations, but he is shocked to discover that Amintor
has jilted Aspatia in favour of Melantius's own sister, Evadne. Apparently the
King suggested it, and once the idea was put into Amintor's mind he thought it a
good one — it is inferred the lady is older than he is, but very beautiful and sexy.

The wedding duly takes place, attended by the weeping Aspatia, and after
much ribald merriment the happy couple are bedded for the night, whereupon
Evadne spells out to Amintor that theirs is to be a marriage in name only. She is
the King's mistress, and he has married her off to make things easier for him and
to ensure there is a 'father' for any children she might have. In fact there is a
bizarre scene the following morning, where the King acts like a jealous husband
and makes Amintor swear he has not made love to his own wife.

Amintor tells Melantius the position, and he then threatens his sister with all
kinds of unpleasant prospects unless she is prepared to kill the King, which she
finally agrees to do in a scene which is worthy of a handbook on strange sexual
practices, as when she ties him to the bed he thinks it is a preamble to some kind of
sexual game. Meanwhile Aspatia (who has given up the idea of dying of a decline)
dresses up as a boy, challenges Amintor to a duel and gets killed by him. Evadne,
on discovering that even though she has killed the King, Amintor doesn't fancy
her any more, commits suicide, as does Amintor, full of guilt. The rest are left to
sweep up the bodies with the observation that this kind of thing can happen if
royalty abuses its prerogative, but that whatever the abuse, regicide is not per-
missible. The latter had to be added, as otherwise the play would never have been
allowed on stage.

The Maid's Tragedy has received few performances in recent years but it can
work if done with sufficient panache; otherwise the welter of corpses at the end
produces giggles rather than awe. But the big scene between Evadne and Amintor
is a marvellous piece of theatre as he ingenuously thinks she is merely coy and
frightened of losing her virginity and she replies 'A maidenhead, Amintor, at my
years!' Almost equally good is the scene in which she assures the King she will be

(left to right) *Anne Dyson (Mother), Judi Dench (Bianca), Derek Smith (Guardiano) and Elizabeth Spriggs (Livia) in the 1969 RSC production of* Women Beware Women. *(Photo: Joe Cocks Studio)*

faithful to him as he is so rich and powerful, and will remain so until someone even richer and more powerful comes along.

Middleton's tragedies are different again. Meticulously crafted, they are fascinating. *Women Beware Women* was written about 1620, and like Webster, Middleton turned to a real-life story. It concerned Francesco de' Medici (there go the Medicis again) who took as his second wife Bianca Cappello. Bianca had eloped at the age of fifteen with Pietro Buonaventura — her family disapproved of the match — and having married him was left to her own devices. She was courted and then seduced by Francesco (who was also Grand Duke of Tuscany), and seems to have felt she preferred what he had to offer to a poverty-stricken marriage with Pietro. So Pietro is conveniently eliminated and she can then marry the Duke. Running alongside the main plot is another which Middleton took from a French romance dealing with the forbidden love of Hippolito for his niece, Isabella. In the original version Hippolito is assisted in his affair by his sister, who is a nun. In Middleton's play the role of fixer is that of Hippolito's widowed sister, Livia, who not only connives at her brother's affair but also arranges the seduction of Bianca by the Duke. She is a truly amoral character, entering into all kinds of subterfuge to procure the niece for the uncle and Bianca for the Duke. But being Middleton, nothing is ever as simple as this, for without meaning to, Livia finds herself falling in love with Bianca's despised husband (who is called Leantio in Middleton's version). When he is killed in order to further the designs of the Duke she decides to tell what she knows, and brings the whole house of cards down with her.

Middleton uses some fine devices. Obviously chess fascinated him — as we know from *A Game at Chess* — and the seduction of Bianca is carried out against a background of a chess game. At the end of the play he goes right back to Kyd's *Spanish Tragedy* with a masque, put on for the Duke's wedding to Bianca, in which the characters who take part actually kill each other or are killed. There are more deaths at the end of *Women Beware Women* than in *The Maid's Tragedy* — Bianca, Leantio, Hippolito, Isabella and Livia — but in this play you can suspend belief. It also has something to say about the buying and selling of women in the commercial marriage market of the day.

In his next play, written about 1622 (though not published till 1653), Middleton collaborated with the actor William Rowley. Rowley is generally credited with only writing the beginning and end of the play, and some of the sub-plot, but he knew what audiences liked and Middleton knew what made excellent theatre, which is why *The Changeling* is compulsive on stage today. The plot comes from a collection of gruesome murder stories written by John Reynolds in 1621.

The main plot concerns a young heiress, Beatrice-Joanna, about to be married off by her father to Alonzo, whom she does not love. She thinks she is in love with the young Alsemero. She is determined to get out of the marriage at all costs — and it is to cost her a great deal.

The family steward, De Flores, has long lusted after Beatrice, and right from the beginning you realize there is something odd about her feelings for him — again and again, to the point of obsession, she tells us and him that he is loathsome, he disgusts her, how repulsive she finds him, how he sickens her. De Flores offers to kill Alonzo for her for a reward he will claim. She agrees, and he does so (bringing along Alonzo's finger to prove it) and demands his reward. Beatrice offers him 3000 gold florins, but this is not what he had in mind. He wants the lady. She doubles the offer. He still wants the lady, spelling it out in brutal terms. He also points out that she who set him on to murder is as guilty as he is: 'Look but into your conscience, read me there, / 'Tis a true book, you'll find me there your equal.' There is nothing to be done, and Beatrice becomes his mistress.

So Beatrice has her own way and is married to Alsemero, but this no longer seems so desirable. Also she has real problems. She is no longer a virgin, she may even be pregnant, and she has discovered that Alsemero seems to be experiencing some doubts about his bride and has devised a set of tests to see if she is a maiden. Having discovered what these are, in a very funny scene, she pre-empts them, but it still leaves her with the wedding night to get through and she decides the best thing is to change places with her maid — a 'bed switch' plot, much loved at the time and used twice by Shakespeare, in *Measure for Measure* and *All's Well That Ends Well*. But then the maid might talk, mightn't she . . . which leaves no alternative but that she must meet with an accident. (Incidentally, Beatrice-Joanna may be 'changed' in the play, but it is the maid, not her mistress, who is in fact 'The Changeling ').

The progression of Beatrice from heedless, egotistical girl to full-blooded

Simon Rouse (Giovanni) and Barbara Kellermann (Annabella) in the 1977 RSC production of 'Tis Pity She's a Whore. (Photo: Joe Cocks Studio)

villainess is not only dramatically sound, it is psychologically right as well. She is a woman who thinks she can achieve a desired end by any means but can somehow remain unsullied by what she does, and at the end she has made a journey into self-revelation to discover a character that horrifies her. Equally well drawn is her growing attraction for De Flores as she realizes that her obsessive loathing is the reverse side of an unrecognized desire. There is nobody else quite like De Flores in the drama of the time, with the possible exception of Iago. In the end the two achieve a strange kind of love, bonded together by what they have done and the similarity to each other that they finally recognize within themselves. It is a most remarkable play.

Finally, it is not possible to leave this brief taste of the range of tragedies without mentioning John Ford's *'Tis Pity She's a Whore*. On the face of it, Ford's drama has more horrors than most, with three plots, all of which end in death and disaster, and a truly horrific and revolting finale. Whether his own heart was in such a catalogue of violence and murder or whether he was writing to please his audience is hard to say, but the main plot of the play is not only remarkable for its subject-matter — incest — but also because we do have sympathy with the protagonists and in the scenes between them see the world through their eyes.

Giovanni and Annabella are brother and sister, and at the outset of the play they discover their love for each other and begin an incestuous relationship, as a result of which Annabella finds she is pregnant. Desperate, she tells the Friar, who persuades her to marry one of her suitors, Sorenzo. Sorenzo discovers he has been tricked and asks his servant Vasques to ascertain the father of the child, which he does. The secondary plot concerns the relationship between Sorenzo and his mistress Hippolita — there is truly a double standard at work here — and her attempts to poison him, which rebound on herself. Even the supposedly comic sub-plot, the pursuit of Annabella by the foolish Bergetto, ends in his death. Having discovered the truth about Annabella and Giovanni, Sorenzo throws a grand banquet to which both are invited. Fearful of what is to come, Giovanni and Annabella make love, he tells her that the only way out is by their death and he stabs her, leaving her on the bed only to make his appearance some time later with her heart on his dagger, his wits having been turned by what has occurred. He too dies at the hands of Vasques after killing Annabella's husband. The last lines of the play do an injustice to Annabella:

> Of one so young, so rich in nature's store,
> Who could not say, 'TIS PITY SHE'S A WHORE.

For whatever Annabella was, she was not a whore.

Ford is thought to have written the play about 1627, but its style puts it within the genre of the Jacobean tragedies. Of the play Ford himself said (in his Dedication), 'The gravity of the subject may easily excuse the lightness of the title.' What makes Ford's play interesting and relevant to today — and played properly it triumphs over the blood and death, partly because it is so fast-moving — is that in his two incestuous lovers Ford is dealing with the problems which have always beset the Outsiders, those who break the rules both of society and of the moral climate of the times. But unlike homosexuality, say, incest remains to this day a taboo subject, and one which rarely provides a plot for drama — even in the most candid Play for Today. It is a mark of Ford's stature as a playwright that we do not turn in disgust or horror from Annabella and Giovanni but look with compassion on two people caught up in a relationship which they did not seek and cannot help.

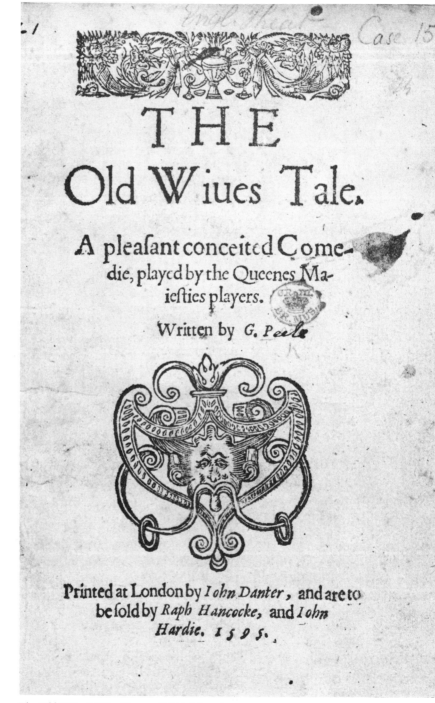

The Old Wives' Tale *title-page (British Library)*

Chapter 9

Comedies

'. . . for nothing is purposed but mirth.'
Dekker

If ever there was a field in which plays are due for revival, then it is in that of the Elizabethan and Jacobean comedies. Some, like *The Shoemaker's Holiday*, do turn up in repertoire from time to time, but there are many others which could be put on and enjoyed today.

When we enter this world of comedy we leave behind the dark corridors and haunted gardens of Spain and Italy, the dungeons of the Amalfi palace, the torches abroad at midnight and the nine coaches waiting of *The Revenger's Tragedy*, and find ourselves in the Isle of Dogs or Billingsgate or the Three Pigeons at Brentford.

Only Shakespeare seemed to feel the continuing need to set his comedies in exotic places — Ephesus, Padua, Verona — although one does feel that while Olivia's mansion in *Twelfth Night* may be supposed to exist in the kingdom of Illyria, in reality it was very close to those great houses Shakespeare would have glimpsed through the trees from the Oxford Road as he rode back and forth to London. Only in *The Merry Wives of Windsor* does he touch on a similar world to that of his contemporaries in domestic comedy.

The world of the comedies is the bustling, thriving, money-making, cheating world of the small merchants and artisans and the low-life folk who lived with and off them. It is the world described so vividly by Dekker in *The Gull's Horn Book*, with eating at the 'ordinary', drinking at the tavern and going in a noisy party to the playhouse.

There are the merchants who are rich and those who aspire to be, the social climbers and their busy wives. There are daughters to be married off with money and land in mind and there are those same daughters pining after poor journeymen and apprentices. Deals are struck, bargains are made, while at a lower level those of the underworld cadge and cheat and con their way through life. There are smart servants who outwit their masters and charlatans who pretend to be doctors or alchemists. There are two languages, the language of the merchants and of commerce and the slang and dialect of the underworld, where anything goes.

Brentford seems to have filled the place Brighton did in the 1920s as a spot suitable for assignations, and the reason The Three Pigeons inn features so prominently in a number of plays was in fact an in-joke of the time, as it was kept by an actor.

While some of the young daughters may pine and fade like their sisters in the tragedies, others most certainly do not, and the wives of the merchants (with a few exceptions) are extremely independent, lively and strong-minded women. They scheme and plot, visit the playhouse, the astrologer and each other while also being very much in charge of large and busy households of family, apprentices, journeymen, craftsmen and servants.

One of the earliest plays in this style actually comes well before this period, and it was written before Shakespeare was even born, let alone Dekker, Middleton and the rest. Nicholas Udall was appointed headmaster of Eton school in 1534 and he had a keen interest in drama. A number of plays are attributed to him, and we do not know the true date of his comedy *Ralph Roister Doister*, but we do know that it was popular by the 1550s, when Edward VI was on the throne. A long quotation from it was published in 1554. It must have influenced many playwrights coming after, not least Shakespeare, for the main character of Roister Doister is a real forerunner of Falstaff — a swaggering, roistering, cowardly buffoon, with an enormously high opinion of himself, most particularly as a ladies' man. The Miles Gloriosus of the Roman dramatist Plautus, and still further back the New Comedy of Greece, were of course original models for the genre.

Although the play is slight and has no complicated sub-plots, the action speeds along fast enough to hide the thin story-line. As well as Doister, Udall also created two other fine characters in Merrygreek, Doister's wily companion-cum-servant who lives off him and his own wits (while keeping the audience informed of the action) and the sparky young widow, Christian Custance. Christian after a marriage to an elderly gentleman is now happily affianced to a young man whom she loves, Gawyn. He has had to go abroad briefly, and while he is away Doister seizes his chance to woo the widow and try to make her his wife.

As he thinks he is utterly irresistible, he cannot understand why she does not immediately fall into his arms. The lady is brutally frank about it. She wouldn't even want her cat to marry him. Merrygreek is sent back to his master with her message, which describes Doister as 'such a calf, such an ass, such a block, such a lilburne [idiot], such a hob ball and such a lobcock' who is so cowardly he could be chased away by a decent-sized goose, and 'who thinks every woman to be brought in dotage, with only the sight of his good personage'. So Doister decides on an abduction to compromise the lady into marriage. However, all finally ends well, but with Merrygreek sounding like Malvolio when he says of Doister, 'he will be avenged one day'.

Before we leave the early plays it is worth also mentioning Peele's *The Old Wives'* [or *Wife's*] *Tale*, published in 1595. This goes back to a very early tradition of story-telling, for it is in fact a collection of tales linked together by an old

THE SHOMAKERS
Holiday.
OR
The Gentle Craft.

With the humorous life of Simon
Eyre, fhoomaker, and Lord Maior
of London.

As it was acted before the Queenes moft excellent Ma-
ieftie on New-yeares day at night laft, by the right
honourable the Earle of Notingham, Lord high Ad-
mirall of England, his feruants.

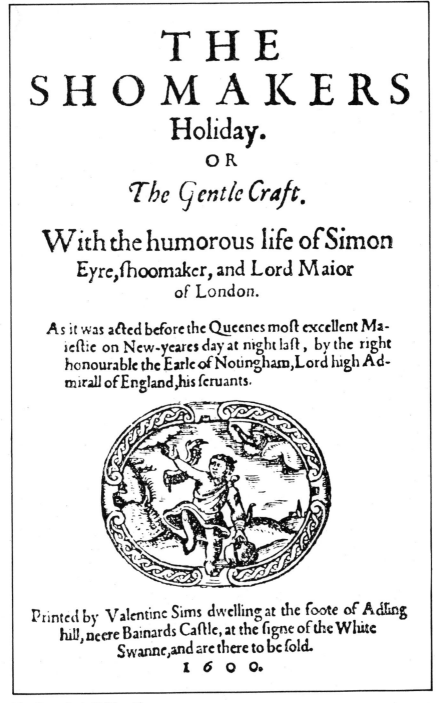

Printed by Valentine Sims dwelling at the foote of Adling
hill, neere Bainards Caftle, at the figne of the White
Swanne, and are there to be fold.
1 6 0 0.

The Shoemaker's Holiday *title-page*

woman who is telling them to two young men. One, the 'Three Heads in the Well', has links with the *Mabinogion*, and the others, 'The Grateful Dead' and 'Jack the Giant Killer', disappear back into the mists of time. It would make a rather pleasant Christmas show today, and it does offer a very early instance of audience participation, for the old woman tells the two young men, and the audience, 'Now this bargain, my masters, must I make with you, that you will say ''hum'' and ''ha'' to my tale, so shall I know you are awake', to which the young men reply, 'Content gammer, that will we do.'

One of the most good-humoured of all Elizabethan comedies is Dekker's *The Shoemaker's Holiday*. It was written about 1598 or 1599, printed 1600 and acted about the same time by the Admiral's Men. The plot is slight. It had the endearing sub-title 'A Pleasant Comedy of the Gentle Craft'. Rowland Lacy, a kinsman of the Earl of Lincoln, falls in love with the daughter of Sir Roger Otely (currently Lord Mayor of London). Nobody likes the match, and he is apparently sent off to the wars but returns disguised as Hans, a Dutch shoemaker, and attaches himself to the Eyre household in order to pursue his suit. But it is not the main plot which makes the play such a delight, it is the comings and goings in the bustling Eyre household, with his lively journeymen, Firk and Ralph, Ralph's attractive wife, Jane, the witty maidservant Sybil and the social-climbing wife of Simon, Margery (Madge). Beside these the 'heroine' Rose is a rather pale figure.

It is a romantic view of the London life of that time, but is none the worse for that. It is full of vigour, has some fine songs and when it is revived proves extremely successful. Simon Eyre really did live; he was elected Sheriff of London in 1434, and became Lord Mayor in 1445. The play also gives us a glimpse of life in a busy craftsman's home in Dekker's own time. The real-life Eyre was apparently very conscious of the status he had achieved, and Dekker has him telling his wife that he is equal to anybody: 'Sim Eyre knows how to speak to a Pope, to Sultan Soliman, to Tamburlaine an he were here . . .'

No round-up of the comedies, however brief, would be complete without a look at the play which landed its authors in gaol — *Eastward Ho!* It is hard to see why this play has disappeared for such a long time. It has a complex string of plots — not surprising with three authors, Jonson, Chapman and Marston — and some very amusing characters.

One concerns Gertrude, the awful daughter of William Touchstone the goldsmith. She is an extremely dim girl, with a head stuffed with foolish ideas and with a desire to acquire an aristocratic husband. She is obsessed by the clothes she would like, and her conversation is peppered with remarks about satin petticoats, taffeta capes, gold lace and so on, and rarely creeps above it. She has her immediate desire and is married to Sir Petronel Flash, who is actually in love with the wife of the usurer Security but is willing to marry Gertrude, take her dowry and then jilt her to run away with his lady friend, Winifred.

Touchstone has two apprentices, a boring prig Golding and a likeable rogue Quicksilver. Meanwhile another plot concerns a group of somewhat disreputable venturers who are preparing to sail off into the sunset for the New World.

Gertrude is sent off in a coach to Flash's non-existent castle ('all the castles I have are built with air'); Flash, assisted by Quicksilver, sets off with her dowry along with Winifred (disguised as a boy), to join the venturers on their trip to the Americas. Before they set off there is an enormous carousal where everybody gets terribly drunk, and finally, in the teeth of a gale, the vessel at last sets sail — only to be wrecked almost immediately on the Isle of Dogs. There follows a very funny scene where the shipwrecked mariners — who imagine they have at least reached Europe — speak to the inhabitants in Franglais, while the residents of the Isle of Dogs imagine they must have been invaded. The whole lot are rounded up and dumped in the Counter Prison, where after much overly obvious repentance all more or less ends happily — although one does not hold out much hope for the marriages of either Gertrude and Flash or Winifred and her husband.

One imagines it was the cheeky Ben Jonson who lifted well-known phrases from other people's work. Quicksilver is given to quotes such as 'Holla, ye pampered jades of Asia' (*Tamburlaine*) and 'I was a courtier in the Spanish Court, Don Andrea was my name' (*The Spanish Tragedy*) while the normally witless Gertrude, made even more stupid by finding there is no castle at the end of her coach journey, is actually given Ophelia's mad song to sing. Such quotation was, however, by no means uncommon in the period. For instance, Dekker has the Kyd parody 'Jieronimo, go by, go by' in *The Shoemaker's Holiday*, and there is the most famous of all, 'Dead Shepherd . . .' in *As You Like It*.

Scholars might not find the text of *Eastward Ho!* worthy of much study but audiences would love it.

Middleton's comedies are more often described as satires, and this is probably true. They are funny but they do bite, as Middleton is very well aware of the avariciousness, social-climbing and cynicism which was behind the jolly artisan world of Dekker. As with his tragedies, Middleton shows a tremendous command of his material: his plots are manipulated with faultless skill, he has a wide variety and range of comic characters and his women again are not only spirited but utterly believable.

To take only two, *A Trick to Catch the Old One* and *A Chaste Maid in Cheapside*, we can easily see Middleton's fast and meticulous stagecraft at work. *A Trick to Catch the Old One* was probably written in 1606, and is quite simply about the gullibility of greedy old men who, however rich they are, want still more. It is also about how they can be tricked by scheming young men and witty women.

Several sources have been suggested for the plot, but it is likely that it was a popular tale which was around in many story books, where a scheming usurer is persuaded to marry a woman he thinks is a rich widow, only to discover she is in fact a lively adventuress who by the marriage gains a name and a fortune and an old man who can't be expected to last all that long.

The 'trick' is set up by the rake Witgood, and his accomplice (known only as the Courtesan) is the lady who entraps the horrid Walkadine Hoard. 'Courtesan' is as unfair when applied to this lady as 'whore' was to Annabella in *'Tis Pity She's a Whore*, for she is a decent girl from the provinces, seduced by Witgood, who has remained faithful to him. In some ways the plot foreshadows the Restoration comedies which were to come nearly a hundred years later. But the action goes at

Clive Arrindell (Jasper) and Lucy Gutteridge (Luce) in the 1981 RSC production of The Knight of the Burning Pestle. *(Photo: Laurence Burns)*

a rare lick, and whatever we might feel about Witgood (and in reality he is a pretty unsympathetic character), the spider's web the two weave — and into which the horrible Hoard willingly walks in his pursuit of ever more money — is a joy to behold. The real winner at the end of it all is the lady. Hoard cannot possibly tell the world what she is and what she has done without making a total fool of himself, and one is left to feel that when he is finally dead and buried she will then look around from a position of substantial comfort for a more amenable mate.

A Chaste Maid in Cheapside was written later than the last play, but there seems no firm date for its first appearance, although we know it was popular at the Swan theatre. Once again the subject is money and what people will do for it, but it is much more of a black comedy. Allwit, a merchant, has been persuaded into letting his wife become the permanent mistress of Sir Walter Whorehound. She regularly bears Sir Walter children who are then fathered on Allwit in return for a promise that when Sir Walter dies — he is presently unmarried — all his money will be left to the Allwits.

The second strand concerns Moll, the daughter of the goldsmith Yellowhammer, who is in love with the younger of the two Touchstone brothers. Her parents have destined her for Sir Walter, who in spite of his promise to the

Clive Arrindell (Jasper) and Lucy Gutteridge (Luce) in the 1981 RSC production of The Knight of the Burning Pestle. *(Photo: Laurence Burns)*

Allwits has decided to marry (Sir Walter is a promiscuous old humbug, as he has a Welsh country girl as mistress as well as Mrs Allwit). The third couple are Sir Oliver and Lady Kix. Their marriage is childless, and Lady Kix is blamed for this by her boorish old husband.

The older Touchstone brother has no such problems. He has virtually only to look at a girl to make her pregnant, and he is continually harried by those chasing him up with the Jacobean equivalent of paternity orders. There are two great comic scenes. One is the christening of Mrs Allwit's latest child by Sir Walter, attended by both the real and spurious fathers and an assortment of citizens, including three Puritans who proceed to get blind drunk. The other concerns the Kixes. The younger Touchstone tells the couple he knows a medical man who can cure Lady Kix's childless condition, and introduces him to his brother, disguised in suitable attire. Touchstone senior proceeds to mix up two nasty potions. The first he gives to Sir Oliver, and when he has drunk it down he then tells him he must get on a white horse and ride it out of London without getting off it for six hours or the potion will not work. And Lady Kix? Ah, now, she has to take hers lying down in a darkened room accompanied by her medical adviser.

At the end everyone gets their deserts. Sir Walter's plan is discovered and the obsequious Allwit realizes his comfortable life and promise of riches is at an end. However, in the ensuing quarrel between the two men Sir Walter suffers an apoplexy and dies, thus ensuring that Moll can marry Touchstone junior. As to the Kixes, well, Lady Kix has her baby. The potion — or something — certainly worked.

When Beaumont and Fletcher could tear themselves away from their tragicomedy, or from the heaped corpses of *The Maid's Tragedy*, they could provide a straightforward comedy which also managed to caricature the other kinds of play from which they made their living.

The Knight of the Burning Pestle (probably written in 1607) actually takes place in a theatre where a company of players is about to put on some grand romance of knightly chivalry. In the audience are a grocer and his wife, George and Nell, and their apprentice, Rafe. The play is called *The London Merchant*, and the plot soon loses George and Nell. In any case, Nell is the kind of woman whom you will all have had sitting behind you in the cinema or the theatre, who interrupts and talks right from the beginning of the show, asks questions about parts of the plot she has missed and fills in the rest of the audience with unwanted observations on the play or film and on others she has seen in the past.

She soon decides that her Rafe could do just as well as any of the professional players, and shoves the unfortunate young man on to the stage to take part in the play, and not any part at that. He must be a chivalrous knight loved by a princess. There are no complex strands of plot as in Middleton, and the humour is of a different kind. The grocer's wife gets more and more caught up in the plot of the play within the play, altering it as she thinks it should develop, while poor old Rafe finds himself in reality in that situation which occurs in bad dreams, when you suddenly wake up on a stage knowing it is your turn to speak but you don't know the words or even what the play is about.

Emrys James as Sir Giles Overreach in the 1983 RSC production of A New Way to Pay Old Debts. *(Photo: Donald Cooper)*

Anthony O'Donnell (Marrall) and Emrys James (Sir Giles Overreach) in the 1983 RSC production of A New Way to Pay Old Debts *(Photo: Donald Cooper)*

The 'text' of the play being performed by the actors enables Beaumont and Fletcher to send up the tragedies of the day, not only Kyd and Chapman but even their own (rather in the way that Chaucer in *The Lay of Saint Thopas* had satirized the popular epic through the medium of himself).

It is hard to make a choice out of so many plays with only limited space, but one which has survived well over the years and was recently revived with great success by the Royal Shakespeare Theatre is Philip Massinger's *A New Way to Pay Old Debts* (about 1625, pub. 1633) — a subject he knew all too much about from hard personal experience. The characters are larger than life and are pretty unsympathetic, with the possible exception of 'the prodigal', Frank Wellborn, but the play is carried along because of the appalling villain, Sir Giles Overreach, and the desire of everybody both in the play and in the audience to see him receive his just deserts.

Sir Giles has ruined everyone who has got in his way, and mostly by trickery and outright corruption, has acquired great wealth. He has wrongly filched the patrimony of Frank Wellborn, who when the play opens is completely destitute and living rough. Frank does admit, however, to having been a rake and a spendthrift and to having been fooled by Sir Giles out of his fortune. Sir Giles is busy with many current plans. He wants to marry the wealthy and widowed Lady

Allworth. As he assumes everything has its price (and everybody), he has also planned to throw his daughter Margaret in the way of Lord Lovell in the hope that his lordship will seduce her (with her willing connivance), get her pregnant, and then be forced into marriage to save her name. He will thus bring a title into the family as well as wealth.

Margaret hates the idea, and anyway has her own suitor, Tom. At the outset of the play, though, it looks as if Sir Giles will get it all his own way as he has in the past, but then Frank works out a plot. He goes to see Lady Allworth and suggests that she pretends to favour him to the point of making it look as if the way to her own heart is through him. By this means Sir Giles is at least persuaded to give Frank sufficient money to clothe himself properly and be entertained in polite society. Lady Allworth and Frank then set about working Sir Giles's downfall. Lord Lovell is alerted to the plot to entrap him, and a scheme is worked out whereby Sir Giles imagines he is furthering the marriage of his daughter to Lord Lovell when in fact she is eloping with her lover. All the twists of the plot finally succeed due to the efforts of Marrall, who is described as 'a creature' of Sir Giles, but who has become disillusioned with him. When Sir Giles discovers at the end of the play that he has been fooled out of his daughter, his Lordship and his money he goes mad and dies.

The 'conventional' happy ending would be for Lady Allworth to marry Frank, as he is attractive and they have grown close during the plotting against Sir Giles, but in fact she accepts a proposal from Lord Lovell. She is conscious throughout of her position and worth, and she and Lord Lovell are from the same class and would not marry outside it. Frank has now got his fortune back and is determined to live a respectable life. Poor old Marrall, who has done so much to bring about the happy state of affairs, is spurned by everyone, even Frank telling him that if he cannot be faithful to one master he is unlikely to be faithful to another.

Massinger's play is unusual for a comedy of this kind, for instead of being set in London the action takes place just outside Nottingham in a country village. What really does make it work, though, is the outrageously villainous Sir Giles, who is just plain bad with no redeeming features whatsoever, and one imagines he was as roundly booed and hissed by the audiences of his day as were his long line of Victorian successors.

These are just a few of the wealth of comic plays of the period, and anyone who looks through them must have his own personal favourite. But it is time they were taken off the bookshelf and put on to the stage, for they are wasted tucked away inside nineteenth-century collections.

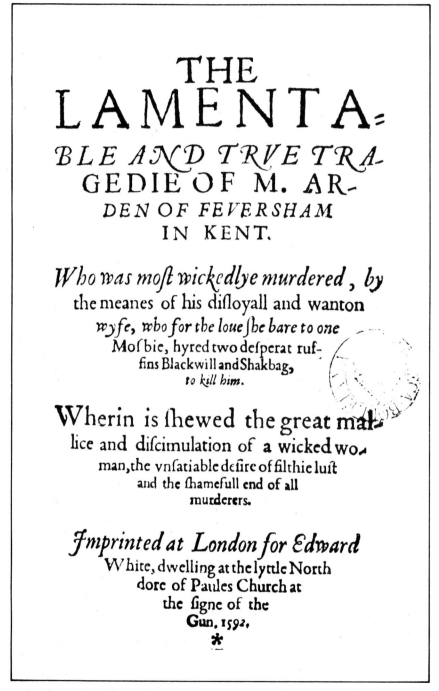

THE
LAMENTA=
BLE AND TRVE TRA-
GEDIE OF M. AR-
DEN OF FEVERSHAM
IN KENT.

Who was moſt wickedlye murdered , *by*
the meanes of his diſloyall and wanton
wyfe, who for the loue ſhe bare to one
Moſbie, hyred two deſperat ruf-
fins Blackwill and Shakbag,
to kill him.

Wherin is ſhewed the great mal-
lice and diſcimulation of a wicked woman, the vnſatiable deſire of filthie luſt
and the ſhamefull end of all
murderers.

Imprinted at London for Edward
White, dwelling at the lyttle North
dore of Paules Church at
the ſigne of the
Gun. 1592.
✱

Arden of Faversham *title-page (Huntington Library – reproduced by permission of Westminster City Libraries)*

Chapter 10

Drama Documentaries

'. . . a style of language so severely simple.'
Arden of Faversham

Drama documentary, the re-enactment of real-life events by actors, is not an invention of television. The Elizabethans and Jacobeans were there long before the notion of television had occurred to anybody. Their playwrights seized on contemporary material with relish — murders, witch trials, the lives of famous or unusual personalities, all were quickly translated to the stage. Plays of famous trials were acted out literally within weeks of the verdict.

I intend looking at just three, *Arden of Faversham*, *The Witch of Edmonton* and *The Roaring Girl*. Each one represents an excellent example of a different type of such a play.

It is impossible to discuss *Arden of Faversham* without the question of its authorship coming up, for it is a mystery. Quite literally, nobody has been able to discover who wrote it. It was probably presented first as early as 1587, was certainly in repertoire with Henslowe's company by 1590 and was first entered in the Stationers' Register in 1592 by Edward White on 3 April. The copyright stayed within the White family until 1624, when it was assigned on 29 June by his widow to one E. Aldie. White had published plays by Greene, Kyd and Marlowe, and also issued the first Quarto edition of *Titus Andronicus*.

Many writers have been suggested — Peele, Greene, Marlowe, Kyd and Shakespeare among them. Some scholars tend to think it was the work of one of the less talented hack writers of the day; or there are even those who think it was written by the Earl of Oxford or the Earl of Derby. But this is most unlikely. *Arden* is, quite simply, unlike anything else of its immediate period. It is certainly not the work of a hack — it is a very fine play, in which a sequence of real-life events is transmuted into a dramatic whole. It is also an intensely domestic tragedy.

The notion of Shakespeare as author was first suggested in 1770 by the bookseller Edward Jacob, since when Shakespeare scholars have taken sides — especially during the nineteenth century, when men like A. F. Hopkinson and A. H. Bullen crossed swords to 'prove' it either way. Oddly enough, the idea that he might have written the play now seems to be seriously considered once again, yet it is a very mature work, far more mature than the earliest works of Shakespeare that we know. Did he perhaps have a hand in editing and rewriting parts of an older play?

Arden appears in all the collections of what are known as 'The Shakespeare Apocrypha', fifteen plays attributed to Shakespeare. Of these only *The Two Noble Kinsmen* and *Sir Thomas More* are seriously considered for inclusion in the canon today, and then it is thought Shakespeare only provided some of the material for them. Most of the rest are so bad that nobody in their right minds could associate Shakespeare with them, even on one of his off-days — *The Yorkshire Tragedy*, for instance, based on another real-life murder story, is just a strip cartoon horror comic, while *Sir John Oldcastle* is obviously some hack's attempts to cash in on the popularity of Shakespeare's Falstaff.

Arden of Faversham is quite unlike anything else in the Apocrypha. It tells the story of the murder of Thomas Arden at his home on 15 February 1551. The play — its original title was *The Lamentable and True Tragedy of M. Arden of Faversham in Kent* — was a real *cause célèbre*, and there was plenty of material available for the playwright, including two detailed accounts. The story caught the popular imagination because not only was a woman involved in the murder but no less than six attempts were made on Arden's life before he was successfully done to death. People have always been fascinated by murder. The most popular barn-storming plays of Victorian times were *Maria Marten and the Murder in the Red Barn* and *Sweeney Todd*. Nowadays people still thrill over accounts of Crippen, Haigh, Christie, the Moors Murderers and the Yorkshire Ripper, which is why the popular press devotes so much space to sensational murders.

The 'Brevist Chronicle' of 1551 notes 'This year on Valentine's Day at Fav. in Kent was committed a shameful murder of one Arden, a gentleman, who was by the consent of his wife murdered whereof she was burnt at Cant. 14 March 1551.' Henry Machyn, a London Merchant Taylor, recorded the execution of Alice's lover, Mosby, and Mosby's sister, as well as the sentences of the other accomplices, and notes he was 'fascinated by the horribleness' of that domestic crime.

The first full account appears in the Wardmote Book of Faversham. It tells of what took place in the living-room of Arden's house at seven o'clock of the evening of the 15th of February, and then details the events leading up to it. Arden was chief controller of HM Customs at Faversham (the Medway was fully navigable then). He was mayor in 1548. He does not seem to have been a very pleasant individual; in fact he was grasping and avaricious. He had acquired much land from the Abbey after Dissolution, and his handsome house (still to be seen) is built out of part of the Abbey gatehouse. He made many enemies by wresting land off them by doubtful means — harsh leases, foreclosed mortgages and so on. He even insisted the annual fair be moved from the still existing Abbey land to his own so he could take profits from it.

When he was fifty-six he married Alice Morfyn, step-daughter to Sir Edward North, the translator of Plutarch. She was twenty-eight, and it seems she had long been involved in an affair with her step-father's steward, Thomas Mosbie, or Mosby. The Wardmote book says 'it was felt desirous by her friends and family' to marry her off, and that Arden knew all about her *affaire* but 'was so greatly given to seek his advantage and cared so little how he came by it that in hope of attaining some benefits of the Lord North by means of this Mosbie who could do much with him, he winked at that shameless disorder'. Alice is said to have told a friend that her husband was so rapacious that 'his old mother was forced to beg in the streets'.

Alice soon tired of her lot, and still in the throes of her affair with Mosby, she decided the only thing to do was to murder Arden. She tried first by acquiring some poison from a local artist which she mixed with his gruel. He realized there was something wrong, and ate only enough to make him ill. Nothing daunted, Alice then looked up a man called Greene who had been badly treated by Arden over some land — indeed, the two men had come to blows — and offered him £10 to kill her husband.

Greene agreed but did not know how to set about it on his own. The true sequence of events from then on is worthy of black farce. Greene first involved a man called Loosebag (later to be known as Shakebag), and it was decided they needed a more experienced conspirator. A neighbour of Greene's, a Mr Bradshaw, introduced Greene to a villain known as Black Will, although he was always to deny that he knew the purpose of this. The trio then made a number of attempts on Arden's life, most of them taking place on a journey to Gravesend. They included an ambush, a shooting and a variety of staged 'accidents'. Nothing worked.

Mosby and his sister were then dragged into Alice's scheme, and finally a plot was hatched involving Black Will, Mosby and one of Alice's servants. Will hid in a closet while Arden was out. When he came home he found Mosby there, who challenged him to a game of chess. As the two men were playing, Will came out of the closet and attempted to strangle Arden but bungled it. During the ensuing struggle Mosby 'stroked him on the head' with a fourteen-pound weight, before Will finally cut Arden's throat.

Mosby, Will and the servant lugged Arden's body out of the house and into a near-by field, arranging it to look as if he had been attacked there. Alice wiped up the blood, and after a suitable time made inquiries as to her husband's whereabouts and authorized a search. His body was quickly found, and the whole crew almost as quickly arrested. It had been snowing when the body was re-moved, and the conspirators had assumed the snow would continue and cover up their footprints but it did not. Also, between Arden's foot and his shoe were found rushes of a kind used to strew on floors. Finally, a bloody knife and a cloth were found stuffed in a barrel by the well.

The aftermath was grim. Alice Arden was burned at the stake in Canterbury on 14 March. Her unfortunate and innocent maid was burned in Faversham 'pitifully bewailing her case and crying out on the mistress who had brought her to this end

Jenny Agutter (Alice) and Robert O'Mahoney (Mosby) in the 1982 RSC production of Arden of Faversham. *(Photo: Reg Wilson)*

for which she would never forgive her'. (The murder of a husband by his wife was then classed as 'petty' — as opposed to 'high' — treason, and punished accordingly. So was that of a master by his servant.) Mosby and his sister were hanged at Smithfield. Michael, the servant, was hanged in chains at Faversham. Greene fled away, but was picked up years later in Cornwall and hanged by the roadside between Faversham and Ospringe. Loosebag/Shakebag was never seen again, while Black Will was supposed to have been executed some time later at Flushing in Holland, but there is no proof. Poor old Mr Bradshaw (whose sole crime was to have introduced Greene to Black Will) was hanged in Canterbury at the same time Alice was burned. A nasty note in the town record says 'for the charges of burning Mistress Arden and the Execution of Geo. Bradshaw — xLIIIs.'

So very strange a story even tempted the famous historian Raphael Holinshed to leave aside his Chronicles of Kings for a while and write up a second and more flowery version of the first account which seems to have been the main source for the playwright. Holinshed gives speeches to his characters, some of which are used in the play. For instance, during the chess game just before the murder Mosby says to Arden, 'Now may I take you, sir, if I will', which is the sign for Black Will to do his dirty work. This version contains many superstitions about the story — most notable is that for two years after the grass never grew on the ground on which the body had lain, and its shape could clearly be seen. Another

Jenny Agutter (Alice) and Robert O'Mahoney (Mosby) in the 1982 RSC production of Arden of Faversham. *(Photo: Reg Wilson)*

was that Alice's guilt was discovered when the corpse's wounds bled as she approached it. It was thought at that time that the wounds of a murdered person would bleed if the murderer came near to him, a superstition used to effect by Shakespeare in *Richard III*.

Holinshed makes Arden and Alice tall, fair and comely people while the villainous Mosby is black and 'swart'. He adds various notions — that Alice sent Mosby a pair of silver dice after one of their quarrels and that after the murder the

Jenny Agutter (Alice) and Robert O'Mahoney (Mosby) in the 1982 RSC production of Arden of
Faversham. *(Photo: Reg Wilson)*

murderers proceeded to throw a party with singing and dancing, accompanied by
Alice's daughter at the virginals. Like the earlier version, he makes the villains
implicate each other after the discovery of the corpse.

There was even a long ballad about it, 'the Complaint and Lamentation of
Mistress Arden of Faversham . . .', which was sung to the tune of *Fortune My Foe*
and is now in the Roxburgh Collection of the British Museum. So the author had
plenty to go on.

He simplified the number of characters involved. Mosby's sister is also Alice's
maid. Shakebag and Black Will become equal partners in crime, with Shakebag as
the sinister one and Black Will as the swaggering and inept fellow who botches
everything. Black Will became so popular with audiences that all too often he
overshadowed everything else in the play.

The artist who mixes poison is offered Susan for wife, and as well as Greene —
who in the play is not only a badly treated man but a man of religious devotion
driven by that treatment to murder — there is also a strange sailor and ferryman
called Dick Reede, whose brief appearance is pivotal to the play. Arden has taken
his land from him also, and Reede curses Arden, wishing he might die on it as he
has left his family destitute. This prophecy and the implication that he is some
kind of ferryman seem to imply that he might almost be Charon. Even the
servant, Michael, is made a rounded person finally racked by conscience.

But it is in the characters of Arden, Alice and Mosby that the unknown author shows a skill unequalled in any other play of the late 1580s. His Arden is avaricious, but nothing like as unpleasant as the real-life Arden, and he is also deeply in love with his young wife. He does not seem to have any knowledge of a previous affair with Mosby and no proof of any current relationship, although he is jealous and even goes so far as to fight a duel with him. Even when he becomes almost certain that there is an affair he does not seek to revenge himself, as would be the case in the typical revenge play of the time.

Mosby in this version is no gentleman steward but a poor tailor who has yanked himself up by his own efforts to run a great household. He is a mixture of arrogance, cunning and cowardice. He is very proud of what he has achieved, and says, 'Measure me for what I am, not what I was.' He is a pretty poor human being, and his treatment of Alice is shabby throughout. At one stage he tells her 'Now the rain hath beaten off thy gilt/Thy worthless copper shows thee counterfeit' but he still cannot keep away from her, nor indeed she from him.

Alice is a remarkable creation, compared by commentators with just about every villainess from Lady Macbeth to Miss Julie, but Alice Arden is very much herself. She is a complex character, misunderstood by her husband, with a superabundance of intelligence and vitality she cannot contain within Arden's household. She is also caught up and driven by an emotion she cannot comprehend and which brings her little pleasure — she and Mosby are either quarrelling bitterly or making love. When he is not there she can see he is pretty worthless and can even feel some real affection for Arden, who is probably a better man, but when she sees him it is all forgotten in a terrible and destructive infatuation. She simply cannot give him up, and she can therefore justify any means to the end — and the end is murder.

Before she is found out she can foresee disaster. As she frantically tries to clean up Arden's blood she says to Susan 'The more I strive, the more the blood appears.' Says Susan: 'What's the reason, Mistress, can you tell?' 'Because I blush not at my husband's death.' Alice cannot be neatly 'explained'.

The very core of the play is the relationship between these three people, all totally bewitched, all locked into a situation from which they cannot escape. Even the long and somewhat ludicrous series of attempts on Arden's life is cleverly done. In the end you become positively irritated that the attempts don't succeed, but it is all leading up to the one which finally does, and it also shows us how blind Arden is. He is given a number of chances and turns his back on them all even though he has prophetic dreams — he sees himself as a deer caught in the huntsmen's nets.

Why did nobody come forward to claim the play? Both *The Spanish Tragedy* and *Tamburlaine* went into First Quarto editions without the authors' names being on them, but Kyd was finally traced as the author of the first and Marlowe soon became known as the writer of the second. (Whoever else wrote *Arden*, one cannot imagine Marlowe having dreamed up Alice Arden.) Perhaps this most remarkable semi-documentary play is the one-off effort of a remarkable playwright who never wrote another word. And yet . . . some of Alice's speeches

Miriam Karlin as the Witch in the 1981 RSC production of The Witch of Edmonton. *(Photo: Donald Cooper)*

do have a ring of Shakespeare. As M. L. Wine says, when all the possibilities have been considered 'of all the cases made for and against various known playwrights, that for Shakespeare emerges as the strongest'. I doubt we will ever know.

The next play poses few mysteries. On 16 April 1621 an old woman, Elizabeth Sawyer, was hanged as a witch at Tyburn. Eleven days later, on 27 April, a pamphlet was published about her witchcraft, the crimes she was supposed to have engineered and her trial. It was called *The Wonderful Discovery of Elizabeth Sawyer, a Witch, late of Edmonton* by 'Henry Goodcole, Minister of the Word of God, and her continual visitor in the Gaol of Newgate'. By 29 December 1621 the Prince's Company were acting a play called *The Witch of Edmonton* before the King and the Court. (This is to be distinguished from the anonymous comedy *The Merry Devil of Edmonton*, which was somewhat earlier.)

Some early editions of the play attribute it to a collaboration between Dekker and Ford, but most later scholars are certain that it was Dekker, Ford and Rowley. While there is some argument as to who wrote the two sub-plots, the story of the Witch herself is credited purely to Dekker.

The trial came at the height of the witch hysteria, when it was all too easy for any old woman to be considered a witch, and the scapegoat for everything that went wrong in a community, from minor mishaps like milk not churning into butter to the deaths of children, miscarriages and sick cattle.

Elizabeth Sawyer seems to have been an unprepossessing old woman. She had only one eye. During her interrogation she was asked why this was and how it had happened and she replied, 'With a stick which one of my children had in the hand: that night my mother did die it was done, for I was stooping by the bedside and I by chance did hit my eye on the sharp end of the stick.'

What means were used to make a lonely, poverty-stricken, terrified old woman confess to witchcraft hardly bear thinking about, but 'confess' she did, down in the depths of Newgate gaol. The report of her questioning still exists:

> *Question:* In what shape would the Devil come to you?
> *Answer:* Always in the shape of a dog and of two colours, sometimes black and sometimes of white.
> *Question:* From whence did the Devil suck your blood?
> *Answer:* The place where the Devil sucked my blood was a little above my fundament and that place chosen by himself and in that place by continual drawing, there is a thing in the form of a teat at which the Devil would suck me and I asked the Devil why he would suck my blood and he said it was to nourish him.

The Devil, the poor old woman told her questioners, had asked for her 'body and soul or he would tear me to pieces'. He had taught her three Latin words as a spell: *Sanctibicetur nomen tuum.* . . .

Witchfinders, expert witch-hunters, searched the bodies of their victims for 'Devil's marks'. As these could take the form of birthmarks, moles or any minor blemish, they were not hard to find.

Almost any 'test' of witchcraft was acceptable. Sawyer had 'long been suspected of witchcraft by Arthur Robinson, a JP who lived in nearby Tottenham', so a 'test' was carried out under his supervision. This was

> to pluck the thatch of her house, burn it and it being so burned, the author of such mischief should presently then come; and it was observed and affirmed to the court that Elizabeth Sawyer would presently [that is, immediately] frequent the house of them that burned the thatch which they had plucked off her house without any sending.

On such flimsy evidence was poor Elizabeth convicted. Asked before her death why she had confessed, she replied, 'I do it to clear my conscience and now having done, I am the more quiet and the better prepared and willing thereby to suffer death, for I have no hope at all of my life, although I must confess I would live longer if I might.'

The persecution of the poor old lady, her supposed witchcraft and her death provide the framework of the play, within which there are two sub-plots, a 'tragic' one and a comic one. There is division of opinion, as has previously been said, over the authors of the two sub-plots. Nowadays Rowley seems to be credited with the comedy and Ford, assisted by Dekker, with the domestic tragedy and romance. One possibility is that the story of Frank, Susan and Winifred was based on an earlier play by Rowley called *All's Lost by Lust*, but another is that this plot too was based on a contemporary murder, details of which are now lost.

Dekker's Elizabeth Sawyer is a poor old persecuted woman. We see her attacked by her neighbours, badly treated, physically assaulted and blamed for everything that goes wrong in the tight rural community which was Edmonton in those days. She is considered to be a witch, a charge which she at first denies. However, in order to try to get her own back and give herself some kind of self-respect she finally decides to go along with the idea, whereupon the Devil appears to her in the form of a Black Dog. The Black Dog speaks and takes a controlling role in the action of all three plots, but it is left open as to whether he is 'real', a hallucination or a focus of evil on which a series of events can be blamed. Obviously Dekker had a good deal of sympathy for Elizabeth Sawyer.

The second plot is also interesting. Frank is a young, rather weak man in service to Sir Arthur Clarington. There is no messing about in the opening of the play: 'Enter Frank and Winifred who is with Child' reads the stage direction.

Frank and Winifred, the lady's maid, are lovers and she is desperate to be made an honest woman and have a name for the baby. Frank is fond of her and does the decent thing; he marries her. But by the next scene we discover it is not in fact Frank's baby. It is the child of her employer, Sir Arthur Clarington. Not only that; he is delighted the child will have a name and Winifred her respectability, and sees no reason why the liaison should not continue, even though Winifred is married to Frank. In fact the proximity of the couple will make it easy. Whatever Winifred might have thought of Sir Arthur before (and the text does not suggest she was averse to his advances), she recoils from this idea, and he threatens to expose their secret. Winifred persuades Frank to hide her away in the country, and Frank goes off home for the weekend.

Here he discovers his father in dire trouble. There are money problems that are preying on his mind. However, there is a solution. Frank can marry Susan, daughter of old family friends and a childhood sweetheart of Frank's, and her large dowry will solve everything. Frank, who had been wondering how to break the news of his marriage, cannot do so; not only that, he eventually gives in and marries Susan, thus having married twice in less than a week.

Winifred by this time has moved near by and made a friend of Susan, neither of them being aware of the relationship of the other to Frank until Susan explains she is Frank's new wife. The unfortunate Frank is at his wits' end. Finally, on a journey with Susan into the countryside he is 'brushed against' by the Black Dog and is tempted to solve his problems by murdering Susan, which he does, and then stages a fake attack on himself. His crime is discovered finally because he is haunted by visions of his murdered Susan and by the Black Dog, and because the murder weapon turns up — still with fresh blood on it. Frank goes to the scaffold but his wife, Winifred, is taken in by her new family.

The third and comic plot concerns a country yokel, Cuddy Banks, who plays the hobby horse in a morris-dance team. He fancies Susan's sister Katherine, and decides to call up the Devil for a spot of assistance. He gets more than he bargains for, and raises the Devil in earnest in the form of the Black Dog. The comedy is much concerned with morris dancing as 'a mystery', a ritual with its place in the scheme of things.

All three plots cleverly intertwine, providing the straight drama of witchcraft, the romantic tragedy of Susan, Winifred and Frank — and Susan is a splendid, rounded creation — and with a laugh thrown in for good measure. The real rat of the play is, however, not the Black Dog or even the pallid Frank but the wealthy Sir Arthur, who as well as triggering off the tragedy is instrumental in bringing in poor Elizabeth as a witch, and who gets off scot-free apart from a fine, causing one onlooker to remark, 'If luck had served Sir Arthur, and every man had his due, somebody might have tottered ere this without paying fines, like it as you list . . .' Dekker was nothing if not a realist.

The Roaring Girl by Dekker and Middleton is a celebration of the life of one of the playwrights' contemporaries, Moll Frith, written with great affection, and indeed admiration.

Mary Frith came from the same background as most of the playwrights we have been considering, but not for her, alas, the grammar-school road to the theatre. She was the daughter of a London shoemaker,

> a fair and square conditioned man, that loved a good fellow next to himself, which made his issue so sociable. Particular care was bestowed on her education for her boisterous and masculine spirit caused her parents much solicitude. A very tomrig or rumpscuttle she was and delighted and sported in boys' play and pastimes, not minding of companying with the girls,

says a chronicle of her life.

Working a sampler was for Mary (or Moll, as she was usually known) 'as grievous as a winding sheet'. Moll had to earn her living to pay her way and was put to service, which she loathed, being a girl of such spirit.

> Household work of any kind was distasteful to her and above all she had an abhorrence to the tending of children, to whom she ever had an aversion in her mind equal to the sterility of her womb, never being made a mother to our best information.

Moll was a forerunner of the feminists. She wore men's clothes much of the time, when it was actually against the law so to do. She smoked a pipe. She consorted with thieves and vagabonds — certainly with actors and playwrights. She kept her own house, and she could certainly look after herself; she was a fine fencer and an excellent shot. She had friends across the social scale, and although she was condemned in one report as being a 'bully, whore, bawd, pickpurse, fortune-teller, receiver and forger' some of this would appear to have been highly libellous. Any woman who acted out of turn then was automatically described as a whore, yet although Moll might admit to forging or various con tricks she was always adamant that not only was she not a whore herself, she had never procured any other girl to be one either. There have been suggestions that she was a lesbian, but she did seem to have had at least two lovers, 'the notorious Captain Hind and one, Richard Hannam, a worthy who constantly wore a watchmaker's and jeweller's shop in his pocket and could at any time command £1000'.

She ended up in court several times, but one of the most interesting incidents is that when she appeared on 27 January 1611/12. As well as being generally accused of taking too much drink (which she admitted), of wearing men's clothing (which she could hardly deny), and being a whore (which she most strenuously did deny), she is also accused of having actually appeared on stage in a play.

It is evident from the epilogue to *The Roaring Girl* that on at least some occasions Moll would appear in it herself, and sit at the side of the stage. The text says: 'For Venus, being a woman, passes through the play in doublet and breeches, a brave disguise and a safe one if the statute untie not her codpiece point' and ends:

> The Roaring Girl herself, some few days hence,
> Shall on this stage give larger recompense,
> Which mirth that you may share in, herself does woo you,
> And craves this sign, your hand to beckon her to you.

For a long time this was felt to mean that Moll might sometimes have got up from her stageside stool and sang a song, maybe even performed the 'jig' which ended the play, but there are a number of suggestions now that she might actually have played herself right through the early performances of *Roaring Girl*. It would have been totally in character, and also absolutely against the law.

The court indictment says she had appeared on stage at the Fortune theatre nine months earlier. A letter from a John Chamberlain to Dudley Carelton dated 12 February 1611/12 (a Wednesday) says

> this last Sunday Moll Cutpurse, a notorious baggage that was used to go in men's apparel, was brought to St. Paul's Cross where she wept bitterly and seemed very penitent but it is since doubted that she was maudlin drunk being discovered to have tippled some three quarts of sack before she came to her penance. She had the daintiest preacher or ghostly father that ever I saw in pulpit, one Ratcliffe of Brazen Nose of Oxford, a likelier man to have led the revels in some Masque at court than to be where he was, but the best is he did so extremely badly and so wearied the audience that the best part went away and the rest tarried to hear Moll Cutpurse rather than him.

We know *The Roaring Girl* was a popular production at the Swan theatre between 1611 and 1625. Moll did not get the benefit of her immediate publicity, as she spent the six months following her public penance in Bridewell beating hemp, but it made no difference at all to her lifestyle when she came out.

Moll lived on the Bankside among the playwrights and actors, she ate in their ordinaries and drank in their taverns: she was their friend. She was about twenty-six years old at the time the play was first put on.

The title of the play literally means a noisy, lively, dashing kind of person — the nearest slang today would probably be a 'raver'. The plot, such as it is, deals with an awful womanizer called Laxton, who has tried to seduce the wives of a number of merchants (to get money off them), a young man who wants to marry the girl of his heart but is forbidden to by his father (who wants him to make a wealthy

Moll Frith, the 'Roaring Girl'.

Helen Mirren as Moll Frith in the 1983 RSC production of The Roaring Girl. *(Photo: Donald Cooper)*

marriage), and of the unfortunate Jack Dapper's attempts to avoid being taken away to a debtors' prison, the Counter. The various assignations of the merchants' wives take place at the Three Pigeons at Brentford. Brentford has been noted before as a suitable place for out-of-town assignations. Using the Three Pigeons was a real in-joke too, for it was kept by an actor called John Lowin who had played the parts of Falstaff and Mahomet. He lived on to old age, running the inn even under the Commonwealth. It remained famous in theatrical circles and plays a crucial part in *She Stoops to Conquer*; it is the inn for which the two young heroes are looking when they are directed to the Hardcastles' house instead, and indeed Tony Lumpkin praises it in a song during the action of that later play.

It is Moll who sorts everything out. Finding that Laxton is attracted to her, she makes an assignation with him. When he arrives he finds he has to fight a duel with her. She is much better than him, and every time she disarms him she tells him just what she thinks of his attitude to women in a splendid funny and telling speech. She persuades the sour father into allowing his son to marry the girl of his choice by pretending to be the son's new fiancée, horrifying him so much that he will do anything rather than have his son marry Moll. She also succeeds in helping Jack Dapper escape the Counter.

If Middleton is responsible for much of Moll, then no doubt Dekker could write at first hand about debtors' prisons, having spent so much time in one. As he was to say of the Counter Prison, ' 'tis a university, a college, where some are of twenty years standing and took all their degrees there from the Master's side down to the Mistress's side, the Hole . . . indeed some are bachelors, some masters, some doctors of captivity. . . .'

The Moll of *Roaring Girl* is delightful. As T. S. Eliot was to say of her, 'She is always real. She may rant, she may behave preposterously, but she remains a type of the sort of woman who has renounced all happiness for herself and who lives only for a principle . . . a real and unique human being.' Even Una Ellis-Fermor — who didn't much like the play — says of Middleton and Moll 'He can see simultaneously the fierce, active virginity in a character like Moll and can draw it clearly without scoffing at it as a pretence or fantasy.' Moll remains absolutely true to herself and her principles throughout the play.

We know a little more of the real-life Moll. When she died a booklet was published about her called *The Life and Death of Mrs. Mary Frith, commonly called Mal Cutpurse, exactly collected and now published for the delights and recreation of all merry disposed persons* — London 1662.

The Civil War was to make full use of her talents. She enthusiastically supported the Royalist cause, acting as a courier and a spy. She is authentically reported to have harried and set upon parties of Parliamentarians, and once actually robbed General Fairfax on Hounslow Heath, shooting him in the arm and killing the two horses on which his servants were riding. She was hotly pursued by some officers and was finally apprehended at Turnham Green, where she was promptly sent to Newgate. One might have thought she would have ended on the scaffold, but not so. Her sheer cheek and spirit so appealed to Fairfax that she was let out on the payment of a fine of £2,000 — a truly enormous sum for those days, and one wonders who paid it for her.

She lived to a good old age, dying at her small home in Fleet Street at the age of seventy-four on 26 July 1659, and was buried in St Bride's church, now the journalists' church. It seems most appropriate. As her last act she willed £20 'so that the conduits might run with wine when Charles II returned'.

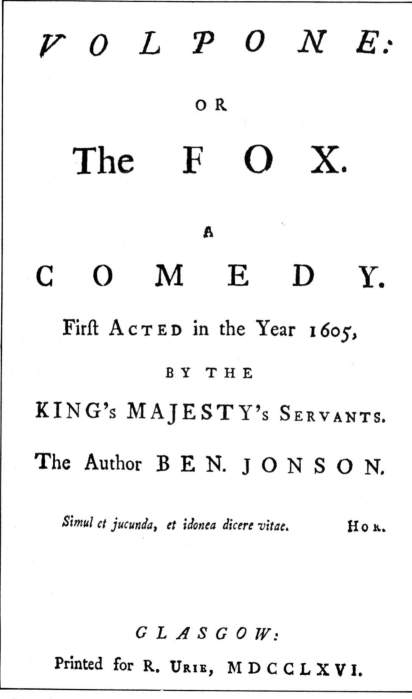

V O L P O N E:

O R

The F O X.

A

C O M E D Y.

First ACTED in the Year 1605,

BY THE

KING's MAJESTY's SERVANTS.

The Author B E N. J O N S O N.

Simul et jucunda, et idonea dicere vitae.   HOR.

G L A S G O W:

Printed for R. URIE, M D C C L X V I.

Volpone *title-page (British Library)*

Chapter 11

The Plays of Ben Jonson

'Name me a professed poet that his poetry did
ever afford him so much as a competence.'
The Poetaster — Ben Jonson

Well, Ben Jonson should certainly know all about that, although most of his own money problems arose from his not being able to hang on to it when he had it. Ben really wanted to go down to posterity as a writer of classical tragedy, with carefully researched plots set in the Senecan mould and written with due reverence and solemnity — this is how he saw himself. His comedies, at least three of which are still popular nearly four hundred years later, he hardly rated at all.

Yet few of us today would really want to sit through the turgid *Sejanus*. We just do not care sufficiently about what happens to him, and even a rash of horrors at the end — his young daughter for instance is raped before execution, as it was thought bad luck for the executioner to hang a virgin — did not make it all that popular in Jonson's lifetime either. *Volpone*, *The Alchemist* and *Bartholomew Fair* remain the Jonson plays most frequently performed, although there are other comedies which ought to be revived as well.

We know that when Shakespeare's company, possibly at his request, in 1598 took on Jonson's *Every Man in His Humour* the budding playwright was very loath to take instruction about what made a play a good piece of theatrical entertainment, not just a piece of writing. Even with his comedies Jonson was very strict about style, though the riotous language bursts through. Jonson was drunk on words.

He did not give his plays exotic settings, he wrote about a world perfectly familiar to his audience, whether it was the inside of the house of a wealthy merchant or the alleyways and taverns frequented by the underworld characters who flit through the pages of *The Alchemist* or *Bartholomew Fair*.

We do not know who suggested that Jonson move the action of *Every Man in His Humour* from Italy to London but it made only a marginal difference, apart from the changing of names. The play begins in the countryside, and then the action swiftly moves into London, where however upside-down it becomes, it all takes place within the framework of the London day. When the actors walk off stage at the end we imagine that day still going on. Cob the watercarrier will continue trundling through the streets with fresh water, the merchants will be buying and selling, the households will carry on as usual. It is a real world. When speaking of an impossibility Jonson says that it is as likely to happen as that 'Drake's old ship at Deptford may circle the world again'. He was writing about things with which people were familiar.

The plot is slight. An old man, Knowell, intercepts a letter intended for his younger son which makes him fear for the lad's morals, and brings him post-haste to London to see what is going on. Two country idiots and one town fool are hoodwinked by the streetwise people with whom they come into contact. A servant, Brainworm, takes the place of his master for the day. A jealous husband, Kitely, is put in his place and almost (but not quite) trusts his wife again. Throughout the day's action strolls the splendid portly figure of the braggart Captain Bobadill quoting chunks of *The Spanish Tragedy* which is his favourite play. (This is an in-joke, in that it seems Jonson himself had updated and re-written some of Kyd's original playscript.) Bobadill is really rather splendid, although one must have some sympathy for those of Jonson's contemporaries who saw something of the author in him. He endlessly borrows money he cannot repay, he drinks too much, he is a prodigious bragger, and he is always telling anyone who will listen what a fantastic swordsman he is. When you listen to Bobadill — as many people are forced to — you enter the world of Superman. There is no foreign battle in which he has not taken a leading part, no attack on a city where he did not lead the troops in through the breach.

Footpads? Highwaymen? No problem at all. As he walks through the streets of Whitechapel or Shoreditch he is often set on, sometimes by as many as 'four, five or six' ruffians at any one time, but it is nothing to him. He drives them back at sword-point along the length of a whole street, 'in the open view of all our gallants, pitying to hurt them, believe me . . . by myself I could have slain them all, but I delight not in murder.'

Jonson followed the play with *Every Man out of His Humour* before becoming involved in the Poets' War. Of this rash of plays, *The Poetaster* stands out for its sheer cheek. Eight classical poets (some famous) grace *Poetaster*, including Horace, Ovid and Virgil, and it all takes place in Augustus's Rome. Most of the action is taken up with a competition to find out which is the best poet, and this not only gave Jonson the chance to show off his classical scholarship but also, as we already know, to attack his fellow poet/playwrights.

Much of the humour in the poets' speeches in the play would be more understandable to the Elizabethan audience than it would to us — at least to those who had got as far as grammar school — for these famous poets all speak as they would have been expected to from the school books of the period. Ovid reads his poems, Horace part of his *Satires*, while Virgil carries off the palm with a stirring passage from the *Aeneid*.

The young hero who wants to be a poet against his father's wishes is Ovid, and the two pseudo-poets whom Jonson ridicules are thinly disguised versions of Dekker and Marston. Probably *Poetaster* would only appeal today to a minority studio audience — although one can see how it could be very entertaining — but the one character who would certainly make it worth the attempt is another of Jonson's splendid rumbustious characters, Captain Tucca.

If Captain Bobadill was prone to exaggeration about his prowess, and draws attention to himself with his bragging, he is nothing to Captain Tucca, who sees the whole of life as a mammoth epic starring himself. Every incident, however ordinary, can be turned into a drama. He is also truly amazing at getting money, from acquiring a few pence when he finds himself temporarily out of funds to a full-scale series of confidence tricks and financial chicanery which takes the breath away. At the end of the play he crashes into the presence of Augustus himself to find two friends facing an action for libel. Not surprisingly (knowing his character), Captain Tucca immediately ditches them both and takes the side of the Court to save his own skin. How much was Jonson influenced here by Falstaff? We can't say. There are certainly similarities between the two characters. Tucca seems to have appealed both to the audience and to other writers. There are overtones of him in the busybody Lucio in *Measure for Measure* and he was seized on with joy by the very playwrights Jonson had satirized as a portrait of the author himself. It would be interesting to see how this comedy would work today.

The first of Jonson's three major comedies is a dark one, *Volpone* (The Fox), and unlike the two which were to follow it is set abroad in Venice. Nor is there a funny or even faintly comic ending, for both Volpone and his accomplice Mosca, The Fly, come to a bad end, one in prison and the other in the galleys. As in *The Alchemist* which was to follow, Volpone and Mosca, the master and man, are mutually dependent while things are going well, and turn and rend each other when things begin to go wrong. It is a decadent world in which Volpone is surrounded by grotesque, almost surrealist, creatures such as a hermaphrodite, a dwarf and a eunuch.

The plot comes from the *Satiricon* of Petronius. Volpone decides it would be amusing to see how people would treat him if they thought he was about to die, what they would do to ensure that they were remembered in his will, and he therefore gets Mosca to put it about that he is terminally ill.

The plot works. Knowing he has a huge fortune, those who want a large share in it are prepared to sacrifice a good deal towards that end, either in the form of gold, jewellery, food and so forth or by prostituting their wives or daughters if that is what the 'dying' man wishes. With very few exceptions, Jonson did not write women well (his opinion of them was pretty low in real life), and the women in *Volpone* are either flattering self-seekers or rather pallid like Celia, whose husband not only ill treats her and happily sells her off to Volpone but exacts complete loyalty from her besides. The world of *Volpone* is a real one but it is highly unpleasant, and shows us one of the nastiest sides of human nature. So awful are the people who attempt to put one over on Volpone that even he in the end does not seem quite so dreadful. All things are comparative.

Sir Ralph Richardson as Volpone in the 1952 Stratford Memorial Theatre production of Volpone. *(Photo: Angus McBean)*

Sir Ralph Richardson (Volpone), Anthony Quayle (Mosca), Siobhan McKenna as Celia in the 1952 Stratford Memorial Theatre production of Volpone. *(Photo: Angus McBean)*

The language of *Volpone* is very rich, and is aptly described by Anne Barton in her book on Jonson as if the characters were forever rummaging through the contents of some gothic lumber room of the imagination 'turning out toothpicks and baboons, oranges, musk melons, apricots, porpoises, frayed stockings and lion whelps, tinderboxes, onions, sprats and Selsey cockles'.

Volpone acts much better than it reads, however, for these grotesque characters need the ability of actors to bring them to life. The play was probably first produced in 1606, and was certainly published the following year.

I make no apologies for saying that my own favourite Jonson play is without doubt *The Alchemist*. Like Volpone, *The Alchemist* (which was first performed by Shakespeare's company in 1610) is about human nature, but it is about its weaknesses and follies rather than its evils. To find why it is still entertaining today you need look no further than the very popular television serial *Minder* with its endless adventures of a rather unsuccessful petty villain, Arthur, and his 'minder' who both assists him in his various shady ventures and has to get him out of trouble when they go wrong. People love an inept villain, and they also thoroughly enjoy seeing others making fools of themselves.

Subtle, the villain of the piece, has dreamed up a marvellous confidence trick. Many wealthy people have had to leave London because of the plague, leaving their houses empty. He makes the acquaintance of a butler, Jeremy Face, who has been left in charge of just such a large London mansion, and he proposes to him that he moves in with his girl friend and sets up as an alchemist. The three will split the proceeds from the money they make duping people, and will move out long before the master of the house returns. People really did believe in alchemists in those days, pseudo-magicians who could produce results by magic, from making love potions to success in business, although their most famous trick was supposed to be the ability to transmute base metal into gold by use of the philosopher's stone.

Before you think how silly the Elizabethans must have been just look through the columns of today's popular newspapers or listen to *Checkpoint* on the radio and you will be reassured that the equivalent of Jonson's Alchemist is still alive and well and living in Britain today. Nor is there any shortage of people willing to buy non-existent villas in Spain, invest in companies which don't exist to make a quick fortune, or find the partner of their dreams.

So the plan is laid. Face will comb the taverns, ordinaries and streets for clients, Subtle will put on a convincing performance as an alchemist. Face is ideal, for he is very sharp, highly intelligent and streetwise. He begins to bring people in, and to really whet their appetites he makes it sound as if it will only be the sheerest luck that the Alchemist will find time to see them. After which they can't wait to be parted from their cash.

First comes Dapper, a foppish young law student. He wants to be a successful gambler. No problem — he has a lucky face, and his aunt is Queen of the Fairies. He didn't know? All he has to do is fetch four gold pieces and his 'aunt' will give him the spell he needs. Abel Drugger wants a cure for worms, but he is persuaded he also needs his horoscope cast to make sure his apothecary's business is successful. Sir Epicure Mammon wants everything: a philosopher's stone of his own to transmute all into gold and total power over all women. Come back later, it will all be arranged.

One client, Surly, does seem rather cynical about the claims of the Alchemist, but he is fobbed off with the promise of a rich wife. He must, however, disguise himself as a Spanish count. There arrives from the West Country a young landowner and his sister. The young man wants to become a famous wit and man about town and a duellist of note. Certainly. And his sister? What about a Spanish count for the sister? No problem at all. Also involved are a group of Puritans who want political and religious power as well as a serum for turning base metal into gold; they are promised all that as well.

It all becomes quite frantic as some of the earlier victims arrive back with their money or come to collect what they have ordered even while new ones are still being attracted in. All must be kept separate from each other, and not only that, but as the Alchemist and Face have suited themselves and their behaviour and even their dress to each client, it also requires constant quick changes of costume as well as pushing people into rooms, up staircases, out of windows and through doors. Like a mad juggler, the Alchemist manages to keep all the balls in the air when suddenly, to the horror of all, the real owner of the house arrives back.

*John Woodvine (Subtle, the Alchemist), Ian McKellen (Face) and Susan Drury (Dol) in the 1977
RSC production of* The Alchemist. *(Photo: Joe Cocks Studio)*

The Alchemist rushes off with his girl-friend, and Jeremy Face, back in his role
of butler, promises to meet up with them at a pub in Stepney later with the loot.
It soon becomes apparent this won't be possible. The owner of the house,
Lovewit, is at first totally bewildered as more and more people pile into his house,
including those who have now discovered they have been conned and are demanding their money back. In the middle of the uproar a faint voice is heard and a
knocking noise — it is Dapper, who has been sitting on the lavatory as he was told
to do, waiting for the Queen of the Fairies, and has been locked in. In a grand
denouement the 'laboratory' at the back of the house blows up.

Face puts the best 'face' on it he can. Lovewit, who is himself no slouch, sees
how he can turn it all to his own advantage. He will take some of the proceeds and
Dame Pliant, thus winning himself a wealthy and attractive young widow.

At the very end Jonson twists the plot for the last time. Face tells the audience
what is really there. Not the mansion we have thought, transmuted into the
Alchemist's office, but only a run-down town house with bare walls, defaced
with graffiti, a few bits of second-hand furniture and some broken pots. The
Alchemist's money-making scheme and the rich widow will be needed to put it to
rights. The audience has been conned as well.

The Alchemist is a most remarkable feat. Jonson has kept seven plots bubbling along together in parallel, requiring constant changes of costume, personality, even of language. It is one of the great comic plays of all time, a true theatrical *tour de force* and a most remarkable creative feat. It does not seem as if Jonson himself rated it very highly, which is ironic for it is one of the finest funny plays in the English language.

For his next great comedy, *Bartholomew Fair*, Jonson remained within that same world. This is the world of the great annual fair held at Smithfield, where the audience participates in the action. In fact Jonson begins with a novelty. The Bookholder — the man who acted as prompter and helped the cast with their lines — appears on stage and makes a solemn agreement with the audience couched in legal terms. The 'Articles of agreement, indented, between the Spectators or hearers, at the Hope on the Bankside in the County of Surrey on the one part; and the author of *Bartholomew Fair*, on the other part; the one and thirtieth day of October 1614 and in the twelfth year of the reign of our sovereign Lord King James . . . .' (Presumably they altered the date to suit the performance.) The covenant is that the people

> do agree to remain in the places their money or friends have put them in, with patience, for the space of two hours and an half, and somewhat more. In which time the author promiseth to present them by us, with a new sufficient play, called *Bartholomew Fair*, merry and as full of noise, as sport; made to delight all, and to offend none, provided they have either the wit or the honesty to think well of themselves.

Then, at great length, it tells the audience what is about to happen.

There is not so much a plot to *Bartholomew Fair* as an endless succession of events which involve one or more of the people concerned — and it is a large cast, with thirty speaking parts. The Fair is the main character in the play, the focal point of all the action, an artificial and ephemeral dream place where anything can happen, where anarchy rules, and where all and sundry are sucked towards its tawdry glamour and adventure with their judgment suspended. It is full of stalls and hucksters and entertainments and cheap goods, and it is the one time of the year when everybody, old and young, rich and poor, can let their hair down. It is a whole world in miniature, a fantastic and unreal world but a believable one, where at least some of those who become involved in it are never the same again.

The delightful *Epicoene; or The Silent Woman* is unfortunately seldom revived. This was first acted by the Children of the Queen's Revels in 1609–10, and printed in 1616. The joke, in brief, of this elaborate comedy is an old bachelor's desire to find a silent woman he may wed. Epicoene is found for him, but after the marriage nearly talks him dead. His nephew (who would have inherited his property) guarantees to rid him of Epicoene, and shows 'her' to be a boy that he himself has trained up for the part. The audience are not in on the secret! Our word epicene, of course, from the Greek, means 'pertaining to both sexes'.

Just a final look at one more Jonson play. He was to go on to Court Masques, as we know, and his later plays while skilled are very different from those of his great period. *The Devil is an Ass* came immediately after *Bartholomew Fair*, and it was first put on by the King's Men in 1616. One of the plots in this play is taken from the third day of Boccaccio's *The Decameron*, where the young wife of a jealous and over-possessive husband is seduced by a clever young man who has permission to speak to her so long as she says nothing. The young man manages to fix an assignation and discover what she feels by phrasing a series of questions which do not have to be answered.

But the character who links the various plots together is a young devil called Pug. He tells Satan that he is bored with minor devilry, souring cream, causing quarrels and such minor mischief. He wants to try his hand at real devilry and cause havoc in the City of London. Satan says he does not think he is up to it — Lancashire, Northumberland, yes, London, no. However, Pug is given his chance, taking with him a Vice called Iniquity to help him, and he duly appears in the City in the body of a young thief hanged at Tyburn that morning.

He becomes servant to Fitzdotterel, whose poor wife is kept locked away to keep her out of temptation. She is loved by Wittipol, and it is Wittipol who plays on Fitzdotterel the trick from the *Decameron* but with one important difference. The lady, Frances, says she will be his good friend and indeed will meet him but will not be seduced by him. Frances alone of Jonson's female parts is a charming, affectionate, very lively and credible woman, and it has been suggested that she might actually have been based on a lady with whom Jonson was emotionally involved at the time. Certainly she keeps her word and fools her husband throughout the play, but it is left slightly open as to just how far she will allow Wittipol to go eventually. He does, however, fall deeply in love with her, and no longer merely wants to get her into bed as just another conquest.

Meanwhile Pug tries his hand at duping City merchants and trying out all his black arts upon them, but he is totally outmatched. So dishonest, so corrupt, so fraudulent are those with whom he comes into contact that he just cannot compete, and in the end Satan has to step in and rescue him with a peal of thunder and take him back to the comfort and safety of Hell. Satan is disgusted, and tells him he is only saving him so that Hell is not shamed by the human beings finding out that they are more than a match for the worst of devils.

Jonson we know had a high opinion of himself. It was in fact justified, for there is nobody else in literature like him. He deserves far more attention than he receives, for he is so vastly entertaining.

Dame Peggy Ashcroft as the Duchess in the 1960/61 Aldwych Theatre production of The Duchess of Malfi. *(Photo: Angus McBean)*

Chapter 12

The Place of Women

'What is better than wisdom? Woman.
And what is better than a good woman? Nothing.'
Chaucer

The women's roles in the plays of this period are fascinating. No single playwright encompassed the sheer range of women that Shakespeare did, but many of them — and most especially Middleton — provided a remarkable cross-section of believable women which reflected accurately the position in which women found themselves at that time.

Up to, and indeed just into, the sixteenth century we know very little about the lives of ordinary women. Only those of the most tremendous importance were considered to be worthy of note — royalty, some women of the nobility, famous abbesses, the rare spirits. A handful of women made the headlines, as it were, for other reasons. They alleged they had the gift of prophecy, for instance, like the Fair Maid of Kent; they were accused of being notorious witches, and suffered the penalty for it; they went to the stake as heretics during the reign of Mary Tudor.

Of the merchant classes or landed gentry we know only what we can pick up, mainly from accounts such as those which appear in the Paston letters, where we gather that Margaret Paston at least was an extremely strong-minded woman quite capable of running a large household and making decisions while her husband enjoyed himself in London. The life of the working women and peasants was hard and unrecorded: an existence of constant toil and frequent childbearing was the lot of most of them.

By the 1520s and 1530s some women from wealthier homes were being well educated; Sir Thomas More's daughter Margaret is a famous case in point. Scholars like Erasmus argued for the proper education of women. The arrival on the throne of an extremely clever and well-educated Queen enabled the women of the nobility to make considerable gains in both education and status, while it would appear that significant strides were also made by their sisters in the ranks of the merchants and artisans. Certainly women in this class began to acquire a notable reputation for independence.

But many of the gains, especially those of the aristocratic girls, quickly evaporated once James I came to the throne. He and his Court circle had little or no sympathy for independent and well-educated women. It became fashionable at Court to denigrate women, to see them as the root of all the vices, assisted no doubt by the fact that James had surrounded himself not only with sycophants but with the kind of homosexuals who are often misogynists.

As has already been noted, just about everything could be bought in a Jacobean Court — titles, places, fortunes and wives. The place of a woman was as her father's chattel, a bargaining piece to be used to acquire wealth or property. The most docile went along with this, even though one imagines there must have been a large number of unhappy marriages. Those who married under duress and refused to accept the double standards took lovers. If this was discovered, then the cuckolded husband would either challenge the lover to a duel or, more often, pay a bunch of heavies to beat up his rival. If he then thrashed his wife within an inch of her life (even though he had several mistresses of his own), then it was considered to be no more than she deserved.

A notorious example of this kind of woman was Frances Howard, Countess of Essex, who had her plans for divorce and remarriage (to the favourite, Robert Carr, Earl of Somerset) opposed by Sir Thomas Overbury. She therefore had him poisoned, using the assistance of a Mrs Turner, a laundress and maker of a famous kind of yellow starch for ruffs which was considered the height of fashion. Frances, being of the nobility, escaped the scaffold, but her unfortunate accomplice went to the gallows wearing, on the specific instructions of the King, one of her famous yellow ruffs.

Yet the wives of the artisans must have kept their independence, because by the end of the period we have considered — that is, by the 1630s and early 1640s — they were actually beginning to take direct political action. Few now know, for example, of the massive anti-war demonstrations by women which took place in the 1640s. On 9 August 1643 thousands of women marched on the House of Commons, surrounded it, held the MPs hostage for hours on end, and were finally dispersed by troops with live ammunition. While one reporter at the time described them as 'for the most part whores, bawds, oyster women, kitchenstuff women, beggar women and the very scum of the suburbs', less biased commentators spoke of their being neatly dressed, wearing white and green favours in their hats and being drawn from the ranks of the merchants and artisans. Some were in fact artisans or shopkeepers in their own right. It is from this class that the playwrights drew their portraits of the women in the citizen comedies, continuing in a satirical vein reaching at least as far back as Chaucer's Wife of Bath.

After Shakespeare, the two most towering figures of the period are, of course, Marlowe and Jonson, but neither of them can figure much here. Marlowe, as has already been said, could not write parts for women at all; Jonson was only marginally better. He could manage satirical portraits of ladies, he could write parts for lively tarts like Dol in *The Alchemist*, who has never been better than she should be. But apart from Frances Fitzdotterel in *The Devil is an Ass* they are not a very interesting or believable collection. Marlowe seems to have actually disliked women, while Jonson had a pretty low opinion of them, and was no doubt one of those infuriating men whose personality and conditioning makes them unable to cope with intelligent women, and who are drawn therefore towards the archetypal whore with the heart of gold. One can well see why he described his wife as 'a shrew but honest'; she no doubt told him a thing or two when she had the opportunity.

Not surprisingly, what came easiest to some of the male playwrights was suffering womanhood, preferably *patient* suffering womanhood. These were the girls who faded away with unrequited love or if badly treated by lovers and/or husbands remained constant to the end. Into this category fall Euphrasia in Beaumont and Fletcher's *Philaster* and Aspatia in the same authors' *The Maid's Tragedy*.

Euphrasia, like Viola and Rosalind, takes male clothing and follows her love, in this case the shallow and rather uninteresting Philaster. So besotted is she with her hero that even when she has helped him to a successful conclusion of his adventures, and he settles down to marry another girl, she is more than happy just to live with them both as some kind of rather superior servant. Aspatia, having been jilted by Amintor at the King's command, settles into a woeful decline, although the authors do give the only truly fine speech in the whole play to her when, looking at a tapestry on the subject of Theseus and Ariadne on which her women are working, she sees herself on the beach of that 'wild island', arms outstretched, hair blowing in the wind and all behind a desert. But she is a lady with whom few of us could identify today.

But in the villainess of the piece, Evadne, Beaumont and Fletcher come the nearest they ever were to approaching a really fascinating woman. For female characters similar to Evadne we would only need to look at popular soap operas on television today like *Dallas* and *Dynasty*. Audiences then, as now, liked an all-out, tough, hard but incredibly attractive villainess, although Evadne is more interesting than her contemporary soap-opera counterparts.

She is, to begin with, quite straight. Marriage is put at its lowest in this play, for her marriage to Amintor is purely for the convenience of herself and the King. When she breaks the news to Amintor that she is the King's mistress she is totally uncompromising about it. It is the reverse of the conventional marriage of the day; she is the one to benefit, not the duped husband. Yet she would not have married just anybody, and when Amintor asks why him — 'there were thousands of fools easy to work on and of state enough within the island' — she replies coolly that 'I would not have a fool; it were no credit to me.' No, she would have an attractive, intelligent, younger man to 'father children and to bear the name of husband to me, that my sin may be more honourable'. She was content to see the proposed bridegroom jilt his fiancée of long standing and take up his role in her scheme of things, in spite of his close relationship with her own brother (in a recent production the inference was that this had been more than friendship, and

Sinead Cusack as Evadne (centre) in the 1980 RSC production of The Maid's Tragedy. *(Photo: Donald Cooper)*

that Amintor was bisexual).

She is equally realistic with the King. Yes, she will refuse to sleep with Amintor, she will keep her part of the bargain. Indefinitely? She cannot promise that. Yet you swore not to enjoy any other man than me, the jealous King tells her. No,

> I never did swear so; you do me wrong . . . .
> I swore indeed that I would never love,
> A man of lower place, but if your fortune
> Should throw you from this height, I bade you trust
> I would forsake you and would bend to him that won your throne.
> I love with my ambition — not with my eyes.

Above everything else, it is the *power* of the King that attracts Evadne; his wealth and his sexual attractions are completely subordinate to that love of power. Not only literature but history is littered with women drawn in such a way, even to men who are utter monsters. Obviously she is also extremely attractive sexually, and would appear from what transpires to have sophisticated skills and tastes in lovemaking. When her brother finds out the true position he tries to kill her. She 'repents' — just how sincerely we do not know — and he tells her that she is in a perfect position to put the family honour straight. She can kill the King.

Possibly a real-life Evadne would talk her way out of this one too, but faced with exposure and death she complies and sets about it with the ruthlessness she has brought to everything else, tying him up on his bed and then flirting in a way which suggests to him that she has thought up yet another strange sexual pastime until it is too late for him to do anything about it. (This makes you think irresistibly of the never-to-be-forgotten 'Mormon and the Beauty Queen' case that made our headlines a few years ago.) She then tells her brother and husband what she has done, and calmly expects Amintor to take her back and live with her. He refuses. She kills herself. It is the one unbelievable action that Evadne takes, but the early 1600s was hardly a period in which a regicide could be seen to have escaped retribution.

The three women in Middleton's tragedy *Women Beware Women* could easily have been ciphers. Bianca, married young against her parents' wishes, could be just the sad seduced heroine of tragedy; Isabella, who has fallen in love with her own young uncle, could be another; while Livia would be the simple villainess. Yet none of them are like that; all are much more complicated, and therefore far more believable.

Our sympathy is all with Bianca initially — a pretty, very young girl whose parents have tried to force her into a marriage with a rich, elderly bridegroom. It is obvious why she is attracted to the young and handsome Leantio, even though he is beneath her in social class. He takes her home to Mother, and she is happily prepared at that stage to live a much simpler life than any she had known hitherto, and without the wealth and comfort to which she had been used. Yet she falls easily enough for the flattery of the Duke of Florence, and is quite prepared to visit him while her new husband is away.

When she first reappears after her seduction — which takes place while Livia keeps her mother-in-law engaged in a game of chess — she certainly puts on the expected show of outraged virtue. How real is it? Probably fairly genuine at the time, although the Duke is no ugly monster; he is an attractive and very experienced philanderer who appears to have fallen genuinely in love with Bianca. So Bianca returns home, but becomes quickly dissatisfied with her simple accommodation and dull life, which could be so much more exciting if she became the Duchess. . . . From there it is a short step to agreeing that Leantio must be put out of the way so that she can legally marry the Duke.

Isabella too appears at first to be a modest victim caught up in an unlawful passion she cannot help, but then Middleton does not leave it at that. She is quite prepared cynically to marry the rich young fool who has come to court her, in order to be able to continue her incestuous affair without fear of the consequences.

Finally, most interesting of all is Livia. She is one of those sensible and highly practical women who would have made a great success in later times in politics, in running a business empire or in holding a high professional post, but who in the seventeenth century had no outlet for her undoubted talents, and thus turned them to intrigue. She is astute, bright and amoral, but her love for her brother is genuine (hence her involvement in his scheming), and the two enjoy a most real friendship as well as being blood relatives.

Diana Quick as Beatrice and Emrys James as De Flores in the 1978 Aldwych Theatre production of The Changeling. *(Photo: Reg Wilson)*

She is only too pleased to put her undoubted talents to work to bring about a number of desired ends. She will assist the Duke to seduce Bianca, she will help her brother in his liaison and organize the match between Isabella and the drunken lout of a fellow known only as 'the Ward'. She has no moral misgivings. But Livia is human too, and unexpectedly falls in love with Bianca's discarded husband, making herself as vulnerable as Bianca and Isabella. She persuades him that

Diana Quick as Beatrice and Emrys James as De Flores in the 1978 Aldwych Theatre production of
The Changeling. *(Photo: Reg Wilson)*

life without Bianca could be very good indeed. It was a secret marriage, let it stay
that way . . . Let Bianca go to the Duke and Leantio come to her. Leantio is torn,
but undoubtedly finds her attractive and agrees.

It is Livia's own brother who decides to kill Leantio. Firstly, it suits the Duke
to have him removed, but the knowledge that his sister has become Leantio's
mistress brings a more important reason — the need to revenge family honour.
But it is a man's reason, not a woman's. When he tells Livia that he killed her
lover for an excellent reason she turns on him and shrieks, 'The reason! That's a
jest hell falls a-laughing at.' Love has turned Livia into a fully realized human
being too late.

Probably the single most fascinating woman in the Jacobean tragedies is
Beatrice-Joanna of *The Changeling* — spoiled, beautiful, capricious, selfish and
determined to have her own way. Throughout the early part of the play we see
Beatrice rather as she sees herself, and it is almost possible to believe in what she
does. We can almost feel sorry for her as she has to pay her part of the sexual
bargain she has made in return for De Flores killing off her unwanted suitor.
Almost — but not quite. For what becomes ever more glaringly apparent is that
Beatrice has absolutely no self-awareness at all. Insensitive and deeply self-centred,
she is the most important point in her own universe, and any means are justified
to bring about her desired ends. It is that lack of self-awareness that draws her in-

Philip Dunbar (Jasperino), Emrys James (De Flores), Diana Quick (Beatrice), Bernard Brown (Vermandero) in the final scene of the 1978 Aldwych Theatre production of The Changeling. *(Photo: Reg Wilson)*

exorably towards De Flores, while maintaining all the time that she finds him repellent.

Why is she so fascinated? He is supposed to be ugly (although he is rarely portrayed as such on stage), unattractive and deeply evil. Perhaps it is because of these things. Actresses who have tried to portray Beatrice as a good girl gone wrong fail to make her convincing.

Like many women of a similar nature, when she has finally achieved what she says she wanted — the husband of her choice — then that does not bring happiness either. Firstly, she is possibly pregnant by De Flores (with all that might mean), and anyway she no longer seems to find her Alsemero as attractive as she did, nor does he seem to be much of a catch once we in the audience see more of him. Inexorably the trail of death goes on — her maid agrees to her plan of switching partners in bed, she taking her mistress's place. So the maid is coolly sacrificed. But very gradually Beatrice becomes aware of what she has done and of what she is. She recognizes that the seeds of her villainy were there from the beginning: she has not *become* ruthless, she always was. She sees that her attraction for De Flores is in part that of true like for like. He has not corrupted her; she was already corrupted. It is he who is the true other half of herself, not the young and foolish suitor she wanted for husband so badly that she was prepared to kill to bring it about.

By the end of the play she has reached the same conclusion as Macbeth when he says he is

> in blood
> Stepped in so far that, should I wade no more,
> Returning were as tedious as go o'er.

'I have kissed poison', Beatrice-Joanna tells her family when she is finally un-masked, and she and De Flores stab themselves to death, united at last in death. It is difficult to think of any modern play which so ruthlessly and relentlessly examines the complex motives of a wicked woman.

But it is the two Webster women, Vittoria and the Duchess of Malfi, who so dominate the plays in which they appear. Vittoria has none of the cool calculation of Evadne, nor does she experience the self-realization of Beatrice-Joanna, and the character suffers as a result. While Evadne and Beatrice are recognizable human beings, however much we might dislike what they do, Vittoria remains a striking character *in a play*. Yet the part is written with great economy, and it is remarkable how strongly she does dominate the action when in fact she only appears in four major scenes.

She is ruthless, she lies without a qualm, she sets out on a course and is deter-mined to carry it through. As John Russell Brown says in his essay on the play, 'In the trial scene she gives no sign of a hidden conscience, save only that she counterfeits innocence with alarming exactitude, as if she knew what it might be like.' Is she, he wonders, just playing a part when she is taken to the house of correction and appears to repent? It is not made clear in the play.

M. C. Bradbrook suggests that the literal-minded Elizabethan audience might well have considered that Vittoria was truly either possessed by a devil or in league with him. When Flamineo says to her near the end of the play, 'Thou hast a devil in thee: I will try if I can scare him from thee', then this might well have been taken quite literally. Witchcraft and demonic possession were accepted by many people then and for a good deal longer. Eighty years after *The White Devil* was written the descendants of those audiences who had moved to the New World could turn on dozens of innocent people and put them to death in the Salem witch trials. While there is no doubt that many who were involved in that persecution had their own reasons for participation, others truly believed that the girls involved had been dancing with the Devil and become possessed.

Vittoria's behaviour is 'unnatural', and perhaps one aspect of her character, whether intended by the author or not, is that she behaves in a way which is more masculine than feminine. Masculine virtues, in women, can become vicious, says the author. When her world falls apart and her murderers come for her she dies bravely, much like one of the male villains of her day — Richard III, Macbeth. Webster gives her a 'good' death, in the way many writers gave their villains a flare of grandeur at their end. (In *Anthony and Cleopatra*, most interestingly, Shakespeare gives Cleopatra a 'good' death while that of Antony is merely messy and inept.) 'If woman do breed man,/She ought to teach him manhood' says Flamineo as she is dying. Only at the very last does Vittoria stare into the dark and

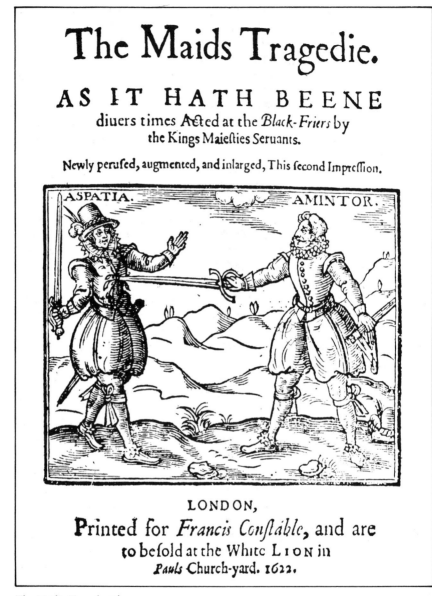

The Maid's Tragedy *title-page*

say, chillingly, 'My soul, like to a ship in a black storm,/Is driven, I know not whither.'

One can stand back and admire Vittoria as a work of creative fiction but we are not moved by her, and there is little with which we can identify. She remains, very firmly, a man's view of a certain kind of woman.

Yet that Webster could portray a woman of a much more sympathetic and believable kind is shown in his portrait of the Duchess of Malfi. She is hardly typical of a woman, either then or now — she is the stuff of which real martyrs are made — but she is drawn as the one truly decent human being in the whole play. Like Vittoria, she too is extremely brave, but she is brave while fully realizing the situation in which she finds herself, and is moving because she is both sensitive and self-aware. The Duchess of Malfi did not seek power, wealth, somebody else's husband, anybody's death. She merely wanted to get on with living her own life in her own way with the man of her choice. Nor was she any kind of a doormat. She has been the mistress of a large estate, and she is capable and strong-minded.

It is she who proposes marriage to Antonio, not the other way around. It is she who persuades him that his inferior rank is immaterial. She is her own woman. Opinions differ as to whether Webster intended to suggest that Ferdinand's feelings for his sister were so extreme that they amounted to an incestuous and jealous love, not just to the arrogance of rank and the shock of seeing his sister married to a man he would consider only as a glorified servant. It is a logical reading of Ferdinand's character, and would explain his total descent into madness at the end of the play.

In fact as the wicked, scheming and calculating villains disintegrate as the play progresses the Duchess, in spite of her sufferings — the attempts of her family to send her mad by locking her up with lunatics, her harsh ill-treatment in her brother's prison — grows ever stronger, meeting death as bravely as Vittoria but with a far more moving effect on those who see it.

Calling this woman only 'the Duchess of Malfi' is perhaps clumsy, perhaps very effective, but she is, as the actress Janet Suzman pointed out, 'the Duchess without a name'. We do not know why Webster never gave her one. Janet Suzman says of the Duchess that her tragedy was that she was born into the wrong world, 'that she wanted to be terribly ordinary, have domestic warmth, babies, a man to love — it was as simple as that — but she gets involved in a terrible duplicity, and so lies. When she loses her integrity she pays the worse consequence. It is amazing that Webster should see such a woman and recognize her needs and then set her in such a class-conscious structure.' Why was she so willing to die? 'It is a mystery.' This actress saw greater similarities between Cleopatra and the Duchess than Cleopatra and Vittoria in the manner of their deaths. 'They both embrace death — for both embrace it as a perfect choice. They wish to make an end. Death becomes a kind of lover and in that embrace, Webster gives his Duchess great dignity.'

But outside such high tragedy, what of the other women? We can get an excellent picture of the women of the citizen comedies in Simon Forman's *Casebook*. If we think the plot of *A Chaste Maid in Cheapside*, with its phoney doctor offering a woman a cure for infertility, is an unlikely one we only have to dip into the cures on offer from Forman. He actually did practise medicine and astrology, and as well as offering a whole range of nostrums for what we would now call women's complaints he too offered a special service to ladies he particularly fancied — and he did not even bother about a potion! Simon Forman went in for what he euphemistically described as 'halecking'. Mostly the women were willing, sometimes it seems to have been in part-payment for other things, and it too was used as a cure for infertility. . . . But we are certainly aware from the pages of his *Casebook* that the women who sought him out led extremely independent lives of their own, outside that of being a wife, mother and housekeeper.

In the earliest play we have looked at, Udall's *Ralph Roister Doister*, there is the sparky, independent widow Christian Custance, her two lively maids — especially Tibet Talkapace — and a tough old nurse, Madge. Set against the women, the rather colourless hero, Gawyn Goodluck, is a poor creature, and their sheer common sense shows up all the more plainly the swaggering conceit of Roister Doister and the cynical manipulation of Matthew Merrygreek, as the women are not taken in by either in the way the men are.

Just as Middleton's tragic heroines and villainesses come across the years as real live women, so also do his women in the comedies. Moll Frith has already been dealt with at length, but all his women behave in ways which are understandable and believable. They are their own people. The woman known merely as 'the Courtesan' in *A Trick to Catch the Old One* is truly sympathetic, while the men are a pretty repellent bunch. As previously noted, the term 'Courtesan' is wrong. All we know of her past history is that she was a decent girl who became mistress to Witgood, whom she still appears to love. Her connivance in the 'trick' which will get her a rich husband is because she is at heart a realist. The success of the stratagem will get her an elderly wealthy husband and respectability, but what makes her so fascinating is that she is (within her own terms of reference) quite honest. She merely sets up the situation and allows the old man to run enthusiastically on to his fate. As she tells him at the end, she never promised him a single thing, never lied to him at all: 'I took a plainer course and told you true I'd nothing.' We can only hope the horrid old man dies off and leaves her a wealthy and brisk young widow able to marry again, if that is what she wants, or if she does not, then to enjoy a lively widowhood.

Apart from poor Moll, the women in *A Chaste Maid in Cheapside* are also extremely realistic. Mistress Allwit is perfectly content to lie in bed without a qualm and greet the christening guests, with her husband sitting on one side of her and the father of the child on the other. Lady Kix surely cannot truly believe that the magic fertility potion will work, especially as it requires a session in the bedroom with the 'doctor', but she has been so abused and insulted by her husband — and it is interesting that even in Middleton's day it was recognized, if not overtly, that it could be the husband who was infertile, not the wife — one can only feel sympathy for her when she is 'cured'. We leave Lady Kix about four months pregnant, smiling quietly to herself in a satisfied way.

The women of the comedies and satires may not be deep — there are no equivalents of Viola, no wits as sparkling as Beatrice — but they show us a very clear picture indeed of women at the end of the Elizabethan era and up to the time of the Civil War.

We see women past girlhood who are intelligent and literate. They make the most of their lives. They are sexually aware and enjoy making love; the inhibitions and guilt were to come later. It is impossible to imagine their counterparts in the reign of Queen Victoria, two hundred years later, speaking so openly and frankly on the subject. While they may not question their position as would today's feminists, they are prepared to scheme and make the best of it. Apart from the young girls married off — or threatened with it — who provide a romantic focus in many of the plays, they are realistic and without illusions.

While some take lovers others are shown as having a genuine affectionate and happy relationship with their husbands — to whom they are more than prepared to stand up, however, when necessary. They are busy people too; not for them the sofa and the boredom of the wives of Victorian businessmen, whose lives were geared to propping up the self-regard of their husbands. On the whole they are without hypocrisy.

Middleton's very obvious feelings for women must have grown out of his relationship with his strong mother and sister and from a happy marriage, but there is no doubt that the playwrights who wrote best about women were writing about women as they knew them.

It was to be a very long time indeed before women were portrayed in such a way again. Henry Fielding's women are either passive sufferers through no fault of their own or larger-than-life females as in *Tom Jones*. Dickens provided a wide range of marvellous character women, often quite bizarre, but his heroines are among the most unreal and vapid in creative fiction, from the dismal Dora in David Copperfield to Little Nell. They can be unbelievable and heartless like Estella, or come to a bad end through their 'immorality' like Lady Dedlock in *Bleak House*. Dickens, while fathering a large family himself before running off with a young actress, shared the general Victorian view of 'fallen' women: Oliver Twist's mother has her presumably illegitimate baby in a workhouse and dies in childbirth; Lady Dedlock pays for her similar sin at a later stage in her life; Little Em'ly, seduced by Steerforth, can never show her face in the country again and so on. In Hardy, poor Tess Durbeyfield is hanged at the end of a sequence of events which begins with her rape. She is not even willingly seduced.

Compared with their Victorian counterparts the women of Middleton, Dekker and Massinger are positively liberated. It was not, of course, to last.

It was to take a very long time indeed for women to regain anything like such a position again, in or out of fiction. In spite of its high tone, the Commonwealth relegated women to a subordinate role, and when they complained commentators of the day admonished them briskly to get back to the kitchen and spinning-wheel where they belonged. The Industrial Revolution sucked in the women of the working classes at the latter end of the eighteenth century and during the nineteenth, while the Victorian age made of them either idealized sexless saints, monsters of depravity or little better than beasts of burden working in the coal-mines and the brickfields.

It is interesting if fruitless to speculate as to what might have been the place of women if they had gone forward at the end of the Elizabethan era rather than first standing still and then going back.

Miles Anderson (Black Dog) and Miriam Karlin (the Witch) in the 1981 RSC production of The Witch of Edmonton. *(Photo: Donald Cooper)*

Chapter 13

Plays for Today

'The man who says 'no' . . .'

However interesting it might be to know something of the lives of those who wrote the plays with which we have been dealing, the playhouses where they put them on, the subjects which excited them, it remains an academic exercise if they are never seen on stage. Somebody has to look at the texts in exactly the same way as he or she would at the script of a brand-new play by an unknown playwright and decide if it will work, how it should be done and what it will communicate to a twentieth-century audience. This is the job of the director, and I went to two young directors who have made a considerable mark in this particular field, Barry Kyle and Adrian Noble. At the time of writing both are predominantly working for the Royal Shakespeare Company, but that was not the reason why I chose them. Both seem to me to have made plays of this period immediate and exciting experiences, while their work is dissimilar.

One of Barry Kyle's most successful productions was the remarkable drama-documentary *The Dillon*, where he translated the reminiscences of an old Stratford pensioner into a show which quite literally used the whole of the town of Stratford and part of the river-bank, including a disused railway line, and employed a cast of hundreds — actors from the theatre and what seemed to be half the population of the town. Funny and harrowing as well, the play offered a harsh picture of a largely uncaring society in which the best that could be hoped by those born poor was that they should somehow manage to survive. Another Kyle production which was deeply impressive was that of Arthur Miller's *The Crucible*, which was toured around a wide variety of different settings from school halls to old churches. I saw it in a large cattle shed in the middle of a rainstorm on Bodmin Moor in Cornwall.

Kyle has directed several Jacobean plays for the RSC — notably *The Witch of Edmonton*, *The Roaring Girl* and *The Maid's Tragedy*. What has drawn him to them?

'There was something in the atmosphere of the theatre after 1612 which reminded me of what had happened in the theatre in the 1960s. I found *The Witch of Edmonton* by accident — I was reading through some synopses of plots and I thought I would read it, as I did not know it and I was terribly struck first of all by the fact that the leading characters were called ordinary names like Frank and Susan. I couldn't believe, as I read it, that it had been written in 1621. The dialogue, rather than becoming more clotted, seemed to be easier. The play had terrific theatrical immediacy and what you were aware of in it was that the playwrights had turned their backs on the joys of versification and were starting to look out of the window into the real world.

'It reminded me of how the poetic drama of the 1940s and 1950s was suddenly supplanted by the working-class theatre of the 1960s. I was interested too because it was a collaboration. Why were there suddenly so many collaborations? Even Shakespeare collaborated at the end of his life. It was rather like that of Howard Brenton and David Hare. They say they found it liberating, the lonely and inward side of writing being replaced by something more immediate, if possibly less subtle and broader. Together they could produce something quite different. When Brenton, Hare and Snoo Wilson collaborated on a play called *Lay-bye* at the Royal Court, Hare turned up on the first day with a roll of wallpaper and started to write things all over it. I felt that Dekker, Ford and Rowley had collaborated in that way on *The Witch of Edmonton*.

'The subject matter is pure documentary, Elizabeth Sawyer only having been executed within the year. It reminds me of instant paperback writing — in a sense they rushed a paperback out, which drew on the sensational circumstances of that trial. Although it did pay lip service to the prevailing anti-witchcraft ethos of the day, at the same time it brought about a sensibility about the poor, actually bringing the poor on stage, which was a new concept. Consequently I became interested in the content in terms of comparing it with, say, *Love's Labour's Lost* some twenty years earlier. It shows how plots could develop during that twenty years and how the language could change. *The Witch* does loosely scan most of the time but there are sections which are so direct, that are bound up with such theatrical imagery rather than the limits of versification, that I was suddenly struck that possibly with Shakespeare dead (something of a relief to some of his contemporaries) something new started to blossom and these rather promiscuous associations developed. Middleton, Dekker, Fletcher, Chapman, Massinger, Jonson all worked in collaboration with others.

'I think that happens when the social atmosphere within which playwrights are writing has become so exciting that that kind of collaboration becomes possible. It's like writing about Watergate or the Vietnam War or the Falklands. They are issues so central that somebody is bound to want to write about them.

'Then there was the emergence of the class issue which is a fascinating one and one that drew me to *The Roaring Girl*, alongside which was the growing independence of women. *The Roaring Girl* needed a hell of a lot of work doing on it — it nearly killed me. It was very, very tough. It is a play you have to do warts and all and the warts are very obvious.

'To make it work you have to get away from the traditional way of looking at that kind of comedy — you know, all thigh-slapping joviality — because when you actually examine the play it is extraordinary what is going on. There is only one real aristocrat in the play and his name is Noland — No Land. It's not much of a part. He is a man who has lost everything and in a way the writers portray him almost with nostalgia for something that is gone, rather as Osborne portrayed the Colonel in *Look Back in Anger*. We know that the values being explained in Osborne's play are Jimmy Porter's. The Colonel's values are what's wrong with England, but at the same time Osborne managed to create in him a kind of regret for the finer things that have gone.

'I think you have some of that in *Roaring Girl*, where the middle classes are the villains and where Wengrave is horrified that his son might make an inferior marriage, but where there is a kind of sympathy between the people who were right at the top and those who were right at the bottom. Noland is the one person who is sympathetic to Moll in the play and I found that very interesting.

'In my opinion, what you see in these plays is capitalism in action. Very few of the selfmade men in them get anything other than satirical treatment. Alongside this there is a respect for simple innocence which dates right back to early Elizabethan times, especially female innocence. That remains untouched. They also showed, indeed became eloquent in showing, the tragedy of people caught up in purely financial catastrophes which were not of their own making like in *The Witch of Edmonton*.

'In that play it is fascinating to see how the subject is treated compared to, say, *Macbeth*. Shakespeare built the supernatural element of witchcraft into his play, but in *The Witch of Edmonton* witchcraft is given the same kind of social explanation which Miller later gives to it in *The Crucible*. The first time you see Elizabeth Sawyer you see a woman saying ''I am not a witch'' and you then see a landowner assaulting her, beating her up. Witchcraft, in that play, is the last resort of the very poor, the people who don't have anything. So the writers were able to show in the play people who embraced witchcraft because they literally had nothing else and they showed those who persecuted them, as did Miller in *The Crucible*, with total lack of sympathy. So there you are in 1621 and the heroine of the play is penniless, illiterate — and female, something which would have been inconceivable back in 1592.

'The way to do these plays is to find a way of releasing the kind of daring that was in them originally, rough-hewn, fast-written, documentary-type pieces with a high ''cock-up'' ratio. You can't allow yourself to be light-wristed over them as they were written so fast. In *The Witch* there are three writers and three plots. I wasn't overmuch concerned over who wrote what, and anyway there is disagreement about it, which I think has prevented critics from giving their literary blessing to it. The play has something better than just literary interest — it has tremendous bravery.

'After I'd tackled *Roaring Girl* I became more and more interested in Middleton. Funnily enough, though, when we were discussing what play I should do, early in 1982, I was equally interested in *A Game at Chess*. I liked the idea of the Black Pieces being the Spaniards and the Whites the English. There's a lot of real chauvinism about Catholics and foreigners. I really kicked myself later when we had decided on *Roaring Girl* because right in the middle of 1982 came, of course, the Falklands War and the play would have hit it at exactly the right moment. If I'd done it I would have had jump jets on stage and all that kind of thing. It would have been such a natural right in the middle of all that Argy-bashing, anti-foreigner, jingoistic fever. When that play was written it was real blazing satire, which makes it all the more remarkable that it was the biggest smash hit of the Jacobean theatre, playing eight days in a row. What a sensation!

'Then Middleton went to prison and the play was taken off. When you read it you are intrigued by the wog-bashing element and the way the White Pieces are presented but the fascination is really in the whole political intrigue of two sides at war. You don't know who is telling the truth, it's the whole *Belgrano* syndrome and there it is, all there in this chess game. The moment has gone, I think, to do it at present. What would have made it so very topical was the fact that in Argentina we had a Spanish-speaking, Roman Catholic country and therefore the political coincidence was very striking. It must have worked in its own day. Only satire gets people thrown in jail. It doesn't happen to writers of plays of con-sensus. It must have been an extraordinary biting, hilarious and above all, dangerous, satire.

'Then *The Maid's Tragedy* is different again. You have two women and it is a moot point to which the title refers, or even if the title should be in the singular or the plural. Both die by the end of the plot. One is the complete victim, Ophelia-like, fragile, very feminine. The other actually says in the text "I'm a tiger". She's an extraordinary, dangerous, brilliant, glittering socialite who has become the King's mistress. She's rather like a film star or pop star might be today who has clawed her way on to the front pages of all the fashion magazines. She has that kind of overwhelming sexy attraction. These two characters sit side-by-side in the play, the second having pinched the potential husband of the first. What is clear from the play is that the most interesting character in it is that of Evadne, the fighting, seeking, ambitious woman, not the loser. That's in Shakespeare as well but he never went quite so far. It was very interesting the way they put these very ruthless women on stage. You had to wait a long time to see it again. Early on they obviously felt the very real problems over having to use boy actors. You notice it in *Love's Labour's*, and even more in *Romeo and Juliet* where you feel par-ticularly irritated there aren't more scenes with them together. Possibly playwrights then felt they just couldn't risk showing such intimacy but as theatre progressed in the early 1600s, writers began to take more risks. Within half a century women were acting on stage, of course.'

Barry Kyle is not attracted personally to the major Jacobean tragedies. 'When Trevor did *Revenger's Tragedy* it made a very strong impact in the minds of audi-ences of what Jacobean tragedy was all about, that malevolent, sinful, brooding, but somehow rather flash kind of society. I just feel there isn't much more to prove in that area. What was interesting to me about the *Maid's Tragedy* was that it seemed so up to date. I set it on a kind of Onassis-style yacht and brought it into the twentieth century, something I didn't want to do with the others. It didn't seem to me to be about dark brooding corridors, it seemed to be bathed in bright, white light. I think there are dangers in thinking of Jacobean plays in terms of two awful clichés — all tragedies are as I have described and all comedies are witty, unbelievable, thigh-slapping stuff.

'It does seem to me that it is more relevant to look at these plays from a more realistic perspective and not in a stylized Restoration perspective; all too often you get Jacobean and Restoration plays lumped together and they are not remotely alike.

'We need to look very hard at the grip a class has on society. Would we had a Jonson around now in the middle of Thatcher's England, all the characters for satire are right here today. Those writers who might have done it seem to have burned themselves out. More than anything what we need now is brilliant, biting, satirical theatre.'

Adrian Noble made his early reputation in Jacobean tragedy, notably a production of *The Duchess of Malfi* for the Manchester Royal Exchange theatre. His first introduction to directing plays of the period under discussion was when he was given *Titus Andronicus* as a very young director. He read it and saw in it a thriller, and a horror story, he says, 'and while I was working on it I was very aware of the audience who would have come to see it who were only a dozen yards down the road from the bearpit and over the river from Tyburn. *Malfi* was my first major excursion into Jacobean theatre and its background affected me a great deal.

'After the Jacobean period, came the Civil War and then our Revolution, yet somehow it is almost as if it has never happened. If you ask a French or a Russian child about their Revolutions they will know all about them. If you ask an English child about ours, it is very unlikely they'll know anything at all. Political events during those years have not been so much misreported as not reported at all. They don't sit central in the syllabus of what children learn in history. Yet those events which took place in England with James I's succession to the throne, and which ended when Oliver Cromwell's son finally gave up, were the vital years for framing bourgeois democracy as we know it.

'The Jacobean period was one of political change. Writers didn't dare write about English politics so they had to find models abroad or all that would happen would be that the theatre would be closed down, so what we see in the tragedies is England at a time of political flux, being expressed through plays very often set in Catholic countries; plays with a high violent context and very often with socially mobile people in them. All those plays like *The Changeling*, *Malfi*, *Revenger's Tragedy*, *The White Devil*, *A New Way to Pay Old Debts* have these kind of people in them and it is not an accident as they are all quintessentially political plays.

'The discoveries I made when doing *Malfi* in Manchester were central to me because it was by doing the play in that particular theatre that I began to understand the style of dramatic writing. It's a period of theatrical transition.

Shakespeare existed as much at the end of the Dark Ages as at the beginning of the Age of Enlightenment. He took into himself a huge amount of mysticism, paganism, the different attitude towards where man stands in nature. It shifted during the Jacobean period and further during the Caroline. When you go right back to the Greeks you have man in the open air. The audience sees man and nature at the same time because of the way their theatres were built. They saw everything, sky, man, earth, in a natural setting. In the Elizabethan period it shifted, but it was still man but not man in nature although he was still seen under an open sky although he was man on a bare stage. By that time the nature was filled in by the poetry, the landscape of the verse, and what I realized with *Malfi* — because there is also prose — is that those writers, initiated by Shakespeare, create whole cosmologies, not just locations as we have subsequently come to understand them — i.e., Act II Scene I The Convent, and so on.

'They created whole universes which can actually change and transform before the audience because what they see with their eyes they are also hearing about with their ears. Then came the next stage, which was moving indoors, and this was the beginning of the move towards bourgeois theatre and that frightful man, Brumante, who invented perspective theatre. So you end up with one seat which has the perfect view and that is the King's seat and eventually the popular theatre becomes élitist theatre as we move first indoors, then into perspective, then scenery and this is the death of popular theatre and simultaneously, the death of a certain relationship between men and society which ceases to be the preoccupation of the playwright. What became the preoccupation after the Restoration was not man and nature but just a few men in a bourgeois society, and the slice of life became ever narrower with less and less interest in man and nature until it virtually disappeared

'During the thirty-year period in which these plays were written, enormous political shifts were taking place. All that is reflected in the drama, and in *Malfi* we found that once we had liberated it from three and a half centuries of theatre architecture, the play revealed itself like a flower we hadn't seen before. You can see that what Webster does is actually to create hell on earth for the Duchess, after which she achieves purgatory and then some kind of redemption because although what we see takes place in prison, what is dramatized is her inner nightmare which could be called hell. This gave me and Bob Crowley (the designer) a whole different view of the play and once we and the actors released ourselves from the locations, we had to start examining the infrastructure of the play which is both physical — how do you present the relationships in the round and reveal the forces within the play — and how one can move from a hubristic society aspiring to Godhead (the Borgias, those astonishingly rich, cultured, interbred people who aspired to heaven), and the socially mobile people that come in, Bosola, Antonio and, indeed the Duchess herself. These are the people who set the cat among the pigeons and the whole aspiration of that hubristic culture is shattered.

'It came very close to James I himself, the God-given, the man at the top of the tree. All that notion was shattered by these mobile people, which is why hell comes on stage. It was a terrible and exciting revelation which we had. Because the drama then was in a period of flux, the play originally must have been done indoors where you could go dark and not see what was going on.

'Of course these plays are violent (leaving aside *Titus Andronicus* which is a special thing, overkill) and what we found is this aspect of them that continentals just cannot understand: that is when you can rub together a laugh and a horror. It's funny and it's also terrible, it's laughter in Auschwitz and that's frightening and it says something very profound about the human condition. Because they were public plays the writers said "Let's put hanging on the stage and discuss it." *Malfi* is, actually, a chamber play, very claustrophobic, something you never get in Shakespeare as it didn't interest him. Webster saw the universe like that.

'As to the comedies, they are very hard work. I'm wary of them but then most directors are terrified of comedy. They vary of course in just how difficult they are: *Eastward Ho!* for example is one of the most acceptable. The people in the comedies are socially mobile as well, but the plays are bastards to do. Yet their language was totally transforming, words were coming into it at an astonishing rate during that period. The English vocabulary bred endless words but when I did *A New Way to Pay Old Debts* I did actually hack the text about. It did pay off too, cutting it. Some of Massinger is just plain clumsy. But the play did work. Sir Giles Overreach is such a marvellous creation — I think it was T. S. Eliot who saw him as a Tamburlaine in a tiny village, "Tamburlaine of three parishes".

'Above all these are actors' plays. We'll never know in some cases though why a certain line works. It must have been because a particular actor pulled it off. Shakespeare does it a lot; for instance he keeps using Welsh characters — Fluellen, Glendower, and so on. They had catch phrases. The actors in those days must have had ways of working them and the playwrights knew how to make the best of their actors and the best of the playwrights were those that not only had genius but who had to do it for a living. I think it is marvellous when you remember that two out of our three national playwrights were either indicted for murder or murdered . . . Only Shakespeare got away scot free. No other country has that. Then both playwrights and actors became more respectable and the material less contentious.

'I think the danger of doing the plays today is to have too much spurious respect for the texts. I say spurious because the texts were not sanctified then, we know they weren't. Apart from Jonson they didn't think they were writing for posterity. I felt when I carved up *Malfi* that Webster wouldn't have minded at all so long as we made the play work. But Jonson would have hated it. I read somewhere a probably apocryphal story about him leaping up and interrupting performances, very much like Joan Littlewood used to do, roaring "You're messing about with my lines." That was when the theatre was a dangerous, rude, coarse and contentious place where people felt so strongly that they would argue it out and fight. It was healthy. Brecht would have liked the Elizabethan and early Jacobean theatre and Joan Littlewood too — Joan was a great Elizabethan.

'I think it is because that theatre had such a great life that audiences are turning back to it, directors and actors always have because the actors have to grow with the plays. It's no good saying Lear's emotions are a bit like I felt when my Dad died. It's far, far bigger. You've got to get bigger all the time, you can't act these plays reductively. Then you've got to find a way of forgiveness and finding grace and it's mind-stretching.

'They alert the audiences' imagination and edify it, not in a smug way but because they are truly big experiences, great epic public experiences. The greatest single experience of the age is Shakespeare where you can have a laugh, followed by a love scene, followed by a battle, followed by a political intrigue in a council chamber, followed by a rough street scene and all within twenty minutes.

'This is the thread which runs through Jacobean plays and the measure of their success is the measure of them as public experiences. If Racine had written *Malfi* he would have started it with the Duchess in prison talking to Bosola and Ferdinand, that's all that would have interested him. When we did *Malfi* in Paris, (a mistake), the difference in response between the English and French audiences was fascinating. The French just could not understand the catastrophe at all, to them all the killings were just barbaric. Nor could they understand the author putting a few laughs in just before a catastrophe. Over there they have become so imprisoned by form that their classical drama is dwarfed by academia. It never had the popular base that ours did.

'What we see therefore is big public issues debated in big public plays. They have a freedom of form because the playwrights virtually invented their own, although they pinched parts of it from all over the place. They were stealers but inventing as they went along, saying ''I'll talk to the audience at this point'' or ''I think I'll bring in a ghost here''. It didn't worry them at all in terms of reality as they were creating, play by play, their own worlds. The audiences would have applauded at the end and then quite possibly, gone off to cheer a public hanging.

'What most of the plays are about is the individual's right to say ''no'', to refuse to conform, to dissent. It's when the collective will comes down and says ''that's enough'' that we identify — if we were all liberated we wouldn't need Jacobean drama.'

Epilogue

The remit of this book was to look at Shakespeare's contemporaries — that is, those who influenced him, those working at the same time, and those he in turn influenced. But it is necessary to round off the period and look ahead a little at what was to come.

The theatre being offered at the beginning of the Civil War was very different from that which had burst into life in the late Elizabethan age. As Adrian Noble has pointed out, it had become far more private and enclosed. There are many reasons for this. The elaborate masques which had become such a feature of Court life, first under James I and then under Charles I and Henrietta Maria, had accustomed the Court and aristocracy to highly artificial performances which used complex and elaborate scenery and costumes. In the Court masques, too, women as well as men took part, right up to the Queen, Princesses and the noble ladies of the Court.

The masques had a definite effect on the presentation of theatre. No longer were theatres built on the old open courtyard principle with a handful of better seats for the better-off. They were expected to provide comfort. Courtiers, used to scenery in the masques, demanded plays with movable scenery. The bare stage of early Shakespeare, where members of the audience filled in what was necessary by the use of their imagination, helped by basic props, was a thing of the past. This in itself set bounds to what the playwright could do.

As to the content, there was a definite turning away from the boisterous comedies of the late Elizabethan and Jacobean period. Romantic and courtly love was the most popular theme, and the robust attitude to sex portrayed in plays such as *A Chaste Maid in Cheapside* and *A Trick to Catch the Old One* was distinctly unfashionable. Nor was it surprising that the biting satirical plays like *A Game at Chess* and *Eastward Ho!* had no successors with a country politically in turmoil, and during a period which was to be a run-up to a bloody civil war. Plays which actually showed the overthrow of a monarch, such as Marlowe's *Edward II* and Shakespeare's *Richard II*, were very definitely out.

Most naturally, all this led to a bloodless and unexciting form of drama, although there was a number of accomplished playwrights writing up to the time of the Civil War. These included Sir William Davenant (who was to continue during the Restoration, and who, legend has it, could have been Shakespeare's own son by the wife of an Oxford vintner, John Davenant, with whom

Shakespeare used to lodge on his journeys to and from London). Shakespeare certainly stood godfather to the child, and Sir William, no doubt, was content to let the rumour run.

The two most professional playwrights of the period were Richard Brome and James Shirley. Brome is described as having been a 'servant' of Ben Jonson, but presumably this could have meant that he worked for him in some kind of secretarial capacity. It seems unlikely that he would have emerged from scouring the pots as a fully fledged playwright. He began writing plays while Jonson was still alive, and Jonson is known to have given his work some rather patronizing approval.

His early works show a strong Jonsonian influence, both in their characters and in their subject matter, but they are much more conventional in form and leant heavily on the romance which was so popular in Caroline theatre. Brome was extremely successful; one play, *The Sparagus Garden* (produced in 1635), bringing the company which put it on over £1000 in box-office takings.

James Shirley was the more accomplished writer. He wrote both tragedies and comedies — as well as masques — but his plays were carefully designed to stay within the bounds of what was fashionable and he was a shameless plagiarist, stealing plots, characters and speeches from earlier playwrights. He wrote his own version of *The Duchess of Malfi*, called *The Cardinal*, but the characters are pale shadows of the original. The fascinating Bosola and the ambiguous, and possibly incestuous, Ferdinand disappear and the Duchess is reduced to a good woman making a choice between two fairly acceptable suitors with neither of whom has she had any sexual relationship. The Cardinal and indeed all the other characters are two-dimensional figures, and although the play ends with a heap of bodies it is stylized and somehow sanitized.

His comedies are far better; witty and inventive comedies of manners which foreshadowed the Restoration comedies of the end of the century. Amusing and in some way reassuring, they were set in the world the Royalist audiences knew and loved. When the Civil War came Shirley fought for the King before retiring to become a schoolmaster. Probably he is best remembered now for the famous dirge 'The glories of our blood and state' which closes one of his masques.

The curtain fell with a clang in 1642, with the edict that all public stage plays should cease. There had always, as we have seen, been a very real division of opinion about theatre and a strong lobby against it on a wide variety of grounds, not the least of which was that theatres were sinful places which encouraged immorality in those who went to watch stage performances, especially women. On the whole the assumption that the Royalists were in favour of theatre while the Roundheads, the Commonwealth, were not is accurate, although the first major closure of the playhouses took place before the resolution of the Civil War and some Puritan writers thought there was a place for plays with a strong moral message.

We know how hard this affected all those associated with the theatre from the pathetic pamphlets which circulated explaining the plight of all those involved in theatrical entertainment who were now without any means of occupation.

Even though the theatre had been banned, it continued sporadically and in a somewhat underground manner until 9 February 1647/8, when a new and draconian ordinance was enacted. This ordered the demolition of all playhouses, the arrest of any actors found performing and substantial fines for each and every person attending a dramatic presentation of any kind. This edict is one of the reasons we have no examples of the early theatres left today. They were quite literally torn down and destroyed, with the exception of the Red Bull theatre.

We know this theatre existed some years into the Commonwealth because there were a number of raids, followed by arrests, during that period when plays must still have been put on. What playwrighting there was consisted of underground-type pamphlets read by very limited numbers of people with, possibly, the odd illicit performance in a remote place. This was hardly an atmosphere in which new young playwrights could flourish. Even if you could find actors of any calibre — who would by this time mostly have been scattered all over the place earning their livings the best way they could — they would need to be very dedicated to face the possibility of long prison sentences should they be found out.

It was the very end of the Commonwealth period before anyone as it were stuck his hat in through the door, and that person was Sir William Davenant. In the mid-1650s he wrote a number of 'entertainments' which he described as being in the 'manner of the ancients'. They consisted of programmes of songs and poetry and were enacted in his own home. In 1656 he got a little braver and actually advertised his newest entertainment with the unwieldy title 'The Siege of Rhodes Made A Representation by the Art of Prospective [Perspective] in Scenes and the Story Sung in Recitative Musick', a kind of opera in fact. Next, having actually ingratiated himself with Oliver Cromwell, he suggested a little entertainment on the marriage of Cromwell's daughter, and he followed this up by a patriotic piece in this genre geared to promote the Commonwealth line on deteriorating relationships with Spain. *The Cruelty of the Spaniards in Peru* (the rest of the title is taken up once again with explaining that it is not exactly a *play*) made a great breakthrough, for the government for political reasons allowed it to be put on in a building in Drury Lane, with all that area's associations with the theatres of the past. *The Cruelty of the Spaniards* was not a play as we would understand the term, but it was a public show; the audience had to pay to see it, and some professionals were used rather than just the amateurs who had taken part in Davenant's home theatricals. Theatre was back.

When it became evident that the restoration of the monarchy was in sight the old players began to return to the capital and rehearse. What remained of the old Phoenix Theatre was restored, and the only playhouse to survive intact, the Red Bull, was reopened. With the return of the King in 1660 theatre was once again to flourish; he did not only authorize it but directly encouraged it.

The theatre to be seen in the 1660s and into the next century was very different from that of the high flowering of the early period. It was the era of mannered comedy. It produced a whole galaxy of new writers — John Dryden, William Wycherley, William Congreve, Thomas Otway, George Farquhar, Sir John Vanbrugh and Sir George Etherege. It gave us our first and remarkable woman playwright, Aphra Behn, who after an adventurous career (which had included a period as professional spy) became a popular and accomplished playwright, often in her work turning the prevailing fashions of the drama of the day on to their heads. In many of Aphra Behn's plays it is the women who manipulate and fool the men, not the other way around.

The single greatest breakthrough was of course that women were finally allowed to act upon the stage in England. (There had been professional actresses in Italy since the 1560s.) The very first were Mrs Hughes and Mrs Rutter, and they appeared in a version of *Othello* presented by Sir Thomas Killigrew at Drury Lane in 1660, playing Desdemona and Emilia. After this there was to be no going back.

As to the Elizabethan and Jacobean plays in the main, they were not to the taste of the new audiences. (The diarist Samuel Pepys, a great theatre-goer, noted the plays he saw, and his reaction to them — invaluable records from an intelligent and cultivated, yet typical, man of his time.) Shakespeare was himself in for a period of severe adaptation and bowdlerization. It was Colley Cibber's *Richard III*, much mangled from Shakespeare, which was to remain the popular version right up to the time of Edmund Kean. It was Dryden's *All for Love*, not Shakespeare's *Antony and Cleopatra*, which was the favourite of Restoration audiences. Garrick in the next century was to make his own versions of *Lear*, *Macbeth*, *Hamlet* and *Romeo and Juliet*, and we owe it to the splendid and eccentric Macready that Shakespeare's plays were finally presented in the middle of the nineteenth century as he himself wrote them.

The plots of some of the Jacobean tragedies were used again by Restoration playwrights, but they make dull reading today. It seems too that the whole burgeoning, lively, remarkable tradition of Elizabethan and early Jacobean acting had been lost; the sense of a company style, the actors who sank themselves into their roles like Burbage. The tragedies of the Restoration were, we are told, presented in a mannered fashion, with the words spoken almost as operatic recitative. Many of the exiled Royalists had fled to Paris and were much influenced by the style of presentation seen there — in fact, style was everything in the tragic pieces, with much attention paid to pageantry and ceremony rather than content, and only Otway diverging from this.

The body of work which has now become known as 'the Restoration Comedies' is of course extremely amusing, but limited. Seduction and cuckoldry were the main ingredients, although put over with great style and much wit. We can laugh with and at the characters, but they do not (with the exception of some of the women portrayed by Aphra Behn) seem very real.

We cannot know what might have happened to our theatre had the country not been plunged into the turmoil of civil war and then administered by a government which was directly opposed to plays, playhouses and players.

There has never again been a period like that of the late Elizabethan and Jacobean stage, that marvellous explosion of words and acting talent, the coming together in one place at one time of so many writers of near-genius, led by one of the greatest who has ever lived, William Shakespeare. We are a strange nation. We consider it patriotic to remember and praise generals and politicians, many of whom fought wars and introduced policies later found to be disastrously wrong. We can treat as heroes those who made whole nations into colonies or whose decisions led to the deaths of thousands. We hold up as shining examples great inventors, explorers, engineers (as indeed we should), but on the whole our children pass through their education without being given any inkling of the skills of those who invented not only the exciting dramatic forms of the period with which we have been dealing but even words themselves; of those who explored the human character and the human condition in a way which has never been surpassed; and those who brought the words and the writers together and by their skills put them on to the public stage.

Select Bibliography

Play texts

For complete collections of plays I worked from editions in the *Mermaid Series*. I also found useful the editions of collected and individual plays given below. The dates given are of the editions I have used, and are not necessarily those of first publication.

Four Tudor Comedies ed. William Tydeman, Penguin 1984
Three Jacobean Tragedies ed. Gāmini Salgādo. Penguin 1965
Six Plays by Contemporaries of Shakespeare ed. C. B. Wheeler. Oxford University Press 1971
The Chief Elizabethan Dramatists ed. W. A. Neilson, Harrap 1911
Christopher Marlowe — Complete Plays ed. E. D. Pendry. Everyman Edition 1976
Jonson's Complete Works ed. H. Herford and P. E. E. Simpson. Oxford University Press (eleven volumes) Oxford 1925–53
A Game at Chess ed. J. W. Harper. New Mermaids 1966
A Trick to Catch the Old One ed. G. J. Watson. New Mermaids 1968
Eastward Ho! ed. R. W. Van Fossen. Revels, Manchester 1979
The Knight of the Burning Pestle ed. John Doebler. Regents Renaissance Drama series 1967
The Maid's Tragedy ed. B. Norland. Renaissance Drama series 1968
Arden of Faversham ed. A. H. Bullen. London 1887 (Includes Holinshed's *Chronicle* and contemporary reports)

Books

J. Q. Adams (ed.), *The Dramatic Records of Sir Henry Herbert, Master of the Revels 1623–1673*. New Haven 1917
Robert Adams, *Ben Jonson's Plays and Masques*. London 1979
John Aubrey, *Brief Lives*. Penguin edition. London 1972
Anne Barton, *Ben Jonson — Dramatist*. Cambridge 1984
G. E. Bentley, *The Profession of Dramatist in the Time of Shakespeare, 1590–1642*. Princeton 1971
  The Jacobean and Caroline Stage. Oxford 1941–1968
M. C. Bradbrook, *John Webster*. N.Y. and London 1980
  The Rise of the Common Player. Cambridge 1962
  The Growth and Structure of Elizabethan Comedy. Cambridge 1961
  Themes and Conventions of Elizabethan Tragedy. Cambridge 1960
G. Bokland, *The Sources of the White Devil*. Uppsala 1957
  The Duchess of Malfi — Sources, Themes and Characters. Harvard 1962

F. T. Bowers, *The Elizabethan Revenge Tragedy 1587–1642*. London 1940
E. K. Chambers, *The Elizabethan Stage*. Oxford 1923
A. H. Cruickshank, *Philip Massinger*. Oxford 1920
John Danby, *Poets on Fortune's Hill, Studies in Sidney, Shakespeare, Beaumont and Fletcher*. London 1952
Thomas Dekker, *Selected Prose Works*. Stratford-on-Avon 1967
T. A. Dunn, *Philip Massinger*. London 1957
A. E. Dyson (ed.), *A Casebook — Webster: The White Devil and Duchess of Malfi*. London 1975
T. S. Eliot, *Collected Essays*. London 1932
Una Ellis-Fermor, *The Jacobean Drama*. London 1936
F. Finkelpearl, *John Marston of the Inner Temple*. London 1969
R. A. Foakes and T. R. Rickert (ed.), *Henslowe's Diaries*. Cambridge 1961
Arthur Freeman, *Thomas Kyd: Facts and Problems*. London 1967
W. W. Greg, *The Henslowe Papers*. London 1907
    Dramatic Documents from the Elizabethan Playhouses Vol. 1. Oxford 1931
Andrew Gurr, *The Shakespearean Stage, 1574–1642*. Cambridge 1980
G. L. Hosking, *The Life and Times of Edward Alleyn*. London 1952
J. L. Hotson, *The Death of Christopher Marlowe*. London 1926
Ben Jonson's Conversations with William Drummond of Hawthornden. Shakespeare Society, 1842
Arthur Kirsch (ed.), *Jacobean Dramatic Perspectives*. London 1972
L. C. Knights, *Drama and Society in the Age of Jonson*. London 1937
Clifford Leach (ed.), *Marlowe*. New Jersey 1964
Alexander Leggatt, *Citizen Comedy in the Age of Shakespeare*. London 1973
Brian Morris (ed), *John Webster*. London 1972
J. R. Mulryne, *Thomas Middleton*. London 1979
Allardyce Nicoll (ed.), *Essays on Shakespeare and ELizabethan Drama*. Missouri 1962
T. F. Ordish, *Early London Theatres*. London 1971
Lois Porter (general ed.), *The Revels History of Drama in English*. London
    Volume III 1576–1613 ed. Clifford Leech and R. W. Craik. 1975
    Volume IV 1613–1660 ed. P. Edwards and K. McLuskie. 1981
C. T. Proutey (ed.), *Life and Works of George Peele*. Yale 1952–70
A. L. Rowse, *Christopher Marlowe*. London 1964
L. G. Salinger, *The Revenger's Tragedy. Stratford-on-Avon Studies I — Jacobean Theatre*
Thomas Seccombe & J. W. Allen, *The Age of Shakespeare*. London 1903
Richard Southern, *The Staging of Plays before Shakespeare*. London 1973
J. A. Symonds, *Shakespeare's Predecessors in English Drama*. London 1884
C. F. Tucker-Brooke, *The Shakespeare Apocrypha*. Oxford 1908
L. B. Wallis, *Beaumont and Fletcher*. Oxford 1947
Glynne Wickham, *Shakespeare's Dramatic Heritage*. London 1969
F. P. Wilson, *Marlowe and the Early Shakespeare*. Oxford 1953

Manuscripts, pamphlets, etc.

Ballad — 'The Complaint and Lamentation of Mistress Arden of Faversham in Kent who, for love of one Mosbie, hired certain ruffians and villains most cruelly to murder her husband with the fatal end of her and her associates. To the tune Fortune my Foe.'
    Roxburgh Collection — BM. Vol III p.156. (1630).
The Spanish Protest Against *A Game at Chess* ed. E. Wilson and O. Turner.
    MLR 44 (1949)

Table of Dates and Events

This table attempts to set some notable theatrical dates and events in the context of the history of the time — no more. Dating plays is notoriously difficult, dates differing by years according to which source is used. We are sure of some, because of subsequent events — e.g., *Eastward Ho!*, *A Game at Chess*. I have picked out the plays mentioned in the text and used the approximate date of first performance as given in the *Revels History of Drama* in English. It should be further noted that to add to all the other difficulties in dating, in this period (and until 1752) England still reckoned dates according to the Julian Calendar, beginning the year on 25 March. For dates in the early part of the year, some scholars will revise forward, some back.

The Monarchies

Henry VII	1485 – 1509
Henry VIII	1509 – 1547
Edward VI	1547 – 1553
(Lady Jane Grey	1553 – 9 days Queen)
Mary I	1553 – 1558
Elizabeth I	1558 – 1603
James I	1603 – 1625
Charles I	1625 – 1649 (executed)
The Commonwealth	1649 – 1660
Charles II	1649 – 1685

	Some political events of importance	What was happening in arts and theatre
1550	William Cecil becomes Secretary of State	*Ralph Roister Doister* – first English comedy
1554	Execution of Lady Jane Grey Elizabeth Tudor sent to Tower suspected of treason	John Lyly born (died 1606)
1558	Accession of Elizabeth I	George Peele born (died 1598) Thomas Kyd born (died 1594)
1559	—	George Chapman born (d. 1634)

	Some political events of importance	What was happening in arts and theatre
1560		Robert Greene born (d. 1592)
1561	Mary, Queen of Scots returns to Scotland	
1564	Robert Dudley made Earl of Leicester War ends between France and England	Christopher Marlowe born (d. 1593) William Shakespeare born (d. 1616)
1566	Birth of James VI (Scotland) I (England)	Birth of Edward Alleyn (d. 1626)
1567	Abdication of Mary, Queen of Scots	Richard Burbage born (d. 1618)
1568	Mary takes refuge in England	
1570	—	Thomas Heywood born (d. 1641) Thomas Dekker born (d. 1638)
1572	Dutch War of Independence Duke of Norfolk executed for treason Massacre of St Bartholomew's Eve in France Parliament demands execution of Mary	Ben Jonson born (d. 1637)
1573	Sir Francis Walsingham becomes Secretary of State	
1574	—	James Burbage granted licence to open The Theatre
1575	Henry III of France crowned	Cyril Tourneur born (d. 1626)
1576	—	The Theatre opens
1577	—	The Curtain, second theatre, opens Publication of Holinshed's *Chronicles*
1578	James VI succeeds in Scotland	Lyly's *Euphues* published
1579	English-Dutch alliance Drake proclaims sovereignty over California	John Fletcher born (d. 1625)
1580	Spain invades Portugal	Thomas Middleton born (d. 1627) John Webster born (d. 1634) Last performance of miracle plays at Coventry
1581	—	Peele's *Arraignment of Paris* performed
1583	Somerville plot to assassinate Queen Throgmorton plot to aid Spanish invasion	Francis Beaumont born (d. 1616) Queen's Company founded Philip Massinger born (d. 1638)
1584	William of Orange assassinated	
1585	Sir Francis Drake attacks Spanish colonies	Edward Alleyn leads the first Lord Admiral's Men

	Some political events of importance	What was happening in arts and theatre
1586	Sir Francis Walsingham foils the Babington plot and proves complicity of Mary, Queen of Scots Babington tried and executed Mary tried and found guilty	John Ford born (d. 1639)
1587	Mary executed	*Tamburlaine* performed (Marlowe)
1588	Defeat of the Spanish Armada	*Pandosto* (Greene) published *Dr Faustus* (Marlowe)
1590	Walsingham dies	*Henry VI* (Pts 1 & 2) – Shakespeare
1592	—	Greene dies. Henslowe begins 'Diaries' *Spanish Tragedy* (Kyd), *Richard III* and *Comedy of Errors* (Shakespeare). Shakespeare appears in cast lists. *Arden of Faversham* published, several years after first production
1593	—	*Edward I* (Peele), *Titus Andronicus*, *Taming of the Shrew* Christopher Marlowe killed at Deptford
1594	Henry IV crowned in France	*Mother Bombie* (Lyly), *Edward II* (Marlowe), *Battle of Alcazar* (Peele), *Two Gentlemen of Verona*, *Love's Labour's Lost*, *Romeo and Juliet* (Shakespeare)
1595	Henry IV declares war on Spain Spanish land in Cornwall and burn Penzance and Mousehole	Thomas Kyd dies *Old Wives' Tale* (Peele), *Richard II*, *Midsummer Night's Dream* (Shakespeare)
1596	Pacification of Ireland Essex sacks Cadiz	Blackfriars Theatre opens *King John*, *Merchant of Venice* (Shakespeare) Swan Theatre opens
1597	—	*Henry IV* Pts 1 and 2. Shakespeare buys New Place
1598	Burghley dies	*Every Man in His Humour* (Jonson), *Much Ado*, *Henry V* (Shakespeare) George Peele dies
1599	Essex made Lord Lieutenant of Ireland, returns and is imprisoned Oliver Cromwell born	Globe Theatre built *Julius Caesar*, *As You Like It*, *Shoemaker's Holiday* (Dekker) *Antonio & Mellida* (Marston)
1600	Essex tried and loses office	*Nine Days Wonder* (Kempe), *Twelfth Night*, *Hamlet*, *Merry Wives of Windsor*
1601	Rising and execution of Essex	'War of Poets' begins

	Some political events of importance	**What was happening in arts and theatre**
1602	Spanish Army surrenders at Kinsale	*All's Well That Ends Well*, *Troilus & Cressida*
1603	Death of Queen Elizabeth Accession of James I Sir Walter Raleigh imprisoned	Henslowe ends 'Diary' *Sejanus* (Jonson)
1604	—	Alleyn retires. *The Malcontent* (Marston), *Bussy d'Ambois* (Chapman), *The Honest Whore* (Dekker and Webster) *Measure for Measure*, *Othello*
1605	Gunpowder Plot. Guy Fawkes and conspirators try to blow up Parliament	William Davenant born (possibly Shakespeare's natural son) *Eastward Ho!* (Jonson, Chapman and Marston; Jonson and Chapman go to prison). *A Trick to Catch the Old One* (Middleton), *King Lear. Don Quixote* published in Spain
1606	Fawkes and others put to death	*Volpone* (Jonson), *A Mad World My Masters* (Middleton), *The Revenger's Tragedy* (Tourneur), *Macbeth*
1607	Union of England and Scotland rejected by Parliament	*Knight of the Burning Pestle* (Beaumont and Fletcher), *Antony & Cleopatra*, *Timon of Athens*
1608	—	*Duke of Biron* (Chapman), *The Roaring Girl* (Middleton and Dekker), *Coriolanus*, *Pericles*
1609	New charter for Virginia	*Philaster* (Beaumont and Fletcher), *Epicoene* (Jonson), *The Atheist's Tragedy* (Tourneur), *Cymbeline*
1610	Arabella Stuart imprisoned Parliament prorogued	*The Maid's Tragedy* (Beaumont and Fletcher), *The Alchemist* (Jonson), *The Winter's Tale*
1611	Dissolution of Parliament	*Catiline* (Jonson), *Tu Quoque* (Greene), *A Chaste Maid in Cheapside* (Middleton), *The Tempest*
1612	Trial of the Lancashire Witches Death of Prince Henry	*The White Devil* (Webster), *Henry VIII*
1613	Marriage of Princess Elizabeth	Fire destroys Globe *Two Noble Kinsmen* (Fletcher and Shakespeare?)
1614	James I's second Parliament	Second Globe built *Bartholomew Fair* (Jonson), *Duchess of Malfi* (Webster)
1615	Trial of Countess of Somerset for murder of Sir Thomas Overbury	

Some political events of importance	What was happening in arts and theatre
1616 Sir Walter Raleigh released to lead El Dorado Expedition	Death of Shakespeare Francis Beaumont dies Jonson First Folio published
1617 James I visits Scotland	*The Devil is an Ass* (Jonson) Jonson made Poet Laureate *A Fair Quarrel* (Middleton and Rowley), *Devil's Law Case* (Webster)
1618 Raleigh executed	Jonson's visit to Drummond of Hawthornden
1619 —	Richard Burbage dies
1620 Pilgrim Fathers leave for America	*The Custom of the Country* (Fletcher and Massinger), *The World Tost at Tennis* (Middleton)
1621 Trial of Elizabeth Sawyer James I's third Parliament	*The Witch of Edmonton* (Dekker, Ford, Rowley), *Women Beware Women* (Middleton)
1622 —	*The Changeling* (Middleton and Rowley)
1623 Prince Charles travels to Spain to secure Spanish bride — and fails	Shakespeare's First Folio published
1624 James I's last Parliament Hostilities with Spain	*A Game At Chess* (Middleton) smash hit. Taken off, company tried, Middleton imprisoned
1625 Charles I succeeds Marries Henrietta Maria, daughter of Henry IV of France	*A New Way to Pay Old Debts* (Massinger). John Fletcher dies
1626 Trouble between King and Commons	*Staple of News* (Jonson), *The Maid's Revenge*, *The Wedding* (Shirley)
1627 Failure of La Rochelle expedition	Thomas Middleton dies *The Cruel Brother* (William Davenant)
1631 Theatres closed due to plague	
1632 —	*The City Madam* (Massinger) *'Tis Pity She's a Whore* (Ford)
1634 —	Probable date of death of John Webster
1637 —	Death of Ben Jonson
1638 —	Probable date of death of Thomas Dekker
1642 Start of Civil War	

Index

Italicized references are to illustrations.

C

D

E